# John Wilcockson's
# *World of*
# *Cycling*

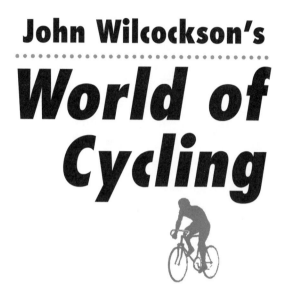

by *John Wilcockson*

VeloPress • Boulder, Colorado

ISBN: 1-884737-50-1

Printed in the U.S.A.

Library of Congress Cataloging-in-Publication Data applied for

10  9  8  7  6  5  4  3  2

1830 N 55th Street
Boulder, Colorado 80301-2700
USA

TEL 303/440-0601
FAX 303/444-6788
email: velopress@7dogs.com

To purchase additional copies of this book or other VeloPress products, call
800/234-8356, or visit our Web site at www.velogear.com

*Book design by Paulette Livers Lambert*
*Front cover design by Erin Johnson*

*For J.B. Wadley*

# Acknowledgments

There are many people and organizations I would like
to thank. First, New York friend James Levine, from whom
came the initial idea for this title. My wife, Rivvy Neshama,
who gave me constant feedback, expert copyediting and
encouragement. San Francisco friend Owen Mulholland and
colleague Charles Pelkey, whose magazine archives I raided
to find most of the earlier work. Graham Watson, for nearly
always being at the right place and time to capture this wonderful sport on film. Evelyn Spire and Dorothy Schuler, for
teaching me the subtleties of American English. The
Kennedy Brothers of Keighley, England, who helped found
*International Cycle Sport* in 1968. John Lovesey of the London *Sunday Times*, for accepting cycling as a mainstream
sport. IPC Magazines of London, which enabled me to edit
*Cyclist Monthly.* Offpress of Brussels, Belgium, which pub-
lished *Winning: Bicycle Racing Illustrated.* Barbara and Bob
George, founders of *VeloNews.* Partners Felix Magowan and
Susan Eastman for helping to establish Inside Communica-
tions. David Walls and Willard Hanzlik, for their help in
relaunching *VeloNews.* Traveling companions Chico Perez,
Robin Magowan, Samuel Abt, Louis Viggio, David Walsh,
Claude Droussent, Franco DeLuise, Rupert Guinness, Steve
Wood and James Startt, for their inspiration and friendship.
And the race organizers, sponsors and athletes that make
cycling the best sport in the world to write about.

# Contents

• • • • • • • • • • • • • • • • • • • • • • • • • • • • • • • • • • • • • • • • • • • • • • • • • • • • •

The sport of cycling changed my life. It brought me incredible excitement and discovery—from a 14-year-old kid who didn't know that bike racing existed to winning the Tour de France three times. The more I see of other sports, the more I am amazed about cycling. It truly is the king of sports, in terms of its athletic challenge and its history. I was just fortunate I was able to stumble upon it.

For me, reading about cycling—going back to the early days of *VeloNews*—had a huge impact. I would say the single biggest factor that created a fantasy—my dream of winning the Tour de France—came about in a little garage in Reno, Nevada, at the home of Roland Della Santa, my first framebuilder. He had stacks of *Miroir du Cyclisme* and *Vélo* magazines there; I didn't read French, but the pictures said everything. And reading about races, reading about the heroes is what draws people into cycling.

Cycling enthusiasts should love all sides of the sport, as cycling is depicted in this book. It has the excitement of the Tour de France and great road races ... and also the thrill of riding a mountain bike down a single-track trail in, say, Colorado. Myself, besides road racing, I've done velodrome racing, even one cyclo-cross race—and I've been riding a mountain bike since 1980.

At the end of that same year, I first met this book's author, John Wilcockson. He began writing about cycling in the 1960s. One thing I've always admired about John is that he has always been a very fair and objective journalist. And his book is one that's going to appeal to everybody who has an interest in cycling. Maybe it will even create a dream for another 14-year-old kid, just like me.

—*Greg LeMond*

**Introduction**

The shortest job interview I ever had turned out to be the most far-reaching, too. It took place February 29, 1968, in a small café in Kingston-upon-Thames, Surrey, the English town where I was working as a civil engineer. The man I met over coffee and cake was John B. Wadley, who had been writing about European cycling since 1934, serving the previous 12 years as editor of Sporting Cyclist, a monthly magazine he founded in the mid-1950s.

Like JBW—as he was known—I had fallen in love with continental bike racing in my late-teens, and crossed the English Channel to see the Tour de France (in 1963). I then raced for a couple of summers with a small team in Brittany, but ended up making as much money writing freelance articles for cycling magazines as I did from winning prize money at the tough races in France. One of those magazines I sent stories to was Sporting Cyclist.

At the 1968 interview, JBW told me that his magazine had just been acquired by a big publishing house, and it would be merged with another title. He didn't want the offered position as editor of the combined weekly, and he said he was going to start a new monthly, to be called International Cycle Sport. Between bites of cake, he asked me if I wanted to be his assistant on a two-man editorial team. "We can't pay much," he added. "It would only be £30 a week."

I was making twice that as an engineer, but I knew that writing about the sport of cycling was something I wanted to do for a living. Within seconds, I had accepted his offer . . . and minutes later, I had my first assignment: "Go to the Continent with your bike and bring back some stories."

Well, I went to the Continent, brought back some stories . . . and that's what I've been doing ever since. This book is one of the results.

For "World of Cycling," I've chosen 22 stories written over the past 30 years; stories that I hope will enhance your understanding and appreciation of competitive cycling—its drama, demands and diversity . . . its history, athleticism and tactics. On traveling around Europe, and later to other continents, I discovered why cycling, after soccer, is the world's most popular sport.

As far as I know, there has never been a book that looks at and explores the many facets of competitive cycling. I've tried to do that here. Not included are the more obscure bicycle-related activities—cycling acrobatics, cycle-ball and trials; and my contact with BMX and down-hilling has been limited. But in the following pages I have included stories on all the other elements that make cycling such a fascinating sport: classic road racing, stage racing, time trialing, championship track racing, hour record attempts, cyclo-cross, six-day racing and mountain-bike cross-country—with the emphasis on the sport's heritage: European road racing.

The book is laid out as a year in cycling, starting in January with an hour record attempt in Mexico, and ending in November with a six-day race in Switzerland. In between, I will take you through the gamut of cycle sport: early-season European road races; English time trials, the spring classics; the grand Tours; world championships in road, track and mountain biking; Olympic Games; and cyclo-cross. The stories are from four different decades, but the thread is the same: This is a sport about people and places, rather than stats and salaries.

Inside, you will find different pieces about the four riders who each won five Tours de France: Jacques Anquetil in the 1960s, Eddy Merckx in the '70s, Bernard Hinault in the '80s and Miguel Induráin in the '90s. There's one story about the very first European race to be contested by an American professional team, 7-Eleven, which was headed by sprinter Davis Phinney; and another about that same squad's success three years later, led by climber Andy Hampsten, at the Tour of Italy (also known as the Giro d'Italia). You'll find a report on Greg LeMond's magnificent world championship in 1989; and on Lance Armstrong's superb U.S. pro title race at Philadelphia in 1993.

Britain's greatest cyclist, Tom Simpson, died at the Tour the year before I began chronicling the sport, but I've included here the moving story of another outstanding British rider of the post-war era, Robert Millar, who rode brilliantly at the 1985 Tour of Spain, in his battle to win the yellow jersey. Irish stars Sean Kelly and Stephen Roche have their place in the book, as do mountain-bike legends Ned Overend and Juli Furtado, six-day standouts Tony Doyle and Danny Clark, and European racers as varied as 1960s standout Belgian Herman Van Springel and present-day German star Jan Ullrich.

Inevitably, I've had to leave out as much as I've included. The biggest classics are here, with detailed accounts of a particularly remarkable Milan-San Remo, Paris-Roubaix and Tour of Lombardy; but the Tour of Flanders, Liège-Bastogne-Liège and Paris-Tours will have to wait for another volume.

Three of the early stories, as JBW requested, were the result of long bike trips: one to the Mediterranean island of Sardinia in late winter; a second to central France in the spring; and a third to Czechoslovakia in mid-summer. Those trips were among the most memorable I've taken. But whenever there is a bike race to watch, examine and write about, whatever the discipline, I still get excited. I hope you do, too.

—*John Wilcockson*
*July 1999*

# THE MAGIC HOUR

**World
Hour
Record
Attempt**

Mexico
January 1994

In the world of cycling, no record is regarded more highly than the world hour record—one man, racing alone on a banked velodrome, attempting to ride farther in 60 minutes than any cyclist before him. The standard was first set in Paris on May 11, 1893, by Henri Desgrange, the Frenchman who would later found the Tour de France. His distance was 35.325 kilometers. A century later, the record stood to a 24-year-old Englishman, Chris Boardman, who rode 52.270 kilometers on an indoor track in Bordeaux, France. This was the mark being attempted in January 1994 by a former holder of the record, Francesco Moser of Italy ... but Moser was now 42 years old!

# Mexico

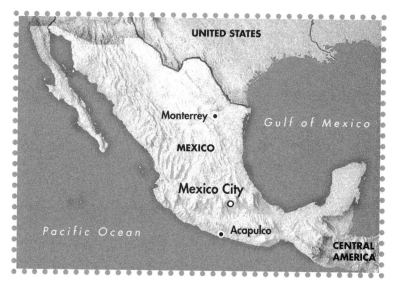

**Olympic Training Center Velodrome, Mexico City**

JUST AFTER MIDDAY on January 15, 1994, a magician was standing at a red light on Mexico City's tree-lined Paseo de la Reforma, performing a trick in front of traffic waiting for the lights to change. He held up a black velvet bag, in which he placed a white ball. Before the lights changed, and with the hope of making a peso or two, the magician had made the ball disappear. It wasn't a great trick, but it needed courage and enterprise to perform—and he did it with considerable panache.

Those same qualities were displayed an hour or so earlier by Francesco Moser, who showed in 60 minutes of racing around the 333.3-meter concrete velodrome at Mexico's Olympic Training Center that even at age 42, and five years into his retirement from competitive cycling, he had lost none of his magic.

The audacity of Moser's 10th anniversary expedition to Mexico City cannot be emphasized too much. In the past, only athletes who were at their prime—or close to it—have attacked the ultimate cycling record. In 100 years, only 22 men have been successful. And the hour-record trail is littered with failed attempts. Why then would Moser come out of a five-year retirement to compare himself, once more, with giants of the sport like Eddy Merckx, Jacques Anquetil, Ercole Baldini and Fausto Coppi?

Since his two successful attempts in January 1984—when he rode 50.808 and 51.151 kilometers in the space of five days—Moser's body weight has decreased from 76 kilograms (167.2 pounds) to 73 kilograms (160.6 pounds); his body fat has increased from just over 5 percent to just under 9 percent; and his anaerobic threshold has decreased from 180 to 170 beats per minute. The only statistic that is still

*World Hour Record Attempt • Mexico• 1994*

the same is height of 1.82 meters (half an inch under 6 feet). Knowing these parameters, however, Moser was still brave enough to expose himself to the powerful glare of media publicity that was inevitably going to follow him to Mexico.

So why did he do it? Well, it started as a private challenge about 18 months ago when Moser was out riding near his home in northern Italy with his friend Professor Francesco Conconi. While climbing the Stelvio Pass, the professor of biochemistry was impressed that the former superstar was still in good shape. Conconi was interested to see if a body, 10 years after its prime, would be able to perform at a level even close to its former maximum. To find out, the friends decided to return to Mexico City and see if Moser could get close to what then was still his world record of 51.151 kilometers.

Even though Moser and Conconi had pioneered the use of disc wheels and heart-rate monitors, they knew that vast technological strides had been made in a decade: wind-tunnel testing has helped create the aero' bar and more-aerodynamic composite wheels; more efficient, clipless pedals have been invented; and heart-rate-monitor training has been perfected. However, could a man of 42 even consider racing again at a level close to what is humanly possible?

That question took on even greater significance when, last summer, first Scotsman Graeme Obree (in his new-fangled riding style), then English rival Boardman (with the ultimate in aero-bar technology)—both men in their mid-20s—raised the hour barrier by 345 meters and 1119 meters respectively. People wondered whether Moser would call off the 10th anniversary project; but the Italian became even more determined to put his reputation on the line.

As an athlete, Moser developed a strict training program with Conconi; as a technology freak, he made tests to deter-

**THE MAGIC HOUR**

mine that the Obree position would prove faster for him than a Boardman bike; and as a bicycle constructor, he went through an evolution of 10 different designs to arrive at the sophisticated "Obree" bikes that he transported to Mexico for tests in early December 1993. Given all that, he still knew that he was taking a huge gamble.

The cost of this fairytale project had taken on larger dimensions. And unlike 1984, he couldn't convince Italian television to cough up the close-to-one-million-dollars it paid to broadcast his hour record attempt. This time, Moser had to settle for about $165,000 offered by the Monte Carlo TV station. Then a pasta company, Barilla, signed up as the main sponsor—but was this far short of the budget provided 10 years ago by the Italian nutrition company, Enervit. Only when Moser finally showed that he was serious, in the week before his January 15 deadline, did Enervit finally come through with some financial support.

In that final week, after six weeks in Mexico—including a week at the high-altitude training facility in Toluca—Moser made a trial run. For 26 minutes, he averaged a speed of 52.304 kph. He and Conconi knew that Boardman's record of 52.270 kilometers was within their grasp....

Then, the day before Moser's attempt, their "guinea pig" Vanni Sanna, a category-four Italian amateur riding one of the Obree bikes, did a trial one-hour attempt. Sanna rode a remarkable 50.205 kilometers in perfect, cool, calm conditions. The whole Moser entourage was hoping for similar, if a little warmer, weather on the morning of Saturday, January 15. It was warmer all right, but only because the sun broke through earlier, when a breeze cleared the Mexico City smog. A breeze could ruin the attempt.

By 9:30 a.m.—when an accordionist set a festive mood for the fans filling the stands of the small, attractive Mexico

*World Hour Record Attempt • Mexico• 1994*

Olympic Committee velodrome—the temperature was 56 degrees F., the humidity 60 percent, and the wind 0.21 meters per second (0.75 kph). It was looking good.

Because of the TV contract, the record attempt was not scheduled until 11:15 a.m. (or 6:15 p.m. in Italy), but Conconi was eager to take advantage of the good conditions at the earliest opportunity. There was the chance of starting a half-hour before schedule, but not earlier, as the blue-painted portion of the track would not dry out before 10:30 a.m.

At 9:36 a.m., Moser emerged from the locker rooms, striding up to the trackside like a gladiator ready for battle. He was wearing training gear and helmet. He seemed nervous ... which was a good sign.

After talking briefly to the driver of his pacing motorcycle, the greying, back-again racer began his warm-up. For 20 minutes behind the moto, he was lapping the 333.33-meter track at a steady 22 to 23 seconds (between 53 and 54 kph). He stopped at 10 a.m.

Ten minutes later, after chatting with Conconi—who had been timing the laps, while his mechanic put in the record attempt wheels (a rear disc and a deep-rim front with bladed spokes)—Moser, still wearing tights, began his final warm-up, without the motorpace.

By now, the temperature had risen to 61 degrees, the humidity hadn't changed, and the wind had risen to 0.59 meters per second (2.12 kph). Despite the increased wind, Moser was looking good on his magenta-colored, Obree-style bike. He warmed up for another 10 minutes, doing a few laps at 22 seconds, or 54.5 kph. There was an expectation that the world record was truly within the veteran's grasp. It was an observation shared by one of the Italian's helpers, who enthused, "This is one of the great moments of our lives."

**THE MAGIC HOUR**

By now, the stands had filled; and there were just as many people on the infield, including Boardman's team director Roger Legeay, Miguel Induráin's coach José Miguel Echavarri, fellow racer Claudio Chiappucci and former record holder Ercole Baldini. Everyone was talking of the possibilities of the morning, while Moser disappeared to the locker rooms before reappearing, to take off his tights, don his white aero' helmet, and begin a final warm-up.

It was 10:35 a.m. The temperature had crept up to 63 degrees, the humidity was down to 55 percent and the wind was still the same, about 2 kph. Moser rode for another seven minutes, while Conconi told reporters that he had scheduled the record attempt at between 22.8 and 22.9 seconds per lap, for a distance of about 52.5 kilometers.

At 10:42 a.m., Moser stopped at the start-finish point, drank a small Enervit energy drink and then a swig of fluid-replacement drink. He adjusted his helmet and sunglasses, and at 10:43 a.m., as the crowd hushed, he accelerated slowly away, standing on the pedals to turn his 62x15 gear. Starting is painfully slow on an Obree-style bike ... until the rider leans far forward in the extreme, aerodynamic tuck.

After the un-aerodynamic first lap of 30.72 seconds, Moser settled in to an incredible rhythm, completing his third lap as fast as 22.14 seconds. In the next 25 laps, his slowest was 22.88 seconds, all ahead of schedule. The Italian zoomed through the first five kilometers in 5:47.85— seven-tenths of a second better than Boardman. At 10 kilometers, his 11:29.29 was 1.5 seconds ahead of the British record holder. And at the 15-kilometer mark, Moser's 17:12.31 was still 1.1 seconds up on Boardman.

But now, the effort of combating the gusting wind was clearly upsetting the former champion. He was already gritting his teeth, and a couple of laps of just over 23 seconds

*World Hour Record Attempt • Mexico• 1994*

crept onto his log sheet. It was becoming obvious that a breeze of 2 kph was probably going to slow Moser by as much as a kilometer over the full 60 minutes.

This became very clear when his 20-kilometer time was noted—22:58.64, 2.2 seconds slower than Boardman (although 23 seconds faster than Obree). Neither of the two Britons had had to contend with wind in their indoor attempts ... although neither had the advantage of making their attempts at Mexico City's 7000-foot altitude.

Moser was not going to give up easily, however. The 42-year-old was now lapping outside the crucial 23 seconds, but tried to lift himself during the 28th kilometer, which he completed in 1:08.76, with laps of 22.86, 22.98 and 22.78 seconds. But the wind was too much and the effort too great. "At 40 kph, such a wind would be no problem," Moser observed later, "but not at 52 kph."

For the last half-hour, the fans were on their feet—chanting, clapping, cheering and waving flags—hoping to shout their man to the now seemingly impossible goal. Their support did help carry Moser onward, but only three more of his kilometer times dipped below 1:09 ... including a final one that featured a remarkable last lap of 22.22 seconds.

The Italian's final distance of 51.840 kilometers was still remarkable, the second-fastest ever, and a distance that is unlikely to be bettered by any cyclist over 40 years old. On coming to a halt, Moser was engulfed by a mob of reporters and photographers toting TV cameras and microphones. It was just like the old Moser-fever days, when he was winning Paris-Roubaix, the Giro d'Italia and Milan-San Remo. In the middle of the scrimmage, Moser calmly answered an Italian commentator, on the live feed to Europe: "I knew I had to go faster, but I couldn't."

**THE MAGIC HOUR**

However, the legendary Italian had beaten by more than two laps his 1984 mark of 51.151 kilometers; he was almost a lap ahead of Obree's record of last July ... and only a lap short of record holder Boardman.

In a press conference that followed, Moser answered every question with candor and humor. When asked if this attempt was more difficult than his hour-record performances of 10 years ago, he replied, "All the other times, I finished by breaking the record. Not today ... so it was not as difficult."

Conconi was more forthcoming. The respected training guru said, "The point is that his aerobic power is good, but his aerobic endurance is not so good. There is a difference between the two, and he lacks some endurance. He said that this was the last time he would race, so there were no gadgets, no heart-rate monitor, no nothing...."

Asked about the Obree position, Conconi said, "There is reduced power, and the power transmitted to the pedals is less, but the aerodynamics is the difference. This position is much more aerodynamic."

. It was hoped that this wind-affected attempt would help Moser in a second attempt four days later. But despite an earlier start, the wind was even worse, gusting to more than 3 kph. Moser did a faster opening kilometer, but he was slower from then on, and came to a halt after 11 minutes. The crowds applauded their hero for his bravado, but no more would we see any magic from maestro Moser.

# THE SEASON OPENS

## Étoile de Bessèges

## France
## February 1985

Opening day of the European road racing season is traditionally in the south of France, at the Étoile de Bessèges, literally the "Star of Bessèges," a five-day race in the barren countryside east and south of the Cévennes mountains. The race resembles spring training rather than mainstream action, but in 1985 it was a big deal for the American-based 7-Eleven team. Not only was it the team's first race in Europe, it also marked the debut of the first-ever U.S. professional cycling team.

# France

Clermont-Ferrand •

Lyon •

**FRANCE**

Bessèges O

• Nîmes

Avignon
•

Lunel O

Montpellier •

Marseille
•

Perpignan •

IT WAS APPROACHING midnight in the tiled and timbered, geometrically contoured bar of the four-star hotel at Le Rouret, an immense sports and leisure complex that sprawls across a rocky, arid hillside in the Ardèche region of southern France. Sitting comfortably at a low, thick coffee table was a young man whose bulging thighs showed prominently through his cherry-red warm-up suit. Recently washed, straight fair hair was brushed across his tanned temples. Over-large, fashionable spectacles accentuated his friendly eyes.

"I can't sleep," said the American, whose identity was revealed as Davis Phinney by the discreet 7-Eleven logo on his back and his famed, well-developed thigh muscles. A few hours before, Phinney had contested a pack sprint for the first time as a professional cyclist. He did not win the finish sprint to the first stage of the Étoile de Bessèges at Lunel, a small wine-producing town close to the Mediterranean coast, and he was not credited with the seventh place in which he had crossed the line. But he was as happy as if he had just won a world championship—or any one of those hundreds of victories that regularly punctuated his amateur career.

Moments after the stage finish, Phinney exclaimed, "A pack sprint finish charges me up. That's what bike racing is all about to me." His eyes were still sparkling from the genuine thrill of sprinting against riders such as Belgians Eric Vanderaerden and Eddy Planckaert, two of the fastest finishers in pro racing. His words confirmed the impression.

"I'm really excited about it," Phinney continued. "I've been building up for 10 years for this trip. I'm just glad to be over here. I love pro racing. For 80 to 90 kilometers you get warmed up, and then it just speeds up until the last sprint.

*Étoile de Bessèges • France • 1985*

"But it was impossible today, competing against the Panasonics. There are 14 of them and only eight of us. Ron Hayman was great. I just got in behind him with a lap to go, but I was left on my own in the last two kilometers. I had a Panasonic rider on both sides, just boffing me. They were saying, 'It's going to be a pack finish, and Phinney's a sprinter. We have to watch him.' My gear was slipping on the 12 sprocket, so I had to sprint on the 13. But it probably made no difference. Vanderaerden was second at the last turn, and another Panasonic rider about four places back eased off and left a huge gap. And that was it," concluded the American.

Another factor he didn't mention until that evening was the bandages he had worn on the two small fingers of his right hand. "I broke them both two weeks ago training in Sacramento. I fell; it was stupid to crash out training."

Phinney was to continue his first pro stage race with placings of fifth and fourth, to be the leading 7-Eleven rider on overall time. He learns quickly, and this is what has made the Boulder, Colorado resident such a successful sprint finisher, and took him to a bronze medal in the 1984 Los Angeles Olympics. But how did he and the 7-Eleven team come to be racing at the start of the European season as full-fledged professionals?

"We had planned to turn pro right after the Olympics," said Phinney, who looked relaxed in an environment that is more familiar to seasoned European riders such as Laurent Fignon, Phil Anderson or Pascal Simon, who were also staying at Le Rouret and were already in bed, probably asleep. "But the Olympics were such a big deal, and such a big ordeal, that we decided to delay things," Phinney explained. "There were receptions for Olympic medalists all over the country. Traveling so much made it difficult to concentrate on training.

 **THE SEASON OPENS**

"Then the threat by the USCF [U.S. Cycling Federation] to stop open racing caused a delay. We eventually filled out applications on the morning of the late January meeting of the USCF board of directors. And now there's a very full season of racing for us in America."

Bike racing is a subject close to his heart—next to his Olympic champion wife, Connie Carpenter—and the 7-Eleven professional talked about it with enthusiasm: "It's everyone's dream to race as a pro in Europe. And here we are doing it on an American team. That's something special. It's not been done before."

Earlier, over a cup of strong coffee in the hotel's pastel pink dining area, Jim Ochowicz, general manager of the various 7-Eleven cycling teams—pro, women and juniors—provided further background on this pioneering trip: "The Southland Corporation [owner of 7-Eleven] is dedicated to cycling. It is developing the sport on all levels, including the top end. This is our fifth year as a team, and it is an inevitable stage in our development to have a fully professional team."

"We have waited until we could do it right," Ochowicz stressed, "and we are doing it right. It depends on how we do on this trip as to when we come back next to Europe. But we will definitely be coming back for an extended stay for the world championships. We may even fit in another trip mid-season." Pressed about his long-term plans, Ochowicz said, "As for the Tour de France, we won't ride it until we can be fully competitive. That will more likely be in 1987 than 1986."

The present limitations in the team's organization and composition were evident in this initial European campaign. To compete in continental classics and stage races, it is necessary to have at least eight riders; to realize this, Ochowicz had to co-opt two G.S. Mengoni riders, Matt Eaton and

*Étoile de Bessèges • France • 1985*

Richard Scibird, who took part in last year's Tour de l'Avenir. For team backup, the squad's Belgian directeur sportif, Richard Dejonckheere, had signed up two Flemish soigneurs and a mechanic. At the last moment he contacted a second mechanic, Englishman Steve Snowling, who had been left without a job when the winter's last six-day race was canceled.

Snowling, a former pro cyclo-cross rider, spoke about his first day with the 7-Eleven team. "Luckily, we had only one wheel to change," he noted. "When I was running toward the rider, I could see him shaking and I thought, 'There could be some problems here,' even though it was a front wheel. He was so anxious that he put his forks through the spokes as I started to put the wheel in. I had to pull his bike up quickly."

On another day, Snowling was amazed by the laid-back attitude of Jeff Bradley, after the tall blond rider from Ohio had crashed on the descent of a long, winding pass in the Cévennes mountain chain. The front forks of his bike were bent 20 degrees out of line by the impact, but Bradley was unhurt.

"He was more concerned with the rider who knocked him off," said Snowling. "Bradley was asking if the other guy was all right. He didn't seem concerned about himself. A European would have just grabbed the spare bike and chased the peloton. But Bradley was more worried about the height of his saddle being right than getting back to the bunch."

Adjusting to the pace of European pro racing is bound to be difficult for an American team. Shipping a support vehicle, bikes and the equipment needed for a nine-man team is no simple matter. (Eric Heiden would join the eight others midway through this first trip.)

**THE SEASON OPENS**

The red Murray bicycles the team had brought from America were well-finished, sturdy machines, but there had not been time to check all of them before traveling. Canadian Ron Hayman's bike was slightly too big; and Snowling described how he had had to file away part of the stem, using calipers and a vernier scale to keep it true, to allow the handlebars to be placed low enough. "Also the wheel clearances were a little too tight," added the experienced British mechanic. "I had to drop the front wheels on two of the bikes."

For an extended stay in Europe, a team needs a lot of equipment. Most of the teams competing at Bessèges had two bikes for each rider, up to four team cars, long-wheelbase vans, and perhaps a bus large enough to carry the whole team and their bikes. In contrast, this first 7-Eleven Euro' team had one bike per rider (plus a few spares), a small equipment van, one car borrowed from the race organizers and another car driven from Belgium. But judging by the professional attitude of the riders and the team personnel, increased backing should be available for their next trip.

The continental teams are furnished with vehicles by Mercedes-Benz (Panasonic), Saab (Fagor), Citroën (Skil), Renault and Peugeot. Motor manufacturers can get year-long exposure to the massive crowds that line race routes throughout Europe. As Ochowicz commented after the first stage of the Étoile de Bessèges, "There's a bike race going on in the front, and a high-speed motor rally at the back."

Wherever they went during the five-day French stage race, the 7-Eleven team received close attention from the public and media alike. A television film crew from the Catalonia region of Spain taped a special report on the team, filming at the hotel and conducting interviews with the Spanish-speaking riders. With such publicity, it should be

*Étoile de Bessèges • France • 1985*

easy to procure the extra sponsorship needed to integrate the team with the European circuit. But the initial aim, as Ochowicz said repeatedly, is to be fully competitive.

They were not without an advantage. Several weeks of training in the California sunshine, sometimes with Greg LeMond, gave the eight Bessèges pioneers a distinct edge on the Europeans, many of whom had ridden less than 1000 kilometers before the race. The Americans' tans and sun-bleached hair made them stand out in the pack. Their early-season campaign was due to end with the 294-kilometer Milan-San Remo classic in mid-March. "That's not a race we expect to win, but we will be building up the miles before it," said Ochowicz. "The riders will be training before and after the races, and in the week before Milan-San Remo comes the Tirreno-Adriatico stage race. We will be ready."

Most of the riders have had extensive experience racing in European amateur stage races on the U.S. national team. The two oldest members—Ron Hayman, 30, and Tom Schuler, 28—have competed in Belgium, where Hayman once rode for a small pro team.

Besides Phinney, the most impressive 7-Eleven performance in the Étoile de Bessèges came from Ron Kiefel, the 6-foot Colorado native. He was prominent in the race's two hilliest stages, with a number of solo attacks on the steepest climbs. When he learns to adapt his enthusiasm and skill to the continental style of racing, he will be a force in any hilly race.

With frequent visits to Europe, together with an American season based on the Tour of Texas, Coors Classic and other events in the 7-Eleven Cup Series, these riders are getting the best of both worlds. It has often been the aim of English-speaking riders to form a pro team of their own in Europe. But until this move by 7-Eleven, the only non-con-

**THE SEASON OPENS**

tinental pro squad to race in Europe was sponsored by a British bicycle manufacturer, Hercules; the team that took part in the 1955 Tour de France.

Thirty years later, the economics and the focus of pro bike racing have changed drastically. Having a team commute across the Atlantic to compete would once have seemed only a dream. Today, it is a real adventure, one that Phinney and friends are pleased to be a part of.

Before returning to his room at Le Rouret, Phinney informed us of some of the other advantages of being an American on an American pro team. His wife was to join him at Palermo during the Tour of Sicily, and she planned to remain with the team through Milan-San Remo. "That's part of the deal of being a pro with 7-Eleven," said Phinney "not like the national amateur team trips, when I'd be away for six weeks and not see Connie."

He could have added that wives are frowned upon in the presence of European pro teams. Last year, Phil Anderson had to get permission from his directeur sportif before he could dine with his wife on the rest day of the Tour de France. The 7-Eleven team is changing these traditional codes of practice, both on and off the bike.

It was past midnight before Davis Phinney was tired enough for sleep. Outside, a pale, almost full moon had risen above the jagged silhouette of the Ardèche hills. Tomorrow, there would be another pack sprint in another town. Another opportunity, perhaps, to beat the Panasonics.

*Étoile de Bessèges • France • 1985*

# ISLAND OF DREAMS

## Giro di Sardegna
## Italy
## February 1969

One of the wildest corners of Europe is Sardinia, territorially part of Italy, but historically an island closer to Africa than Europe, and peopled by Iberians and Phoenicians rather than Italians and French. It has notoriety for bandits in the mountains, and is famed for its beautiful scenery. In the summer, it welcomes a growing numbers of tourists; but in the late winter of 1969 it played host to Europe's top professional cyclists—at the Giro di Sardegna, Italy's first race of the new season.

# Sardinia

FRANCE

Genoa

Nice

Livorno

ITALY

CORSICA

Bonifacio

Olbia

Rome

Sassari

Nuoro

SARDINIA

Cagliari

*Mediterranean*

*Sea*

SINCE CHILDHOOD, the name of Sardinia has held a special fascination for me, a place of mystery and imagination. And so it was with a definite air of excitement that I boarded a huge white ship in the darkened harbor at Nice, France on Friday, February 21, 1969. There was a cold nip in the air as the appropriately named "Napoleon" steamed slowly out into the night—destination Ajaccio, capital of Corsica and first stop on my way to Sardinia.

The night was as black as ebony, so I soon tired of looking out over the dank waters of the Ligurian Sea to the already distant lights of the French coast, and went below decks to my allotted berth. Sleep was only intermittent and I was glad when it was time to climb the stairs again, to find the first light of a new day beginning to creep into the sky.

The silently throbbing ship was already slipping effortlessly into the Gulf of Ajaccio … and what a view! Corsica is smaller, and even more rugged, than Sardinia. The eastern sky was a riot of bold reds and blues, gradually raising the orange tints of the sun over a skyline of snow-capped peaks as jagged as can exist anywhere. The mountains rise to well over 8000 feet, on an island no more than 30 miles across. Not surprisingly, it has become a paradise island for the French, and in winter is particularly popular with skiers.

I would have loved to join the tourists, but I had to reach Sardinia that evening; and I found out that the only means was by a small ferry that afternoon from Bonifacio, the southernmost town on the island, some 80 miles away. It may have been possible to reach there in time by bike, yet I knew from the map that the road climbed and descended from sea level to over 2000 feet on three occasions in the 80 miles. I was told that a bus was leaving from around the corner at 7:45 a.m.—so bus it was.

*Giro di Sardegna • Italy • 1969*

With my bike strapped on the roof alongside a car's exhaust system bound for a Bonifacio garage, we were soon bumping our way past the docks and up the hill past the isolated soccer pitch (French Division One). The near-five-hour journey was one of those experiences of a lifetime, as the driver proceeded to fling the long vehicle around the never-ending series of bends with reckless abandon. Traffic was almost nonexistent; therefore, it mattered little if blind bends were taken on the wrong side of the road, although the driver reassured himself with the occasional blast on the horn. At times, nothing could be seen from the side window except the distant prospect of cork oak and scrub far below in the valley. On the long climb to the Col St. Georges (2451 feet), we had a dice with an overloaded lorry, the driver inching his way by, up the narrow road. At one point we took to a dirt track, climbing up to a small dead-end village, that was like something out of the Wild West.

There were also some outstanding views, as when descending toward the turquoise waters of the Gulf of Valinco. At Propriano, there was a longer halt than at most towns, because the load in the back of the bus—about 30 ornate wreaths, standing four or five feet high—had to be transferred to the undertaker's office. And a little later on I had to climb up on the roof again, to pass down my bike and the exhaust system, to put them on a new bus; the other one turned off to Porto Vecchio. We eventually came to a halt besides the little port of Bonifacio at 12:30 p.m., just a couple of hours before the Sardinia ferry was due to leave.

Drizzle had fallen for most of the morning, but it had now cleared and there was a lunchtime calm in the air. The old town of Bonifacio stands proudly atop a 200-foot-high ridge of undercut limestone cliffs that separate the long, narrow harbor from the sea. The silence was broken only by the

**ISLAND OF DREAMS**

breeze rippling the water, or the bark of a dog echoing around the white cliffs.

The fare across to Sardinia, including the bike, was just $2, leaving me about 40 francs to change into lire. The snag was that there was no bank; but I was directed to Colombo's grocery store as likely to undertake the transaction! That done, it was full-steam ahead on the ferry boat across the straits of Bonifacio. The sun had come through, and a stiff breeze was lifting the clouds from the distant peaks of my island of dreams: Sardinia.

It took 50 minutes to reach San Teresa Gallura, and at last I was awheel on a smooth road headed for Olbia, on the east coast of the island. The first impression was of an almost deserted landscape, with wide grassy plains and jutting rocks and boulders worn into odd shapes by centuries of wind. Occasional hamlets added to the frontier feeling, with their motley collection of shacks and children playing in the road. And the motorists were obviously not used to meeting other traffic, as their method of driving was to speed down the very middle of the road, only making for the side when another vehicle was about to meet them from the other direction!

It was dark when I reached Olbia, where all of its 12,000 population seemed to be out walking the streets—a custom more common in Spain than in Italy. They were still walking up and down when I went out after finding a room, and having had a wash and change. I bought a newspaper, went for a meal, and when I came out of the restaurant everyone had disappeared, leaving the cobbled streets deserted. And it was still before 10 p.m. I was to find that Sardinia was indeed full of surprises!

In the paper I had seen the details for the Giro di Sardegna that was due to start on the morrow. That day,

*Giro di Sardegna • Italy • 1969*

there had been the 20th annual cycling classic from Sassari to Cagliari, the only major cities on the island; all the Tour teams were down to ride the event. I learned next day that world champion Vittorio Adorni had succeeded in this first important race of the Italian season, a race that was just a high-speed romp down the only real motor road on the island, 140 miles long.

The Tour itself was to last seven days, the final two being on the mainland, to finish at Rome. For the first time, a time trial stage was to be included in the event, and this would be from Sassari to Porto Torres on the last day on the island. Most of the big names were on the list of starters—except for Eddy Merckx, although his Faema team was there. Rik Van Looy has been a "regular" in Sardinia, but he had pulled out at the last minute, and taken the rest of his team with him.

Ten Italian teams had entered, with such names as Adorni and Adriano Durante (Scic), Franco Balmamion and Dino Zandegu (Salvarani), Michele Dancelli and Giancarlo Polidori (Molteni), Franco Bitossi and Italo Zilioli (Filotex), Gianni Motta (Sanson), Claudio Michelotto (Max Meyer), Ole Ritter (Germanvox), Imerio Massignan and Aldo Moser (GBC) and Giuseppe Beghetto (Ferretti). In the foreign teams were stars such as Jacques Anquetil and Jan Janssen (Bic), Guido Reybroeck and Martin Van den Bossche (Faema), Derek Harrison and Jean Jourden (Frimatic) and Walter Godefroot (Flandria). Quite a line up for the first big race of the year, although the majority would be using it only as their preparation for later events like Paris-Nice.

First stage of the Tour was to be a flat 115 kilometers (72 miles) from Oristano, on the other side of the island, to Cagliari (again) on the south coast. I would be joining up with the route at the end of the second day at Lanusei … and that meant "my" first stage would be over 100 miles

**ISLAND OF DREAMS**

long, and would take in the 3300-foot Genna Silana climb. I reckon the professionals had the easier task! And, in fact, I learned next day that stage one had been rather surprisingly taken by three-time world track sprint champion Giuseppe Beghetto, fresh from the Milan Six.

My stage start at Olbia is the main center of the Costa Smerelda, a coastline of exquisite beauty dotted with luxury hotels, all built as a millionaire's paradise. This was why the roads were so well surfaced, I presumed, because as I headed south the road surface gradually deteriorated. The first 40 miles were pleasant enough, the road playing hide-and-seek with the sea, with the scene dominated for some time by the 1850-foot-high mass of the Isle of Tavolara, that rises straight out of the water. Before Siniscola, I turned left on to a side road, just as the sun came through after an overcast morning. I stopped awhile at the little coastal village of la Caletta, completely unspoiled, with its own sandy beach and the distant view of mountains inland. It was difficult to remember that it was still February!

It was clear why Sardinia is chosen for the season-opener, and tales of ice and snow when Merckx won the race a year before seemed difficult to believe.

Contrarily, it started to rain within a few kilometers, and my yellow plastic cape was on as I dropped down to Orosei, an oasis of green fields and orange groves in a land of bare moorland and mountains. This was where the climbing began, and I was soon more than 800 feet up, looking down to the sea far below. The weather cleared for a time, but after the hill through Dorgali, the clouds closed about me for the rest of the 15 miles of anti-gravity work to the Genna Silana summit.

By now, it was late afternoon: The Tour riders would have finished their stint for the day. For me, though, the bat-

*Giro di Sardegna • Italy • 1969*

tle against the elements was still in progress. The mist was such that it occasionally drifted from the roadside pine trees to reveal a deep valley on my right, with impressive crags beyond. But the most memorable scene came a few minutes after the tumbling descent had begun. I had just topped a small crest, when through a freak break in the cloud, I looked down to a brilliantly green valley, some 1500 feet below, which was just like a corner of Switzerland with its own village and cultivated fields. Just as quickly, the dream-like image was gone, as I plunged into a thick bank of cloud. I looked the place up on the map that evening, and found the little "Garden of Eden" was called Urzulei, 20 miles up in the barren mountains.

The surprises were not yet over for the day, and just before sweeping down the last series of bends on wet roads, I passed through the almost medieval village of Baunei, clinging to the rocky mountainside. I was looking into the distance (I had hardly seen a car all day), toward the coastal plain and the sun setting over the hills to the right. It was a picture of incredible beauty, but suddenly I was pulling on the brake levers; the road was completely blocked. It was Sunday, and the whole town was climbing the road toward the church, led by nuns and old women in black with shawls over their heads. It was just like another world up there.

Down below, it was warm and dark, and I was glad to find a large hotel at Tortoli called the Victoria. The manager said it would be filled next day with teams and officials of the Giro di Sardegna, but I almost had it to myself that night, and I have rarely appreciated a hot shower as much. It had been quite a day.

Stage two of the Tour was to finish at Lanusei, only seven miles away (13 by road) but 2000 feet higher. It would be a tough stage finish, and the Italian sports papers were

 **ISLAND OF DREAMS**

predicting a battle between Bitossi and Gilbert Bellone, the Frenchman who had just won the G.P. de Cannes on the Riviera; both of them are noted *escaladeurs*. From Cagliari, the race would cover 80 undulating miles, before reaching the final 11-mile climb.

Thankfully, I had only the climb to do, and it was delightful to sit awhile in the warm sunshine sheltered from the breeze. I was in a little valley, with Lanusei visible on the hillside high above. There had been more orange trees growing near Tortoli, but here there was only scrubby grass, with children looking after the occasional flock of mountain sheep. A bullock cart rocked along a stony track to a distant house, and yesterday's rain grumbled angrily down the wide bed of the Corongiu creek.

Lanusei was an odd place for a stage finish in an important international stage race, being no more than a village, although it did have a bank and a hotel. When I arrived, the finish *banderole* was being strung up just up the road from the hotel, and a quantity of fencing had been erected as crowd barriers. I found out that the race was being sponsored by the newspaper *Il Giorno di Italia,* and organized by the Audax Cagliari club.

The town was an odd collection of ancient pastel-washed buildings, with new, often only half-completed blocks of flats littered down the hillside. A narrow-gauge railway clung to the contours, and donkeys grazed on rough ground next to terraced vineyards. It was lunch time when I arrived and a line of students was ambling back from their place of learning. Seeing a stranger, one of them stopped to try out his French on me. His name was Bruno, and he said he would help me find somewhere to stay for the night.

We went along to the hotel, which was booked with race personnel, but one of the waiters knew of a vacant room

*Giro di Sardegna • Italy • 1969*

in the town. So he went out to his car, and told me to follow him on my bike. The destination was at the other end of the town, an old building; but the room turned out to be clean and modern, and when I opened the shutters, there was a wonderful view to the east, right down to the sea where I had stayed the night before.

The people of Sardinia are certainly very friendly, not having to rush about to the demands of the modern world; and I was to find this out again the next day, very much to my benefit!

Lanusei was now ready to greet the Tour of Sardinia. There were dozens of posters up saying: "Long live the journalists" ... "Long live the Tour of Sardinia." People were streaming up the hill from the town center to the finishing area, although the older citizens—grizzled gents in gossip groups and black-clothed ladies in ankle-length garb—were content to watch the world go by from their habitual haunts on stone steps and shop doors. Leather-booted Polizia Stradale were roaring up and down on motorcycles, ensuring that the roadway was completely clear.

There was also a considerable publicity caravan, with the rival firms of Salvarani and Scic (pronounced Shick) advertising their kitchen fittings; Faema, their coffee machines; Ferretti, their furniture; Max Meyer, their paints.... And finally, it was time the race itself was due.

From the loudspeakers I knew that two men were 22 seconds up on the bunch, with 5 kilometers to go. And in no time, those two figures emerged from the main part of the town below, one in the orange Bic jersey (Bellone), and the other wearing the brown of Molteni. This was Polidori, the young Italian who had worn the *maillot jaune* of the Tour de France at Amiens in 1967. The uphill sprint should have been a cinch for Frenchman Bellone, but when Polidori

**ISLAND OF DREAMS**

challenged, it was soon obvious that Bellone had done most of the work on the climb; and I later learned that he had been quite aggressive on an earlier climb, the Campu Omu (1417 feet).

However, Bellone just managed to counter the challenge of Polidori near the barriers, and he survived a subsequent appeal to win the 30-second stage bonus and take over the white jersey (with red and blue bands) of race leadership, the first of his career. Former leader Beghetto finished in 77th place, 2:19 down (all lost in the final miles), in a small group with old Tour star Massignan and French six-day man Alain Van Lancker (Frimatic). Classics stars Reybroeck (Faema) and Ward Sels (Bic) were even further behind.

When the main bunch passed me (10 seconds behind the two leaders), 300 yards from the line, it was being led by Jan Janssen. But he was jumped out of it by nine others by the line, with third place going, not surprisingly, to fast finisher Franco Bitossi from Marino Basso, Dancelli, Motta, Zandegu and Ritter. Quite a selection of top riders.

An intermittent drizzle had begun just before the finish, and as the cloudy sky suddenly turned summer back to winter, I was glad to go up to the hotel in the evening to see English rider Harrison and his Frimatic colleagues. I had met their Italian-speaking team helper in the town where he had been doing some shopping, and arranging for a barber to go up to cut some of the riders' hair. First one to undergo the ritual of the scissors was young Frenchman Van Lancker, just starting his first season as a professional. His even younger friend, and today his firmly established six-day partner, Jacky Mourioux, was also there—both of them having traveled at the last moment when regular team leaders Joaquim Agostinho and Jiri Daler were unable to start.

*Giro di Sardegna • Italy • 1969*

Agostinho had broken his renowned, and ancient, Portuguese frame the day before coming, and he could not get a replacement from De Gribaldy in time. And it was discovered that Daler's visa was sufficient for travel in France, but not in Italy. These small details showed that the Frimatic organization was not of the highest standing.

It may appear strange for track racers like Van Lancker and Mourioux to be riding a race as tough as the Tour of Sardinia; but like Beghetto, who had taken the first stage (and who was to take the penultimate one, on the mainland), they were both accomplished road men as amateurs. Beghetto was champion of his country on the road, at the Italian equivalent of both schoolboy and junior.

I first met Alain Van Lancker in Brittany in 1965. He was a student from Paris, spending his holidays racing on the Breton circuit. He was still a 2nd category amateur then. The race where I met him was on a hard little circuit near Pontivy, and the big field was drastically sorted out early on by a narrow sandy track that had to be ridden along each lap. It was raining heavily, and wheels were sinking in above the rims in that sand. There were many good men riding, but Van Lancker stormed away solo, took most of the primes on the 60-lap race, and won on his own by about two minutes! He was then 18 years old.

I also rode against Alain in a one-day, two-stage event at Malestroit, a week later. In the morning, he had taken most of the primes in the 50-mile stage, having broken away with my teammate Lloyd Coward right from the start. They were caught well before the finish, but Van Lancker went away from the start of the afternoon's more hilly stage. There was a good climb after only three miles, which he took, chased by myself. I caught him over the top, and then tried to outsprint him for the next town prime—ha-ha! He

**ISLAND OF DREAMS**

beat me by several lengths without really trying. He thought it was a great joke, and his mischievous face was one broad grin when we joined up again to continue our two-up break.

It wasn't till later that I learned that Van Lancker was the French collegiate sprint champion. And now he has established himself as one of the fastest men, and most popular riders, in the six-day circus, having already won a race (the Montreal Six) with Mourioux.

The bespectacled Harrison was the other one to have a haircut. He said he had been down south since January 15, and that his knee had healed well from the serious operation he had had after the 1968 Tour de France. He was not feeling overly ambitious for this race, because he was still being treated for a heavy cold contracted on the French Riviera; but team boss Louis Caput said that Derek should do better than the others next day in the mountains.

Yes, stage three was to be the hilliest day of the Tour of Sardinia, although only 78 miles long. It also turned out to be the most significant of the week: The four riders who occupied the first four places on the stage would be the same four in the leading four places in the final general classification. This was the stage during which, in 1968, Eddy Merckx had frightened all his star rivals by recklessly breaking away on a long descent on roads made icy by snow and frost. That weather was to be repeated in this 1969 stage, and the results would be just as catastrophic to the bulk of the field, with men like Dutch star Jan Janssen destined to finish more than 22 minutes in arrears at the finish in Nuoro.

The day began with bright sunshine, followed by lashing rain, and then more sunshine when I called at the hotel to wish the Frimatic team good luck. There were few signs

*Giro di Sardegna • Italy • 1969*

of the drama to come as they left on their bikes to freewheel down to the start at Tortoli, 12 miles away.

Those miles, uphill, would be the first of the stage, with the high point coming 23 miles later at the summit of the Arcu Correboi Pass (4088 feet). It took me most of the morning to reach that summit, but the ride and the continuation to Nuoro was one of the most unforgettable of my life.

Away from Lanusei, the road continued climbing steeply for three miles with a series of hairpin bends. There were even a few fir trees here, sheltering the road from the savage wind that was bringing the bad weather. There was still some blue sky over the distant sea, but dark clouds were gathering in the mountains ahead. The prospect was even less palatable when I reached the last part of this initial rise, as I was almost stopped in my tracks by the gale.

The next 13 miles looked fairly flat from the map, with a rise of only 18 meters (58 feet), but they turned out to be up and down the whole way, with several steep hills and innumerable bends. On the first long rise, winding away from a grey reservoir that was rather grandly named the Lago alto de Flumendosa, I stopped to eat some of my iron rations: sweet biscuits, cheese, chocolate and fruit.

I was momentarily sheltered from the wind by a fold in the grassy hills and it was quite warm sitting there on a convenient rock. There was hardly a sound to be heard in this desolate spot, and there was a peculiar, unreal appearance about the odd publicity van that would go past to advertise the race. They were an intrusion in this pristine landscape.

On my way again, I shortly passed through a little valley that was just like a transplant from Scotland; but the two wild boar scrubbing around by the road were true Sardinian, just like the rifle-touting shepherds I later saw sitting around a brushwood fire. On one bumpy descent, I was

 **ISLAND OF DREAMS**

surprised to pass through a small frontier-like village called Villanova Strisaili, which was a collection of timber-built houses, huge piles of lumber and a line of faces out to see the *coridorri*.

Shortly afterward, the drizzle that had started to fall turned to a blinding shower of rain and hail. I was toiling through this storm, up a long hill, with the road already shining wet, when a carload of overweight Italian journalists cruised by in the luxury of their heated limousine. In contrast (and I could not really say I envied them), I took to the shelter of a huge rock, huddled cross-legged under my cape. I thought of Shakespeare's "Macbeth" and how this scene would make a perfect "blasted heath" for the Three Witches. The wind had become even stronger, the rain heavier, a strange mist was hanging over the stunted growth of gorse and oak ... and suddenly there was a flash of lightning, and a long, low rumble of thunder to break the silence.

The storm quickly passed, and the weather improved enough for me to de-cape after another few miles along this wildly beautiful road. Six miles remained to the summit of the pass, which was now climbing again in earnest up the right side of a desolate valley. Across the ever-deepening chasm rose a wall of rocky scree, with the peaks of the Gennargentu Mountains (the highest on the island) showing themselves above, when the clouds allowed.

There was snow lying at the edges of the road, and halfway up there was a renewed attack by the wind and hail. The cape was donned once more, and I plugged on into the tempest as fast as I could, half expecting Bitossi or Bellone to come by at any minute. But the race, too, was suffering from "weather sickness," and it was well behind schedule.

*Giro di Sardegna • Italy • 1969*

The final stretch doubled back across the side of a ridge. There was deep snow on the roadsides here, and 200 yards from the prime banner I stopped and pushed my bike into the snow to prop it against a post. There was a big shout from the hardy group of spectators above, so I continued up to where they were.

It was a surprise to see so many people at this godforsaken spot. There were khaki-clad police and cassocked priests, oil-skinned road workers and muffled pressmen. One of them gave me two swigs from a flask of cognac, another said that they thought I was a racer by the speed I had been climbing (ha-ha!). By the time I had fished my cameras from the saddle-bag, the hail had turned to snow, which soon put a white covering over the bumpy road.

The riders themselves could not be long now, and there was an expectancy among the tifosi when judges and time-keepers drove up. A keen sprint was hoped for, because there were time bonuses of 30, 20 and 10 seconds for the first three. Eventually, two figures appeared from the gloom to contest the sprint. It was a very closely fought affair, but little Giuseppe Fezzardi (Sanson) just held off the taller Claudio Michelotto (Max Meyer); 50 seconds later came a pursuing figure in brown. It was Polidori, who had come second the day before. Soon the minutes ticked away— where were the others? Two, three, four ... it was finally five minutes before the expected Bellone came by, vainly defending his leader's jersey.

It turned out that the Frenchman had been in the stranglehold of the largely Italian bunch, from the moment Fezzardi had attacked after that initial steep climb through Lanusei. Bellone had only been released a mile from the top, and he had already dropped them for nearly a minute. The bunch itself was led over by Derek Harrison, obvious-

**ISLAND OF DREAMS**

ly riding up to his manager's forecast. But he would have a difficult task to maintain his position on the descent. Thick snow is very difficult to see through for a man wearing glasses.

It had been a bizarre experience to watch a cycle race in these conditions. The first three men still had their regular team uniforms; the rest, however, were indistinguishable in their woolly hats, racing capes, tracksuit tops and thick gloves. Only two or three were off the back; the others had already packed it in and came by in the sag wagon (Sels, Reybroeck and Jourden among them).

By the time I was ready to go, the snow had thickened steadily, and half an inch had already settled on the steep descent, where a deep valley fell away to the right. The wind was even stronger on this windward side of the pass, blowing the snow hard into my face. In order to see, I had to close one eye, leave the other only half open and screw my head around at an angle. I thought how lucky the race had been to have crossed before this ultimate tempest. Feet, hands and face were slowly freezing, and I was beginning to wonder whether I would ever get down from these rugged heights.

Suddenly, there was a great booming sound from right behind me, and a huge wall of metal loomed into view. It was a snow plow, attached to the front of a massive truck. The driver slowed down and waved me over. My bike was in the back in a trice, and I was sitting snugly in the warmth of the heated cab. There were already three others there, and they said they had seen me riding up the pass earlier.

The cold and danger were soon forgotten, and my mind was on watching the race once more.

The wipers were having a hard job keeping the windshield clear of the snow that was still teeming down. But I

*Giro di Sardegna • Italy • 1969*

could tell that the riders were not far in front, as their wheel tracks were clearly visible in the snow. They made a crazy criss-cross pattern all the way to Fonni, 10 miles from the top, where the snow was still falling. This was as far as my "rescuers" were going, so they dropped me off, giving me my bike from the back, and I was soon the center of a group of curious villagers.

A well-dressed businessman came up and said he could speak French. He took me (bike and all) into the bar opposite and gave me another tot of brandy! He told me that this was the highest village on the island (1000 meters, or 3100 feet high) and that there had been 50 centimeters (20 inches) of snow lying in the village just two weeks before, with a two-meter (6 feet 6 inches) covering on the top of the pass. When I told him I was going on to Nuoro (20 miles away), he assured me that there would only be rain below Fonni, and that the road was wide and well-surfaced all the way. This proved to be correct—except that rain turned to hail on one occasion, and the wind hardly eased the whole 10 miles.

I heard later from the riders that conditions were just as bad on the more indirect route they had taken. Derek Harrison said the bunch completely split up just after Fonni, where Anquetil himself was leading the chase for teammate Bellone. They had hit a particularly bad stretch of road, and only the strongest were left in contention. Jean-Claude Lebaube added that he finished at the back with Jan Janssen, who had stopped several times to clean his glasses, and scrounge a pair of woolen gloves at another point. He said they had been further delayed by a brief storm that covered the road an inch deep in hailstones. Eventually, the Anquetil group (with Bellone, Dancelli, Motta, Adorni, Bitossi, Ritter and Basso) had finished 4:29 down on the stage winner, while Harrison had finished in the main bunch at 12:26.

**ISLAND OF DREAMS**

Alain Van Lancker had done the best of the Frimatics to finish 28th at only 5:11—an excellent performance.

Out in front, Polidori caught the other two leaders on the descent, as their lead was cut to less than three minutes. But the gap widened again on the mainly uphill miles to the finish, where poor Fezzardi lost contact, losing 2:44 before the line. The two leaders fought a close tussle up into Nuoro, where Polidori just gained the edge to make up for his disappointment of the day before. But it was Michelotto who took over the race leadership, because Polidori had lost almost two minutes on the first stage, when there were several mass pileups in the closing miles. In fourth place, 30 seconds in front of the Anquetil group, was Flaviano Vicentini, the world amateur champion in 1963.

It was still raining when I reached Nuoro myself, and I envied the riders who could go straight to their warm hotels, a hot bath, massage and meal. I eventually ended up in the "one-dollar-for-the-night" Ristorante Toscano, but at least it was dry, and my memorable day was over. I had covered only 48 miles, as against the 78 of the pros. But they had not been much faster, for the winner had completed the stage in 4 hours 6 minutes 11 seconds (18.9 mph), while reigning Tour de France champion Janssen had taken 4:28:57 (17.5 mph).

Two other Tour winners, Anquetil and Aimar, had time problems the next morning, when they both arrived late for the start. They probably got fined for not signing in, but they were safely in the pack as it disappeared in a barrage of police whistles and hooting car horns, destination Olbia. My destination was Sassari, 80 miles in the other direction.

Starting out under a watery sun, my journey was another one punctuated by hurried rain showers and thunder. After a few miles through a deserted landscape, I saw two

*Giro di Sardegna • Italy • 1969*

big dogs standing in the road in front of me, at the top of a short rise. On spotting me, one dog mounted the bank to the right, the other to the left. It was an ambush! My only recourse was to sprint as hard as I could out of the saddle, and try to get to my top speed before the baying hounds ran down the grassy banks. They were close, but I just managed to beat them to the start of a long descent, and they eventually turned back, defeated.

A little later, I was merrily churning along a smooth highway when there was an almighty bang from behind my left ear. I turned, and saw that a van, which had just passed in the other direction, had abruptly lost a rear wheel. The wheel was bowling along up the road, while the van, loaded with boxes of market produce, had thudded to a dead stop in a shower of sparks and clouds of dust!

The rest of the day was less dramatic—just varied images of windswept main roads, high mesa country and wide, green plains, modern road viaducts in construction and grazing sheep. The one final surprise came at the end of miles of wide modern highway, when, with Sassari (a town of 65,000 inhabitants) only four miles distant, the road suddenly turned to the right and I had to tackle a series of seven steep hairpins lifting the N.131 to 1000 feet within a couple of miles.

The next morning, I had plenty of time to look around the town, in the sunshine at last, although the northwest wind was still blowing. Sassari was an interesting mixture of new blocks and paved patios at the top of the hill, and ancient shops and narrow passages at the bottom. To find out about the race, I bought a copy of the *Gazzetta dello Sport,* which had a report of the previous day's stage. I learned that it had been downhill and fast most of the way to Olbia, where the bunch was still grouped. But on a final,

**ISLAND OF DREAMS**

20-mile loop around the Costa Smerelda, there was a complete upheaval. The big stars, demoralized by their time loss the day before, simply allowed a group of, first four riders, then 13 others, to ride away and do some racing, while the peloton finished nearly nine minutes behind them! Caught out by the attacks, Bellone fought well to limit his personal loss to 3:30, while the race ahead developed into a pursuit match between the four leaders (including Polidori) and the 13 chasers (containing Michelotto). A gap of more than a minute was reduced to just eight seconds at the line, leaving Michelotto with 50 seconds still in hand over Polidori.

This day, the last on the island, was split into two; with a morning stage of 83 miles from Olbia, and an afternoon time trial of 12 miles.

Along with thousands of others, I walked out to the eastern suburbs of Sassari, to where the finish of the hilly stage from Olbia was due to finish at about 11 o'clock. This was more in keeping with the image of the Tour of Sardinia, a race that has been won three times by Rik Van Looy. The straight, wide finishing road was lined with palm trees and a shirt-sleeved crowd out to cheer their racing idols. And the sprint turned out to be fast and furious, disputed by 10 men, with 25 more 200 yards back, and the rest of the field 1:20 down.

It looked to be a comfortable win for Gianni Motta, who entered the final 50 meters several lengths clear; but Dino Zandegu (Salvarani) came through with a tremendous rush right between Motta and the barriers. Nobody knew who had won, and both riders climbed the fence to see the photo-finish film. The result was 1. Zandegu, 2. Motta.

When I got back to my hotel, I found it had been invaded by the whole race entourage. The riders were having

*Giro di Sardegna • Italy • 1969*

lunch here, and mechanics chatted in the sunshine as they worked on the machines. I left them all behind and rode out along the road the others would be racing on two hours later.

The first part was on a divided highway, mostly flat, then came two long drags, and a final swoop down to Porto Torres, before skirting the town to finish on a headland to the east. The wind was mostly unfavorable, and fast times were not expected at this early point in the season. The one redeeming feature was the springlike sunshine, and the incentive to the riders (especially Italian-sponsored) to get their team name into the television limelight.

Porto Torres is a sort of shanty town, its extensive docks being the reason for its existence, because Sassari (the city in the north of the island) is 12 miles inland. There is a huge oil refinery, with some ugly industrial buildings, at one side of the town; while the eastern end has fine sandy beaches and modern blocks of flats. Therefore, the crowd watching the time trial (it was Thursday afternoon) was made up of a mixture of schoolchildren, off-duty workers and dockers, and the usual cycling-mad enthusiasts. Where I watched from, on the road into town, there were also two coachloads of involuntary spectators—the police having stopped their Sassari-bound buses when they closed the road at 2:30 p.m.

The important issue in the time trial was the battle between Michelotto and Polidori, who were separated by just 42 seconds. And with two more stages to complete on the mainland, Polidori was expected to have the better chance, mainly because of the greater strength of his Molteni team over Michelotto's Max Meyer formation.

On my section of road, there was a long right-hand sweep followed by a short, steep rise and a right-handed corner. The early starters (lowest placed on G.C.) mostly

**ISLAND OF DREAMS**

came by in gears too big for them, having to get out of the saddle for the hill, and struggle around the bend. There were one or two notable exceptions, the first being Jan Janssen, no less.

He was the best so far, but the elegant neo-pro Giovanni Cavalcanti (Gris 2000) beat his time by about 20 seconds. The next good ride was by the surprising Beghetto, world sprint champion at the time, who equaled Janssen's time.

Not all the riders had following cars, and the only man in the Frimatic team to have one was Derek Harrison, even though he was well down on general classification (42nd). Manager Caput was expecting a good ride, and Derek was going very smoothly (possibly too smoothly), and he barely rose from his saddle up that hill. His time was pretty good: 15 seconds better than Janssen, to give him an eventual position of 16th. However, there was a surprise in store three minutes later, when an "unknown" Italian came storming by. It was another 25-year-old from the experimental Gris 2000 outfit, Arnoldo Spadoni, a big man who has represented Italy in team pursuits at world championships. He was almost a minute clear of Harrison, for a time of 24:48. Not a bad time for 12 miles!

The next "performance" was expected from Motta. He passed by going very fast, but some three minutes later than expected. In fact, his time was next to last, the explanation being that while warming up, he had ridden into some chickens wandering on the road. He had fallen, bent a wheel … and had a four-minute late start. In real time, he would have beaten Spadoni by 12 seconds!

By now, those delayed bus passengers were getting impatient, and one of them asked me how much longer there was. I told him "15 more," which seemed to satisfy

*Giro di Sardegna • Italy • 1969*

him. In fact, Jacques Anquetil was next along, as masterly as ever, but not flat-out and falling 10 seconds short of Spadoni's time. Then came three riders, one after the other, who were riding beautifully, greatly encouraged by the crowds, and especially by their managers in the team cars. First along was Bitossi, who beat Spadoni by 5 seconds; then rainbow-jerseyed Adorni—even better by 10 seconds; and finally, it was the flying figure of Danish ace Ole Ritter, turning a huge gear, but very comfortably. Ritter was well ahead of the rest and it was clearly a winning ride: 24:12, even 21 seconds faster than Adorni, and an incredible average of more than 30 mph.

The Polidori-Michelotto tussle was all that remained, and to show their equality once again, Polidori won the match by just 10 seconds; he still had 31 seconds to pull back if he were to win the Tour of Sardinia—but he would have to win it on the mainland, just as Eddy Merckx had done on the first stage of the 1968 event, when he rode away to a solo six-minute stage win.

Nothing of the sort happened this time, though, and there were two rather monotonous stages to Sienna (won again by Beghetto) and to Rome (won by Casalini, Scic). The only outstanding incidents were the withdrawal of the Frimatic team—protesting the disqualification of Harrison for a positive dope test on the snowy stage (the drug was one prescribed to him for his cold treatment); the re-routing of the last stage to avoid a demonstration of striking miners; and the shipping of the whole race from Porto Torres to Livorno....

The ship scheduled to transport all the race vehicles and personnel was the "Caralis" of Naples, the regular car-ferry running between Sardinia and Genoa. As a result, it had to make a special call in Livorno to drop everyone off. I

**ISLAND OF DREAMS**

was also traveling on the boat, but going all the way to Genoa, before riding along the Italian Riviera to complete my round trip that had begun from Nice more than a week earlier.

I don't remember much of the boat trip to Livorno, as I had a very comfortable bunk, and the sea was calm under a starry sky; but the complicated loading and unloading operations are still clear in my mind. In fact, the race's Livorno-Sienna stage started two hours late because every car had to be taken off individually, a crane lifting each one away from the ship's car deck to the dock, a long way below. It was like seeing a model stage race being assembled.

The departure from Porto Torres the night before had been just as absorbing, with the final car being winched aboard just as the sun set in a blaze of red, with jet-black silhouettes being my last view of Sardinia. Right before the ship pulled away, there was a little family drama being enacted on the quayside. There was a black-clad mamma, who had been remonstrating with port officials and the captain for some time, delaying the boat sailing. She had obviously been waiting for someone, who had not arrived. In the end, a taxi drew up, out stepped the daughter (I presumed), who went on board to take off two large suitcases. The mother was arguing—as only Italians can—the whole time. The daughter arguing back. Still gabbling away at top pitch, the daughter bundled the mother into the taxi, and the voices died away into the dusk. Everyone disappeared from the cobbled quayside, except for a courting couple in the shadows, and a small dog left forlornly wagging its tail in fond farewell to the friendly ship. The tall, white "Caralis" slipped silently away from the shore, with great gusts of wind sweeping the dock in the space it had left behind. Then the scene rapidly became quiet, dark and deserted;

*Giro di Sardegna • Italy • 1969*

the final zephyr blowing the dockside clean, sending an odd newspaper and dust swirling into the cold, black water. For me, the Giro di Sardegna was over; Olbia, Lanusei, Nuoro and the Paso Arcu Correboi were now memories ... memories of Sardinia, my island of dreams.

 **ISLAND OF DREAMS**

# ALONE AND UNASSISTED

## North Road
## Hardriders
## Time Trial
# England
# February 1985

**While competitive cycling** had its origins in France, with a race in a Paris park in 1868 and a first road race the following year, racing in Britain followed a different path. At the same time as classic races like Paris-Roubaix and Liège-Bastogne-Liège were being founded in Europe, road racing had been banned the other side of the English Channel. The result was the birth of the individual time trial, an event in which competitors race against the clock, not against each other. The first-ever time trial was promoted in 1895 by the North Road Cycling Club on roads north of London.

# England

EARLY-MORNING SUNSHINE was breaking through a mist still clinging to the water meadows beside the silent Hertfordshire lane. Wild geese were gliding down to a splash-landing in a reed-bounded pond. Cattle were taking their first munches of dewy grass at the start of another day. And on a lawn at the road's edge, 84 numbers were laid out awaiting the 84 entrants in this typically English time trial. Soon the silence was broken by the first competitors arriving from the changing rooms a mile away. They talked about the weather, how mild it was for the time of year. It was going to be a lovely day.

They chatted about training rides and the new equipment they had bought at the bike shop the day before. One rider was having his best lightweight frame resprayed and was concerned that he might have some problems with the brakes on his older machine. There were a number of sharp turns and steep descents on this early-season 25-mile time trial, organized by the North Road Cycling Club.

This is the centennial year of the North Road CC, the club that organized the world's first cycling time trial in October 1895. The decade before that event, there were no bicycle races on British roads. Road racing had been banned by the sport's administrators, because of complaints by the public and interference from the police. At that time, bicycles were the fastest vehicles on the highways, and an early road race must have been a formidable sight to people used to the pace of horse-drawn coaches and carts. Each racer was paced by a team of other riders, which multiplied the problems caused by a group of cyclists racing through villages on the dusty roads of that era.

*North Road Hardriders Time Trial • England • 1985*

Once those road races were banned, the events were transferred to the many velodromes that existed in Britain. The only form of road riding that remained was that conducted by the Road Records Association, a body established in 1888 to sanction and approve record attempts on place-to-place and set-distance rides. These were not really races, because only one rider was allowed to attempt a record on a single day. One man who did well in this type of cycling was F.T. Bidlake, who set records on a tricycle for the London to York route (about 200 miles), and at 50 miles, 100 miles, 12 hours and 24 hours.

These records were all straight-out, point-to-point rides, often assisted by strong following winds. It must have been during these rides that Bidlake—a member of the North Road CC—had the ingenious idea of introducing a more competitive element to this form of riding, but without the hazards caused by direct racing and pacing. A number of racers would be invited to ride, unpaced, over a set course on the same day, with each rider starting alone, separated by an interval of at least one minute.... The road time trial was born.

The first North Road CC time trial was held over 50 miles on a straight section of the Great North Road, the main highway connecting London with the North of England. It was simple to mark out the course: The competitors raced 25 miles north, made a U-turn and raced 25 miles back to the start-finish point. The event was a great success, with no complaints from the public or the police, because they didn't even know it was taking place.

The cyclists were pleased to be racing on the open road again, unrestricted by the tight turns of a velodrome. They were not bothered that there was no publicity for their sport,

**ALONE AND UNASSISTED**

and no spectators other than the few club cyclists who knew about the time trial.

In many respects, the time trial is the same today. At the North Road "Hardriders 25" this year, there were just three people watching—besides the starter and timekeeper—when the first competitor, A.K. Kennet of the promoting club, started his time trial at 8:37 a.m. Another similarity with the original race against the clock was the presence of tricycles in the event. Bidlake would have been pleased to see that his favorite machine was still being raced.

There were two "trikes" among the first 20 starters, both ridden by men from the local Hertfordshire Wheelers club, K.A. Jiggens and R.A.J. Akers. Listing competitors with initials rather than first names is another tradition that has continued in British time trialing.

Once the plastic start number had been pinned to a racing jersey or skinsuit, a rider took his place in the short line behind the timekeeper. Before reaching the front of the line, some would check to see if they had picked up any flints on their tires; others would lift the back of the bike and shift to a different gear for the start; and most would think ahead to the first part of the course.

When one rider had started, the next would freewheel to the line chalked roughly on the road. The starter—the pusher-off—held up each rider as toe straps were tightened and pedals positioned, ready for the strongest possible starting effort. After a few words of encouragement from the starter came the timekeeper's "five, four, three, two, one ... go."

The ritual of a time trial start is the same today as it was 90 years ago. Those first lungfuls of cold air are memorable. And there is the mental thrill of challenging other riders in front or behind you, each experiencing the same sensations.

*North Road Hardriders Time Trial • England • 1985*

This is what made time trialing popular in Britain when the only competition alternative was track racing.

As more and more clubs eventually began to organize open events, most had different rules and methods. Twenty-six years after the first North Road time trial, the clubs met to discuss the problems, and in 1922 they formed the Road Racing Council. It was named that and not the Time Trialing Council because, at the time, there was no other form of road racing.

The sport flourished through the 1920s and 1930s, but with increasing numbers of riders and changing traffic conditions, it again became necessary to discuss the situation. The result was a change of name in 1938 from the Road Racing Council to the Road Time Trials Council (RTTC). The newly named body was opened to all cycling clubs in England and Wales, instead of being restricted to the clubs that organized open time trials.

Many rules and regulations have been added or altered since that time, but the fundamental rule of time trialing remains: "Competitors must ride entirely alone and unassisted. They must not ride in company with, nor take shelter from, any other rider or from any vehicle on the road."

The language of time trial start sheets also remains the same. For the North Road Hardriders 25, the course instructions began: "Proceed along the B.158 through Essendon and Wildhill to join A.100 at Brookmans Park (M). Turn left (Care) on to A.1000 and then first left on to B.157 (M)...."

For the competitors, this formal wording was soon translated into a bagful of mixed impressions. On the winding, sometimes narrow B.158, there were obstacles to avoid: a jogger running with his dog, a deep puddle, a parked car. There was a first gradual climb—the first of 10—to Essendon, a pretty village with a half-timbered pub called

**ALONE AND UNASSISTED**

"The Rose and Crown" and a war memorial that lists the village's sons and daughters who were killed in the two world wars, "For God, King and Country."

The first of the tricycle riders was caught by his minute man as the hill was crested. The physical effort was hard, but the mental pleasure real. Feeling the wind in your hair and hearing damp tire treads singing on the tarmac is the same if you are pedaling at 20 or 30 mph. And if you do not have expectations of winning, you probably have time to peek at the distant views filtering between bare oak and beech trees. You can hear the birds singing. And on this morning you might catch a few words from the radio of a parked car: "It's going to be a mild, sunny day with a high temperature of 12 degrees Centigrade...."

There has always been an insularity about time trialing in Britain. Until World War II, all competitors—men and women—had to wear black tights and black jackets to preserve the sport's anonymous nature. Until the 1960s, all start and result sheets for the events required the words "Private and confidential" printed on them. Even today, the courses are not described by their actual location, but by code numbers. The latest version of the 50-mile course used for the first time trial is called the F.1. Each district of the RTTC has its own key letter; the North London district's is F.

In the early part of the 20th century, most districts had only one or two courses at the various distances—25, 50 and 100 miles—using the straightest highways in the area, and always on an out-and-home formula. The exceptions were courses for 12- and 24-hour time trials, which used loops as well as straight legs. There was great prestige attached to breaking a course or event record, but when riders were able to travel more widely, the competition became nationwide and the aim was to get the fastest record in the country.

*North Road Hardriders Time Trial • England • 1985*

As a result, the RTTC worked out a system of competition records that was started in 1944. This altered the concept of time trial course designing, which was already becoming difficult with the increase in motor traffic. U-turns were a problem, except at times very early in the morning. In search of faster times, districts began using the highways that were being built to satisfy the boom in motor vehicle production, during the 1950s and 1960s. It was not a coincidence that from a pre-war 25-mile record of one hour, the competition record broke the 55-minute barrier in 1962, and was taken below 50 minutes a decade later by Alf Engers, a man who has become legendary in British time trialing.

The main attraction of this year's North Road Hardriders 25 had been a possible clash between Engers, now a veteran [over 40], and Darryl Webster, the current British 25-mile champion. Unfortunately, Engers called the event secretary two days before the event to say he couldn't ride because of a flu.

In Engers's absence, the main challenge to Webster—who had won this event in 1983 and 1984—was expected to come from the 1982 winner, Martin Pyne, and Webster's new Manchester Wheelers teammate, Peter Sanders. Both Sanders and Webster have been members of Great Britain's world and Olympic team time trial squad for the past two years, and both are fine performers in road races. This is unusual in Britain, where time trials have become the domain of the average club cyclist who does not want to compete in criteriums and road races, because of the extra training and expense required, or because there is total satisfaction in racing against a personal best and competing with friends, week after week.

"You get out what you put into it," said Webster. "I find it very enjoyable. It's a pastime as much as a sport. l would

**ALONE AND UNASSISTED**

ride time trials all the time if they got you anywhere, but they don't mean anything internationally."

It was interesting to contrast the versatile road racing approach of Webster and Sanders, who finished the event first and second, with the more restricted styles of the pure time trialists. Pyne and the members of his CC Breckland team wore black skinhoods for aerodynamic advantage. But on this untypically difficult course, with an average of one 90-degree turn for every mile, they were not riding the low-profile "funny bikes" that many British time trialists now use.

On this springlike morning, Webster was 2:18 outside his event record of 1:00:38, set last year. "I'm not so fit this year because I have done less training," he explained. It wasn't a day or a time trial that set records. We had returned to the spirit of the 1895 event, when taking part was what mattered. This spirit was perhaps best expressed in the rides of the two tricyclists. Jiggens pedaled, leaned and dragged his trike around the acrobatic circuit in 1:22:51. Akers's time was 1:22:29. The closeness of their performances is something they would probably talk about all week, until the next time trial—alone and unassisted.

*North Road Hardriders Time Trial • England • 1985*

# THE GREAT RACE

## Milan-
## San Remo
# Italy
# March 1970

**Every year,** spring is celebrated in the cycling world at the classic one-day race from Milan to San Remo. The Italian event was first held in 1907, following a near-300-kilometer course that remains almost the same to this day: south from Milan across the Lombardy plain, over the Apennine chain to the coast near Genoa, and west along the Mediterranean coast to San Remo, the city of flowers. Milan-San Remo has always been the year's first big international classic, which today opens the series of World Cup races. In 1970, this beautiful bike race was expected to be won by a rider who was winning everything at the time: Eddy Merckx of Belgium. Who could beat him?

# Italy

IT WOULD BE HARD to find grander and more classic surroundings for a bike race than those of Milan-San Remo, the race that *is* the national holiday (St. Joseph's Day, March 19) to most Italians. The signing-on takes place in an imposing medieval castle—the Castello Sforzesco; the race passes the famous Milan Cathedral in the neutralized zone; midway along the marathon 288 kilometers route, the snow-capped Apennines are crossed through Tour de France-like conditions on the Passo del Turchino; and then comes the 130 kilometers along the Riviera di Ponente—the blue Mediterranean on the left and misty mountains on the right—before the last sprint into San Remo along the Via Roma.

In 1970, there were "only 236 starters" (according to the race radio) that set out to battle from Milan at 9:27 on a bright morning in March, with victory in this season-opening classic the dream of them all, especially the 108 Italians in the line-up. To emulate countryman Lorretto Petrucci, the 1953 winner, and end a grim record of 16 successive wins by foreigners, would make them immortal stars overnight.

The 236 professional riders from 27 different trade teams had traveled from all over Europe for the great race, 10 nations being represented. The race preliminaries took place the previous afternoon in the splendid grounds of the Castello Sforzesco. Tables for the issuing of race numbers, car plaques, programs and official passes were laid out in a romantic inner courtyard, its floor paved with rounded cobblestones, and so distant from the bustle and noise of the traffic-laden streets of Milan, on the other side of the high castle walls.

Among the first to arrive, causing a commotion among the inquisitive fans outside the gates, was the Zimba-GBC

*Milan-San Remo • Italy • 1970*

team with former race winner Rudi Altig of Germany, and bespectacled Aldo Moser, the veteran Italian rider who is even older than Altig. With photographers about, there were inevitably a few publicity stunts for the morning papers. The flamboyant Altig was soon laughing as a couple of champagne bottles were popped open, with the august president of the Union Cycliste Internationale, Italian "godfather" Adriano Rodoni, somehow getting himself in the pictures.

Many of the riders had come straight from Paris-Nice, the eight-day stage race being ideal preparation for the *Primavera* (Italian for "spring," which gives Milan-San Remo its alternative name); while most of the Italians had finished their own equivalent (Tirreno-Adriatico) three days before. As for the Belgians, the best classics riders, they had been content to persevere in the cold of their home racing: men like 1968 Tour of Lombardy winner Herman Van Springel; the very successful De Vlaeminck brothers, Roger and Eric; and the stone-faced one-day specialist, Frans Verbeeck.

As more teams (most of them clad in warm-up suits), pressmen and race followers assembled, so the peaceful courtyard became filled with people and talk of the morrow's big race. A lot of the talk was whether Eddy Merckx, winner at San Remo in 1966, '67 and '69, was going to start or not. He had just won Paris-Nice more brilliantly than in 1969, but even he had suffered from the bad weather, and was troubled by a painful saddle sore. Obviously, his absence would be a great relief to most riders and team managers, as they could then transfer their efforts from watching (and being watched by) the Merckx team, to more attacking moves on their own behalf.

Among the last to arrive, as the shadows lengthened, was the French Sonolor team with the only Englishman on the long start list, Barry Hoban. Paris-Nice had left him

**THE GREAT RACE**

with a strain below his left knee, but he seemed confident enough. The "injured" Merckx also put in a smiling appearance and seemed likely to be on the starting line the next morning.

Alongside Merckx and the other favorites on the start line would be a host of unknowns, many of them on low-budget Italian teams such as Civitanova Marche, Cosatto Marsicano and Zonca. These are the men who help to bolster the size of the field to such huge proportions, and also make the job of forecasting the outcome so difficult.

In modern times, it is normal to look for a sprinter as a prospective winner, as the race finish is mostly disputed by a small breakaway group or even the whole bunch. The only solo winners in recent years were Poulidor in 1961 and Merckx in 1969, both of them crossing the line at San Remo with the peloton in sight behind them. And the last time that a really long-range break had succeeded in staying away to the finish was in 1960, when Frenchmen René Privat and Jean Graczyk came first and second.

This year, the names most frequently cited as danger men were Jan Janssen (Bic), Patrick Sercu (Dreher), Cyrille Guimard (Mercier), Franco Bitossi (Filotex), Verbeeck (Geens-Watney), Guido Reybroeck (Germanvox), Daniel Van Ryckeghem (Mann), Eric Leman and the De Vlaemincks (Mars), Gerben Karstens (Peugeot), Walter Godefroot (Salvarani) ... nearly all of them Dutch and Belgians. One name that was missing was that of Molteni's Marino Basso, possibly the most rapid sprinter of all, but not starting because of an injury. This meant that Michele Dancelli would be sole leader of the Molteni team, with young Davide Boifava its other "protected" rider.

Speaking to Barry Hoban before the race in the mobile Faema coffee bar, parked in the Castello Sforzesco grounds,

*Milan-San Remo • Italy • 1970*

he predicted: "No Italian's going to get away in a break without a skiving Belgian sprinter in it … or perhaps a skiving English one," he added, with a twinkle in his eye.

Hoban's view was probably shared by most of the riders and race followers gathered on this bright, crisp Thursday morning, so it seemed unlikely that this was to be the year that the Italian successor to Petrucci would be found. And whatever they actually thought about their respective chances, it was certain that Eddy Merckx was going to be danger man No. 1. As one team manager who had been on Paris-Nice said: "Merckx is capable of dropping everyone on the hills, he can outsprint them all, he can even go faster downhill, and he also has the strongest team!"

THERE WAS QUITE A CRUSH in the Sforzesco castle on race-day morning as a never-ending stream of cars and people came through the Barchio gate between 7:30 and 8:30, team cars and officials being directed to the right, press cars to the left. The vehicles lined up facing each other on either side of the main Filarete gate, after making their way between the lawns and flower beds. It was an imposing sight.

The early-morning sunshine had warmed everyone up by the time the man on the microphone had finished reading through the roll-call of names: 248 on the list, but only 236 starting. Before the riders formed a solid phalanx, the police motorcycles and the scores of press cars managed to escape over the castle drawbridge and follow the neutralized route through the city along the Via Dante and the Via Orefici, to pass below the huge and ornate facade of the Milan Cathedral.

It was St. Joseph's Day, the national holiday, and there were massive crowds lining the streets to see off the big race and its convoy on their way to San Remo, almost 200 miles away on the Mediterranean coast. There were white-helmeted policemen at every intersection and traffic light. On the road out through the southern suburbs of Milan, the crowds were just as dense.

I was traveling with an experienced journalist from the ANSA news agency, who had a well-tried method of reporting the race. To get his story to the office as quickly as possible, he typed out the details of any breaks while they were in progress, and then handed the sheet of paper to the four correspondents waiting along the route at Voghera (60 kilometers), Voltri (155 kilometers), Savona (185 kilometers) and Alassio (235 kilometers). In this way, 80 percent of his work would be done by the time he had reached San Remo!

As we cruised out to the real start, we passed several groups of club cyclists, soaking up the atmosphere and getting the chance to see their idols in the flesh. I was told that one little chap we saw following behind a veteran was only seven years of age—they certainly start young in Italy! There were also the usual placards being held aloft to the praise of Felice Gimondi, Gianni Motta and other Italian stars. But I was surprised to see a similar number (written in Italian) for Eddy Merckx, such as "Viva Merckx—to your 4th victory" and "Eddy will win." Apparently, not all Italians mind that the incomparable Belgian beats their own heroes so frequently.

The sky was lightly clouded when we reached the proper start on a long, straight main road that heads south toward Genoa. Looking back over the city, the snowy peaks of the Alps could be made out, indicating a fine day, as did the distant bands of blue sky between the clouds.

I was glad it was to be good weather, as the mountains and the Riviera road would be at their best on the Milan-San Remo route that has hardly changed since French cyclist

*Milan-San Remo • Italy • 1970*

Lucien Petit-Breton won the race's first edition in 1907. In those early days, the rough road conditions, combined with the three climbs of the Capo Mele, Capo Cervo and Capo Berta, always caused a selection. Coppi used these climbs in the final 40 kilometers to send him minutes ahead for his hat-trick of wins in the 1940s. But when the road surfaces became smoother, the gears became bigger, and the race started to end in bunch sprints, the organizers (the *Gazzetta dello Sport* newspaper) introduced the Poggio, a two-mile climb that then descends into the streets of San Remo itself. Never had the Poggio proved of more benefit than in 1969, when Merckx literally sprinted to a 10-meter lead on the very summit of the hill, and swooped down to the finish on the Via Roma alone, to win by 12 seconds. Everybody was wondering if he could do it again this time.

THE OFFICIAL STARTING TIME was 9:30, but Signor Rodoni, the UCI boss, dropped the checkered flag (yes, it signifies the start in Italy) at just 9:27 a.m. and The Great Race was underway. No sooner had the race radio reported this fact than the numbers of the first attackers were called out. "The first break, straight from the start, numbers 247, 144, 179 and 78." Translated into names, that meant a four-up attack by Lievore (Zonca), Sonck (Hertekamp), Pecchielan (Molteni) and Tamiazzo (Ferretti). Three Italians and a Belgian, and already one of the Molteni riders. And seconds later, two more Molteni men had joined the leaders—175 and 170, Santambrogio and Dancelli.

Breaks at this early stage count for nothing, and after six kilometers, the field had regrouped, charging along the flat, straight highway at a steady 45 kph. Through the roundabout at Binasco, I timed the gap between the front and the back of the compact assembly of over 200 riders.

**THE GREAT RACE**

It was almost 20 seconds; and when it stretched out into a long line passing through towns, perhaps the time gap was twice that.

The importance of keeping near the front to observe the attacks and avoid the crashes is very obvious, and this maxim would be proved many times during this long day on the road.

Next man to attack was another Molteni rider, Luxembourger Eddy Schutz; but he was soon back, before finding himself off the front again in the company of a fellow called Eufronio Sahagun Santos (La Casera), as well as Soave (Sercu's Dreher teammate), Hellemans (Hertekamp), Van Loo (Willem II teammate of Van Looy) and Carniel (another Zonca). The bunch quickly reacted, and then there were three more finding themselves clear—Huysmans (Faemino), a Merckx man; Ballini (Dreher); and Delisle (Peugeot), a Frenchman. They, too, were soon back; and then it was French pro Serge Lapebie (Sonolor), son of the 1937 Tour de France winner, who showed momentarily in front, before Polidori (SCIC) suffered the same fate.

This was pure road racing. No hills to interfere, few bends and an infernal pace set by the massive pack echeloning into a slight breeze from the left. There always seems to be a thoroughbred quality about a big race in Italy, and this was no exception. Perhaps it is the police motorcycles that help to create this staccato atmosphere: In France and Belgium, the police use big, almost cumbersome BMWs and Triumphs; but in Italy, they ride excitable little Moto-Guzzi's, smaller and buzzing up and down the road to see that the race proceeds smoothly.

With the leafless trees, a canal running alongside the straight road, and the flat fields stretching out to the horizon on either side, the scene resembled Flanders more than

*Milan-San Remo • Italy • 1970*

Italy; and so it is no surprise that Belgians are expected to do so well in this rough and tumble of a race.

A tumble in Milan-San Remo usually means a crash, and it was less than 20 kilometers before the first of many took place this time. It was nothing serious, just leaving unfancied Italians Tartoni and Ballini struggling off the back. At the same time, another Italian, Lucillo Lievore (the first attacker), was away at the front again, gallantly staying there for the next 20 kilometers with never more than a half-minute's lead. He was only doing his job, by showing the Zonca name to the public massed in the streets of Pavia, the first big town on the route after Milan. His attack would also get in the local papers (good advertising), as the Zonca headquarters are at Voghera, first dropping off-point of my friend's agency report. But there was plenty more action before we reached that 60th kilometer....

Just as Lievore was being absorbed, the road had risen a few feet to cross a long viaduct over the Po River and its wide flood plain, and it was then that the radio announced a puncture for Roger De Vlaeminck, runner-up in 1969 and a favorite this year. Curiously, at that moment, I looked out of the car and saw one of the many club-rider spectators dressed in a 1958-vintage track-suit—Faema-Flandria. The two firms were then allies; but now, in 1970 they are big rivals. 1 do not think that Merckx (Faema) would have thought much of going back to help De Vlaeminck (Flandria) in these times. However, the old wearer of the F-F colors, and winner in 1958 of this race, Rik Van Looy, was going to play a big part in the story of this, his last Milan-San Remo.

With the first hour gone and more than 45 kilometers covered over these flat, straight roads, the countryside at last started to change, as hills loomed ghost-like out of the mist

**THE GREAT RACE**

of the plains. There were tall factory chimneys on the left and equally tall poplar trees on the right, and still those dense crowds lining the roadside. They now saw Belgian Kerremans (Hertekamp) and Italian Cortinovis (Ferretti) on the attack for a mile, before the 200-plus bunch concertinaed back together again into a remarkably compact formation. An impressive sight, as I looked back and saw them come thundering over the skyline of an *autostrada* bridge.

The Molteni riders were still very prominent at the front, their chocolate-colored jerseys attacking and defending in turn, as the thin line at the front swished its vicious way back and forth across the macadam. Cortinovis tried another sprinting attack on the right, but this time it was the red-and-white Faeminos who were the first to counter him. And that is how the race continued: small attacks constantly forming and foundering; the attacks causing the high speed, and that speed spelling an end to the attacks. A vicious circle of events.

The first signs that the pattern was to change came as the route turned right at Casteggio (50 kilometers) onto a road running parallel to the hills, now on the left. It was not like Flanders any more, for the Italian landscape made itself known by the vineyards on the hillsides, the sun-baked clay tiles on the houses, and the peeling plaster on the walls. For the first time there was a break without an Italian, when Riotte (Sonolor), Krekels (Caballero) and Pfenninger (Zimba)—a French, a Dutch and a Swiss rider—attacked after Montebello della Battaglia. And when they were caught, it was Belgian Willy In'T'Ven (Mann) making a move.

At Voghera, with the sun again breaking through the white, puffy clouds, it was still an integrated group. And they treated the really huge crowds—two deep both sides all the way through the big town—to an impressive display of

*Milan-San Remo • Italy • 1970*

speed, as the town prime was won by Van der Vleuten from Ward Sels (both of the Willem II team).

After this rapid sprint, the next bit of excitement came from the armada of press cars in front: The *Direttore Corsa* decided the riders were getting too close, and so there were a couple of kilometers of klaxoning and roaring of engines as drivers carried out the instructions to move forward.

The incident emphasized the continuing fast pace of the race, with the car-borne drivers tiring more quickly than those born to pedal. With the warm sunshine inciting more and more attacks, it seemed inevitable that there would soon be a proper breakaway. In less than an hour, the gradual, winding climb up the Turchino pass would begin ... and end the hopes of the many riders not really fit enough to tackle it at this early stage of the season, after 80 miles of hanging on to their fitter companions.

An indication that things were about to boil over came as the race neared Tortona (77 kilometers), at the end of half an hour of bunched riding. There was a long drag up around the town's modern bypass, and a rider in black-and-white had managed to move clear when I had a look down the road—before the road turned right under another motorway and over a river. It was an Italian in the SCIC team, No. 213, Luciano Armani. This could be the start of something big, for Armani had won two big races already that month: Genoa-Nice, in which he outsprinted Gimondi and Leif Mortensen, and Milan-Turin, a solo victory.

He was moving very well, and as he turned left onto another straight, but bumpy highway, he was joined by fellow Italian Primo Franchini (Cosatto). Glancing down at my watch, I saw that the race had covered the first 50 miles in under 1 hour 43 minutes ... and when I looked up again the two breakaways had been absorbed. I saw the reason

**THE GREAT RACE**

why. Most of the Faemino team—the Merckx riders—were gathered at the front, with young Joseph Bruyère riding so strongly that he was soon off the front, looking around for others to help him force a break. Nobody came, and next it was his Belgian colleague, Frans Mintjens, having a go— together with Emilio Sanantonio, another Cosatto man.

We then passed a sign on the left of the road that said "200 kilometers al arrivo," only 125 miles to go! A rather forbidding sign to see at this stage in the proceedings, but it was not daunting the two attackers, who had now been joined by seven more—Soave (Dreher), Erik Pettersson (Ferretti), Aldo Moser (GBC), Chiappano (Molteni), Borghetti and Favaro (both Sagit) and Jotti (SCIC). The biggest break yet, but even they were not strong enough to withstand this unrelenting pace on the flat roads: 91 kilometers (57 miles) had been covered in two hours.

However, there is more to bike racing than flat-out speed and fitness; there is also experience and incentive, both of which were now used to their fullest by 36-year-old Aldo Moser, one of the oldest men in the field. Sensing a slight slackening of the pace as his nine-up break was caught, he immediately went away again to a 50-meter lead, knowing that there was a big prime to be contested just three kilometers up the road at Novi Ligure, hometown of the late Fausto Coppi. This prime was to play a large part in the story of this Milan-San Remo ... as would another one in three hours' time.

Moser did not take the prime, having been joined by seven other riders—two Italians and five Belgians. The names: Carlo Chiappano (Molteni) and Marco Simonetti (Ferretti); Jos Huysmans (Faemino), Eric De Vlaeminck and Eric Leman (both Mars-Flandria), and two Willem II men, Rik Van Looy and Herman Van Loo. This was clearly a very

*Milan-San Remo • Italy • 1970*

important attack, as it included the two most experienced veterans (Moser and Van Looy) and two of the strongest finishers (Leman and De Vlaeminck). Even so, it would probably not last long, if no more Italians could get up to the front.

It was appropriate that all this action should take place in such a famous town, where really huge crowds had gathered, the same crowds that had probably cheered in the past their for own townsman, Fausto Coppi. They were not to be disappointed, as they soon saw a group of 10 more riders (half of them Italians) chasing 150 meters behind the leaders, with the front of the gargantuan peloton coming through another 150 meters later. The Italians in the chase group were Italo Zilioli (Faemino), Franco Bitossi (Filotex), Luciano Soave (Dreher), Adriano Pella (Germanvox) and Michele Dancelli. There were two more Belgians—Godefroot (Salvarani) and the other De Vlaeminck brother; two Dutch—reigning world champion Harm Ottenbros (Willem II) and Karstens (Peugeot); and the German Rolf Wolfshohl (Fagor-Mercier).

The first critical stage of the race had been reached after two hours of fruitless endeavor, but it was still uncertain whether these two important splits were going to be consolidated, and that we were at last going to see a definite break succeed. The next news was that Van Loo (the protégé of Van Looy) had left the front group with Chiappano (henchman of Dancelli), both of them working to ensure that the speed was kept at breaking point.

At points like this in a race, I prefer to see what is happening personally, rather than get the information from the race radio, and so I was glad to see our car slow down on a long straight. We looked back to the corner and, in a moment, a big group of riders came streaming past a line of

**THE GREAT RACE**

tall poplars, with no breakaways ahead. The two front groups had joined up! And it was half a minute before the main bunch came into view. The break was on: Eighteen men had eluded 200 others.

It was the perfect moment for this first real break, because the plains had at last been left behind, and the road was dipping and twisting along a valley into the hills. The breakaways were already out of sight, the 30 seconds became 42 in another five kilometers, and 1:10 after two more. Probably more than half the main bunch did not even know that a break had become established.

There were plenty of people who did know, of course— all the pressmen and directeurs sportifs, for a start. They would now be writing down the numbers from the radio announcements, converting the numbers to names and teams, and then digesting the information. This is what they would have found: that 12 out of the 27 teams were represented, with only four of the bigger teams having missed out. Most of the race favorites were in the group ahead, including Bitossi, Leman, the De Vlaemincks, Dancelli, Karstens, Godefroot. As for Merckx, he was being represented in front by Zilioli and Huysmans (his two lieutenants), while Sercu had Soave there, Altig had Moser, Reybroeck had Pella (who had won the last stage of Paris-Nice), and Gimondi had Godefroot.

On paper, therefore, the chances of the break staying away were very good; although with more than 100 miles still to race, no forecasts could be made whether the break was strong enough to stay clear until the finish. But things were also looking good on the road. The break was about to reach Ovada, starting point of the Turchino climb, when a radio flash reported a big crash in the peloton, with at least 30 riders involved. Adorni and Janssen (both unrepresented

*Milan-San Remo • Italy • 1970*

in front) were among those who had been delayed the longest.

It was just the impetus the break required, and there was even worse to come for the men behind. Within 10 minutes, most of those involved in the crash had fought back to the bunch, which was then starting the climb. But Vittorio Adorni then punctured, causing him to chase once more, and 10 minutes later he was in another big crash! It was also Jan Janssen's misfortune to fall again, this time breaking his spectacles and putting him in the hospital, where he was joined by Spaniard José Lopez-Rodriguez, another victim. News was given at the same time of the forced retirement of Patrick Sercu—his team car had not spotted him in the crash and he was left standing by the roadside without a spare wheel.

The disappearance of both Janssen (third in Paris-Nice, after his Mont Faron stage win over Merckx) and Sercu was a particular disappointment. Former world track sprint champion Sercu was at last showing his true form as a roadman, having won the Tour of Sardinia a few weeks before, and then followed up with sixth place (and a stage win) at Tirreno-Adriatico. But one must always expect bad luck stories when so many riders are competing in a race like Milan-San Remo.

As a result of the crashes, first Pecchielan (Molteni) and Ballini (Dreher) had taken up the chase, 200 meters up on the bunch, then Sanantonio and Guidali (Mobel-Huser) had gained 15 seconds. But by this time, after only six kilometers of gradual climbing, the break's lead had shot up to 2:40.

Our car had dropped back to be with the break on the climb, and it was frightening to see the speed with which they were progressing (it was too fast to call it "climbing") toward the Passo del Turchino. Out of crowd-packed Ovada, a typical hill town of tall, rectangular buildings, the 18 riders were in one long line, threading their way from bend to bend, as three consecutive rail crossings passed below them on the way to the heights. The road was now tight to the hills, with their cover of bare trees and patchy snow; and the lazy river of the plains had become a fast flowing stream, tumbling down the steep valley to the riders' left.

The upward gradient was not steep, but the riders were out of the saddle at times, because of the fierce pace being set at the front. On the flatter parts, two lines were in operation, with the whole 18 working as one unit, really charging along. On the steeper parts, young Pella was usually struggling to hang on, while Bitossi, Huysmans, Moser, Wolfshohl and Chiappano formed the vanguard; but the most ardent worker was little Eric Leman, who took the lead for long periods, hands on the drops and not looking around for any assistance. It seemed an unusual action from a rider who had been previously considered what Hoban described as a typical "skiving Belgian sprinter" ... but I thought back to Paris-Nice a few days before, when we had seen Leman sustain a solo break for an hour on the hilliest stage of the race. Here was the explanation: He was after his first classic win.

Only the climb's final slopes were steep enough to give the impression of a major col (the Turchino is only 1745 feet high), although there was plenty of atmosphere. The roadsides were jammed with people, cars and packed snow, police whistles blew, car horns sounded, the crowds clapped and cheered ... and then the leaders sprinted for the summit prime before disappearing into the dark, narrow tunnel beyond. It was Bitossi who pocketed the prime, just beating Dancelli, Moser and Wolfshohl; not a surprise. What was startling was the time they had now taken out of the bunch—4:50; nearly five minutes!

*Milan-San Remo • Italy • 1970*

This information was not given on the race radio until the dangerous descent had been completed, right down to sea level and the Mediterranean Sea near Genoa. It was like being transported into another part of the world. The halfway point of the race had been reached, and the wintry landscape of the northern side of the Apennines had been left behind; ahead lay the corniche road along the Riviera, with its palm trees and bays bathed in warm sunshine. Such a transportation must be a tremendous incentive to a break-away, particularly during the 12 kilometers of descending, with the mountains behind and the blue sea becoming closer and closer down the narrow valley.

Our car had overtaken the break on only the last part of the climb, and so we had the racers on our heels for the first part of the descent, swishing around the hairpin bends. The driver then accelerated away to the coast at Voltri, where the second agency man was waiting to take the Italian journalist's up-to-date race report, which he had finished typing coming down the mountain. It was like a piece of espionage, with the journalist holding up a little sign that the other man had to spot. He saw it, and came running out of the dense crowd—just as the break swept around the corner to start the 133 kilometers along the coast to San Remo. On seeing the riders come through, the local man could add another sentence at the end of the report: "Carlo Chiappano led the break through Voltri (155 kilometers) from Aldo Moser and Rik Van Looy, with Rolf Wolfshohl bringing up the rear, taking a drink from his bidon." And if he had his wits about him, he could have also added that the big bunch came through four minutes later.

Yes, the main field had pulled back almost a minute of its deficit on the downhill stretch. When the pack came along, it was one long line, spearheaded by the yellow Mann

**THE GREAT RACE**

and white Watney jerseys, both of these teams (working for Van Springel and Verbeeck, respectively) having missed out on the break. They were traveling very fast, and it looked like they would soon be reeling in the breakaways even more quickly.

The next time check was 3:50, still going down, but that was as low as it was to become for the next 50 miles—the reason being that there was now a strong tail wind, giving the 18 fugitives even more encouragement. It was a very blustery wind that I first noticed at Arenzano, where the thickly leafed palm trees were blowing vigorously, outlined against the blue of the sky. There were other evergreen trees—cypresses, pines, cedars—whose shade tempered the heat of the strong sunshine. And everywhere there were crowds, hundreds of thousands of them all the way to San Remo gathered in the succession of towns, tourist resorts and fishing villages: Cogoleto, Varazze, Albissola Marina, Savona, Spotorno, Lido di Borgio…. Was it to be a long procession to the finish, ending in a sprint on the Via Roma between the remains of this 18-up break?

It appeared that the best policy for those in front was to work together so that the bunch would not catch them, for the chances of success were very high with such a strong back wind. However, the composition of the break did not favor this policy. Among the 18 leaders, there were two teams with three riders each: Mars-Flandria (Leman, Eric and Roger De Vlaeminck) and Willem II (Van Looy, Ottenbros and Van Loo). This numerical superiority and sprinting prowess should have meant a sprint finish with one of their number winning; but this break had already been striving mutually for two hours, and there were about another three hours to go. By then, all of them would be very tired, so that the sprinting factor would not be so important. After the

*Milan-San Remo • Italy • 1970*

Mars and Willem II teams, both Molteni (with Dancelli and Chiappano) and Faemino (with Zilioli and Huysmans) had two riders there; none of them noted sprinters, so they would undoubtedly try to get a splinter group away before the finish. And among the individuals, there was another cross-section: Godefroot, Bitossi and Karstens would be happy to contest a sprint, while Wolfshohl, Pella, Soave, Moser and Simonetti would probably try to join any break-away attempts.

It was an interesting situation, and we soon saw that the policy was going to be one of attack after attack, until the decisive one eventually came.

THE RIVIERA ROAD between Genoa and San Remo falls into three distinct parts: from Voltri to Savona (30 kilometers) there are a series of hills rising about 200 feet with many twists and turns; then from Savona to Alassio (50 kilometers) the road is flatter and straighter, but with several narrow stretches through towns and villages, as well as six tunnels where the road cuts through coastal headlands; and the last and most famous section is from Alassio to San Remo (also 50 kilometers), offering the varied climbs of Capo Mele, Capo Cervo, Capo Berta and the Poggio (which is the highest at 500 feet above sea level).

There was plenty of action on the first stretch to Savona, where the breakaway had regained its former lead of 4:50. Several small attacks had contributed to this success, the main one being by Chiappano, Wolfshohl and Moser. All experienced riders, they understood the urgency to stop the break from stagnating. Their attack, on a section that dipped and turned around a rocky part of the coast, caused a split in the break that was mainly closed by Eric De Vlaeminck, who was clearly working in the interests of his two sprinter teammates.

**THE GREAT RACE**

They regrouped on a flat section of road, high above the turquoise-blue sea before Varazze, a charming little town with yachts bobbing in the harbor, and heads bobbing in the crowd to see the action. There were no more attempts to upset things before Savona, because this was the first feeding zone (the second was at Alassio); and all 18 men would be needing fresh drinks and food if they were to stay away to the finish, especially in the summer-like temperatures that had materialized.

Savona is a big shipping port, and I wondered if anyone else spotted the big Norwegian ship tied up in the docks as we went by—it was called Long Hope!! It would be a good name to give to this superb 18-man break: the Long Hope Break. That long hope was looking much more possible, the odds now being much shorter that they would finally succeed.

To see how the chase was progressing behind, we stopped for some hurried refreshments on the road out of Savona, grabbing a coffee and getting away just as the peloton came ambling through. Yes, there was little hurry about the giant group, now 5:35 in arrears, typified by the figure of Raymond Poulidor at the front, who was looking around to see if anyone else was interested in chasing. It seemed that the defending riders (in the majority) had killed off most of the urgency shown earlier, so the initiative was back with the riders up front—if they could keep their speed up, they had a very good chance of lasting out the 100 kilometers that still remained.

While we motored back up to the break, the radio announced that Huysmans, Zilioli and Godefroot were piling on the pressure, causing another split in the break, which had closed again by the time we reached them at Spotorno (198 kilometers). News had also come that three riders had gained 20 seconds on the bunch, 5:20 down on the

*Milan-San Remo • Italy • 1970*

break. Their names? Conti (SCIC), Crepaldi (Salvarani) and Monseré (Mars-Flandria), the last two more likely to be defending than attacking. It showed that the experienced men in front were justified in their efforts to keep the pace high; and soon, four more men were 100 meters clear: Zilioli and Moser again, with Leman defending and Pella also there, having recovered from his earlier falterings. It was another split, and this time it was loners Bitossi and Wolfshohl who caused the regroupment.

This activity seemed bound to throw up some successful attacks before long, despite the absence of hills on this Savona-Alassio section. It remained to be seen whose ambitions were the greatest, as nearly all of the 18 seemed to fancy themselves as winners. This is why the break was so interesting. In a similar break in a stage race, they would all be working for a common cause and there would be none of these repeated attacks; and if there had been, there would have been less urgency in bringing them back.

Another five minutes and there were two more pairs opening up gaps, and this time Godefroot led the chase to neutralize them. And the radio gave the time gap as 4:40. Were the larger numbers in the bunch at last having their say? It seemed that way, for the break had clearly slowed down, as emphasized by an incident that moment when young Pella punctured and rejoined the others with no trouble.

It looked as if this Savona-Alassio section was finally going to cause the break's downfall, most of the 18 now looking tired after being away for 120 kilometers. Chiappano was still active, and Van Looy was also attacking, but the men from Mars were on the alert, working toward a hoped-for sprint finish.

And then it happened: a break so unexpected that everyone was taken by surprise.

**THE GREAT RACE**

We were coming into Loano (218 kilometers), a typical small village with crowds jammed solid both sides of the winding main street ... and there was a prime to sprint for. A prime that was to cause the second decisive move of the 1970 Milan-San Remo. Alassio (and the start of the final hilly section) was not far away, and so our car had just overtaken the break. Looking back, I saw that Chiappano was sprinting away for the prime, which he took in his stride. Several bends then interrupted our view, before I saw the brown Molteni jersey again, now well clear of the others. I wrote down in my notebook: "Chiappano 0:20 up. Out of sight of break."

It had happened very quickly, but it was quite a surprise to see on dropping back that it was not Chiappano ... it was Dancelli. Yes, the two Molteni men had worked a very subtle ploy that only one or two of the riders in the break could have spotted. Dancelli had asked his teammate to lead him out for the prime; but Chiappano was first over the line, and then immediately eased, allowing his leader to continue at full speed, giving him a huge lead in no time at all.

The break had been riding in a jagged single line through the town, and so the view of most riders of the incident was this: They saw a Molteni rider attacking for the prime, before seeing him drop back after taking the cash prize. A team car (Molteni) then passed the riders, obviously moving ahead to the last feeding station at Alassio. It was another of the never-ending series of incidents that would continue all the way to the finish. Nothing to worry about.

The few riders who had seen that Dancelli had gone away were probably of the same opinion. Nothing to worry about. One man like Dancelli would have no chance of staying away for the remaining 70 kilometers from such riders as Godefroot, Wolfshohl, Zilioli, Huysmans, De Vlaeminck ... it

*Milan-San Remo • Italy • 1970*

was out of the question. Few people would have disagreed with this opinion—except, of course, Michele Dancelli.

He was riding as if the finish were only a mile away, his big gear turning on the flat, smooth road, eyes alert and concentrating on the goal ahead—to become the first Italian to win the Primavera for 16 years. Things were going perfectly so far, and, after he had been away for only five kilometers, I timed his lead as 1:10 over the others.

The wind was blowing more strongly than ever from right behind, and there were no signs of a chase materializing.

The deeply tanned, pint-sized 27-year-old Italian had every incentive to keep riding at maximum speed. The beautiful corniche road started again before Alassio, with the wind whipping up white caps on the turquoise sea. The sun was warmer than ever and the crowds were cheering for Dancelli all the way, having heard from the radio of his attack. Conditions could not have been more perfect.

Down into Alassio, where big rollers crashed on the sandy beach to the left, news came through that Roger De Vlaeminck had attacked from the group and was chasing Dancelli on his own. So they had found out that the Italian was away, but they couldn't have known that he was now two minutes clear. In fact, the first race-radio information concerning the attack was at 2:58 p.m., exactly 40 minutes after Dancelli had gone away. It was the sort of thing that could only happen in Italy, and even then, they gave facts that were 15 minutes out of date, saying that at Laigueglia (239 kilometers), Dancelli was 1:35 clear of De Vlaeminck, 2:25 clear of the other breakaways, and six minutes up on the pack.

Since even that message was garbled on our radio, we stopped at the 40 kilometers-to-go sign, after watching Dancelli climb the steep Capo Mele and flatter Capo Cervo in

**THE GREAT RACE**

impressive style, still riding with the impetus of his initial attack. The gap on the chasers was now 3:30 and he was still gaining, De Vlaeminck not having been strong enough to pursue his effort. The 17 were riding without conviction, looking at each other to do something about the situation. Ahead lay the Capo Berta, an unrelenting climb that rises from sea level at Diano Marina to just over 400 feet.

Would this prove the downfall of Dancelli? It seemed unlikely as we cruised up the hill, with the break ambling along behind, led all the way up by Jos Huysmans. There was no snap in the riding, just a sort of resignation, although we discovered later that many of them (including Karstens) had not been informed of Dancelli's break. Only at the summit (where the deficit was 3:35) was there any action. Godefroot jumped away suddenly, with Eric Leman glued to his wheel, and Wolfshohl chasing on the descent.

The acceleration was enough to split the group into three, with Ottenbros and Pella being dropped, following in the wake of Chiappano who lost contact on the actual climb. It also cut Dancelli's lead by a minute, although there was but 20 kilometers to bring back the other two-and-a-half minutes. The flatter roads after Imperia caused a regroupment, and Leman then took up the chasing for the Mars team, proving that Paris-Nice had really brought him to a high degree of fitness.

The finish was now at the front of all our thoughts, and it seemed that only a disaster could rob Dancelli of the victory he had set out to conquer six hours earlier on the outskirts of Milan. Our car was also heading for the finish, which meant passing Dancelli after another slight climb. There were vehicles everywhere, most of them press cars that had been cruising in front for the whole race. The race director was again panicking, shouting for the cars to move

*Milan-San Remo • Italy • 1970*

forward on the descent. Dancelli was almost riding along in our trunk, which he didn't seem to mind, but the man in charge did. So our driver pulled over to let them pass, and the situation was again back to normal.

It was another incident that was bound to encourage Dancelli, and there was only the 500-foot climb of the Poggio left in the last 10 kilometers that could possibly defeat him. It did not. And at the summit of the two miles of 5-percent grade, he was still 2:00 clear of Leman, and 2:30 up on the others headed by Karstens, Simonetti and Wolfshohl; while Van Looy and most of the other escapees were in the process of being absorbed by the bunch that was still more than 120 strong.

This information came from the loudspeakers strung along the Via Roma at the finish, all the press cars having bypassed the last hill by continuing along the coast road instead of turning right up to Poggio village. The truly enormous finish crowds cheered every announcement as if Italy had just won the World Cup. In fact, it was more important than that. It was their own Michele, who would now be known affectionately as Michelino, who was coming in, to win the Primavera after a gap of 17 years. The noise was deafening as he came freewheeling down that famous street, his arms raised in pleasure, honor and emotion, with his rascally face a mass of smiles and joyful tears. He had won the greatest victory of his life.

If this were not drama enough, the next piece of action would have amply sufficed. It was the stupendous finishing effort of Gerben Karstens, who had gained 50 seconds on the winner in five kilometers to catch little Leman in the last yards and fling his bike over the line in front, and throw his arms up in victory. This could only have been the action of a man who really believed he had gained another classic

**THE GREAT RACE**

win, an opinion that was quickly confirmed by the Dutchman as he spoke with the journalists beyond the line. As I said, it could only happen in Italy.

The final picture could have been even more dramatic, and would have given Eddy Merckx his fourth victory in the race, because the main bunch was but 17 seconds behind Karstens at the line, and it was Merckx who spearheaded a superb line of sprinters to take eighth position, just ahead of Verbeeck, Reybroeck, Van Ryckeghem et al. And just as they had been winding up this sprint, there had been a massive pileup in the bunch, with bikes and bodies littering the street. It had been a long way to come for a crash, and I will always remember the bulky figure of Spaniard Carlos Echevarria strolling the last yards, dragging his bike behind him.

Another race was over, the sun was shining and the people were happy.

So happy that they were still mobbing "their" winner, shouting out "Ecco, ecco, Dancelli, Dancelli...." Had it been a "hollow" victory, I mused, considering the final action of Karstens? No, it was a win that fully warranted all the fanatical furor of the tifosi and deserving of the highest praise from the sportswriters of Europe. It had been a splendid way to carve the name of Dancelli into the Italian history books: winner of The Great Race.

*Milan-San Remo • Italy • 1970*

# CRITERIUMS FOR THE STARS

## Châteauneuf-la-Forêt and St. Claud

## France
## April 1968

Easter weekend in France is the traditional time to open the country's season of criterium racing—multi-lap races on short circuits where fans pay to watch the action. Until there was a huge stepup in pro cyclists' salaries in the late 1980s, the star riders earned most of their income from appearance fees at these criteriums. In the 1960s, $750 was huge start money for a top rider, and is equivalent to perhaps $10,000 today. Among the few earning big bucks in the 1960s were French standouts Jacques Anquetil and Raymond Poulidor, who fought many epic battles at the Tour de France from 1962 onwards. They earned top billing at two criteriums in April 1968.

# France

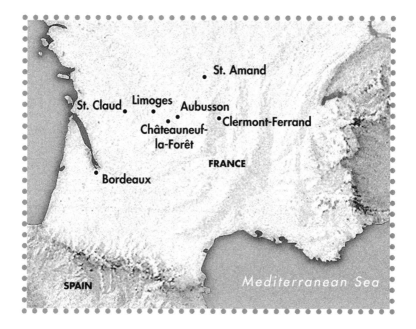

CRITERIUM RACING originated in France, where most towns and villages around the country stage an annual bicycle race. The most popular ones are those to which the top professionals are invited, enabling the organizers to charge spectators entrance money, so that there is enough cash to pay for the stars' appearance fees. In 1968, the season's opening pro criteriums were held on Easter Sunday and Monday. The first was at Châteauneuf-la-Forêt, in the Haute Vienne, local region of the popular Raymond Poulidor, while the second was held at St. Claud, another small village, 65 miles to the west in the Charente region, where Cognac brandy is produced. My own cycling journey to see these events began more than 300 miles away in Burgundy, where the best French wines come from.

Luckily for me, a northeast wind that had been blowing for more than two weeks was still rampant, giving me a strong, but cold, tail wind that was mitigated by bright sunshine from dawn to dusk. Central France in springtime is a delightful place to be. The roads are empty, the leaves are just beginning to show in the trees, and violets and cowslips abound on the roadside verges. It is also warm enough to stop and enjoy a lunchtime picnic.

The 91 miles I covered the first day of my journey ended in the pleasant town of St. Amand-Montrond, the last mile of which I rode sedately behind a friendly gendarme! No, I was not that tired; it was just that there was a network of narrow streets between the police station and the youth hostel, and I was told in the genadarmerie that the easiest way to find the hostel was to follow the gendarme on his bike.

The next day, I was soon in the hills of the Massif Central, and I will long remember the road between Montluçon and Chambon as one of the hilliest I have encountered in France, especially since I was loaded up with touring gear.

*Châteauneuf-la-Forêt and St. Claud • France • 1968*

The rolling countryside, however, with fir-lined valleys and busy streams, was ample compensation; as was the final exhilarating swoop down to the tightly enclosed town of Aubusson, and a welcome meal of *truite meunière* followed by *steak maître d'hotel*. The town, population 6000, is famous for its tapestry and carpet industry, and it was a joy to see the window displays in every other shop. The tapestries were all brightly colored, with every conceivable picture or pattern depicted on them.

Aubusson is also famous, in cycling circles, for having organized the French pro road championship there in 1967, and for a criterium at nearby Felletin, where 25,000 would see the hilly 1968 edition won by Frenchman Gilbert Bellone. Bellone, who won the stage into Bayonne at last year's Tour de France, was also the winner of the first, and only criterium previously held at Châteauneuf-la-Forêt, in 1966. From a local paper, I saw that Bellone would be riding again; but it seemed unlikely he would repeat his success, because among his Mercier teammates was local hero Poulidor, along with three other French riders, Christian Robini, Robert Cazala and Francis Campaner, and new British pro Graham Webb, the 1967 world amateur road champion.

Against this strength in depth, the Bic team of five-time Tour de France winner Jacques Anquetil also included 1966 Tour winner Lucien Aimar and Spanish climber Julio Jimenez, who has won the Tour's King of the Mountains title for the past three years. Other interesting elements among the scheduled 27 starters (all of them paid start money) were Bitossi and Mugnaini of the Italian Filotex squad, local professionals Daunat, Rabaute and Samy, and half a dozen *hors-categorie* amateurs—including the classy Paul Gutty from Lyon.

It was drizzling when I left my Aubusson hotel the morning of the first race, but it was only a short 70-kilometer ride to Châteauneuf. There was, however, a stiff little hill to climb

**CRITERIUMS FOR THE STARS**

out of the Vienne valley at Eymoutiers, and it must have been used in some recent races, because "POULIDOR" was scrawled in paint at various points up its length. Châteauneuf-la-Forêt is a small hillside village a couple of miles off the main road to Limoges, and I was probably the first spectator to arrive. The race was not due to start for another four hours.

Road blocks were not yet in place, and the entry booths stood waiting for their first customers (Entry 7 francs; 6- to 14-year-olds 3 francs—or about $1.50 and 50 cents). I took the chance to ride around the circuit, but came to an abrupt halt at the top of the 600-yard-long hill when my rear tire blew out … just a few yards from the "Arrivée" banner that was going up. The men erecting the crowd barriers on this stretch stopped work for a minute to see what had happened, as I changed the tire. That finished, I was glad of the shelter offered by a temporary "buvette" canopy, where the "landlord" was stocking up with crates of beer and orange soda. The rain had suddenly become heavier, and I wondered if this would affect the size of the afternoon's crowd.

Well, it didn't. The countless Poulidor fans of the region do not have many chances of cheering their hero in the flesh—especially in a race against Anquetil. And they were not going to worry about rain. With an hour to go before the start, a long line of cars stretched up the hill across the valley. And the thousands of passengers were massed around the 1.8-kilometer (1.1-mile) circuit, most of them on the 7-percent hill that had to be climbed 60 times. This would certainly be no easy "fish-and-chip" criterium, even though it was only 67 miles long.

Before the main event, there was a 15-lapper for local youngsters, who arrived in an assortment of football shorts, sneakers, trade jerseys and helmets too big for them. These were certainly not pampered French amateurs, and they showed as much enthusiasm as schoolboys anywhere. The

*Châteauneuf-la-Forêt and St. Claud • France • 1968*

winner was an incredibly spindly legged youth, who knew how to get up that hill quicker than the others. A similar event would have been against the rules in Britain, where the federation handbook says that a schoolboy cannot compete in a road race until he is 14.

The "Prix des Jeunes" took place in the dry, as the rain eased just before the start; and it was still dry when the pros emerged from the local school, where the main classroom served as a makeshift changing room. But the rain soon started falling again, getting heavier as the race went on. Not that it really affected the crowd's entertainment. The non-stop speaker, Jean Tamain, had plenty to say, with the bunch lapping every two-and-a-half minutes and in sight for much of that time. He certainly kept the 15,000-strong crowd on its toes—as did the race, which was constantly on the move.

One of the first attackers was Italian star Franco Bitossi, who had a 35-second lead by the end of six laps. His restless style was well suited to this tough little circuit. Basically, it was triangular in plan, with one side downhill, one side flat and the other side uphill to the finishing line. In fact, the hill made the race into a battle of the climbers— remember that former winner Bellone is a renowned *grimpeur*, having won the hilly stage of the French Critérium National at Revel in 1966.

On the seventh lap, Jean-Pierre Ducasse (hero of the Tourmalet stage in last year's Tour) took up the chase, which brought an immediate reaction from Poulidor, momentarily splitting the bunch. Ducasse was brought back, and straight away Mercier's Francis Campaner started a counter move. By lap 12, he had latched on to Bitossi and the two were 45 seconds ahead. With several primes under his belt, the Italian decided to slip back; but the energetic Campaner pressed on and maintained his lead for the next 15 laps. This boy from Bordeaux is also an accomplished climber.

**CRITERIUMS FOR THE STARS**

Half-distance here was reached in one hour, 18 minutes (26 mph), and Aimar and Poulidor were now chasing hard through the torrential rain. I suspect they were glad that they had not had this weather a week before in Paris-Roubaix, although the mud-spattered bunch was beginning to look like fugitives from the "Hell of the North." Within two laps, the Aimar-Poulidor tandem had bridged the 40-second gap, but the rest of the field was also becoming more active, with Bitossi again stirring things up. With Poulidor out in front, the locals were all happy and the race had come to life. In road racing, the decisive moves often happen very quickly, and this race was no exception.

After a closing-up of the leading riders, a clear break emerged with 15 laps to go. In one lap, Poulidor came cleanly away, but with the aggressive Paul Gutty in his wake. It would be an interesting struggle between these two resistant riders, both good climbers. Gutty, like several top French "amateurs," is a gypsy in the summer, traveling all over the country riding in pro criteriums and the richer amateur races; he consequently makes a better living than some professionals.

Gutty did not look out of place in his two-up break with the revered Poulidor, and they were soon a minute up on a numbed and struggling pack. Meanwhile, Anquetil was not having a brilliant day. He has never liked the cold and wet, yet he proved that he was prepared to suffer in search for form by figuring among the 18 finishers.

With five laps left, the two leaders still had 55 seconds in hand on the strung-out peloton, and a two-up sprint finish seemed in the cards. But Poulidor was not going to let a chance to shine slip away in front of his own fans, and he attacked vigorously on the 59th climb to leave Gutty groveling in his wake. The crowd cheered their hero even louder, quite happy to be standing in the rain for a couple of hours

*Châteauneuf-la-Forêt and St. Claud • France • 1968*

to see their own Pou-Pou win at Châteauneuf "en solitaire." Gutty lost 43 seconds on that last lap to take second place, while the unexpected Christian Robini outsprinted Aimar for third place another half-minute back.

The race over, the thousands of fans streamed up the hill to cheer the immensely popular Poulidor, as he received his winner's bouquet and was interviewed by the speaker. An hour later, there was still a big crowd gathered in the school hall for the *vin d'honneur*. Everyone had a glass or two of champagne, and helped themselves to petits-fours; and then the mayor of Châteauneuf made a typical mayor's speech, saying what a nice day everybody had had, and how they would be running the race again in 1969. Both Poulidor and then Anquetil said a few words of thanks, each receiving an equally enthusiastic reception. Farewells were said and the riders adjourned to the nursery school next door to receive their contract money: Anquetil was first in line, followed by Poulidor, who was carrying his small daughter, and then Aimar … it was a very friendly assembly.

Most of the pros were competing the next day at St. Claud, so they were soon roaring off into the night heading for home or hotel. By chance, I came across one of these hotels the next morning. When looking for a place to have lunch on the way to St. Claud, I spotted a sign pointing to an "auberge" down a side road. It led down a bumpy lane, over a small stream, past some old wrought-iron gates and up a tree-lined drive to a vast old château and its gravel courtyard. It had a beautiful, manicured lawn and flower garden; and there, sitting on a small dado wall, was a track-suited Julio Jimenez polishing his wheels that glinted in the bright spring sunshine. I have rarely been to a more peaceful spot, and the chirping of the song-birds and the rustling of the leaves in the beech trees seemed to be coming from another world.

**CRITERIUMS FOR THE STARS**

The silence was broken momentarily as a big Mercedes-Benz drew smoothly up, its wheels crunching eloquently over the gravel. Out stepped French pros Raymond Riotte and Jean Stablinski; and I learned from the bow-tied waiter as he showed me into the polished, wood-floored banqueting hall, with acres of white linen covering the long oak tables, that "Monsieur Anquetil" and "Monsieur Poulidor" were also expected for a lunch appointment at noon.

Bottles of red Bordeaux were uncorked in anticipation of the two honored guests, whose public rivalry is well-known, but their private friendship less so. The two French stars are at different phases in their careers—five-time Tour winner Anquetil, 33, soon to retire, Poulidor, 29, still a Tour de France contender—but their popularity has never been greater. They regularly command the fattest fees in the annual round of French criteriums, and every organizer is happy to have the pair topping their bill, as they are bound to draw a big crowd on reputation alone. It is because of this popular rivalry that Anquetil has not yet retired. How can he afford to when every appearance on the starting line in a criterium means another $750 in the bank?

Anquetil and Poulidor work hard for this kind of money. Besides the vast amount of traveling entailed, criss-crossing the country in the busy post-Tour criterium season, they have to maintain good form to give the public their money's worth. Crowds attracted to the race by the big names expect to see their favorites battling as hard as in a Tour de France or Paris-Nice epic. In this 1968 season, they would keep the fans happy, with Poulidor winning 10 criteriums, Anquetil six.

Socially, the two mix in different circles. Although Anquetil grew up in a family of strawberry growers, his home was near the city of Rouen. He had cycling success in

*Châteauneuf-la-Forêt and St. Claud • France • 1968*

his late teens, and soon earned enough to buy a manor house overlooking the Seine, only an hour outside of Paris. A man of feline grace, coiffed blond hair and sophisticated tastes, he enjoys playing cards and drinking champagne with his Parisian friends. Poulidor's broad country accent immediately sets him apart, and he still lives in a modest home near his parents' farmhouse in rural Limousin. That's what makes him an underdog, popular with the masses, as does his stubborn determination and often terrible bad luck.

At the château restaurant near St. Claud, Anquetil fit right in, while Poulidor was clearly uncomfortable. He'd rather be sitting at a country inn, eating a cheese-and-ham *casse-croûte*, than feasting on a *déjeuner* of local fish and game. But he knew that this pre-race get-together was necessary to discuss how the afternoon's criterium would be played out. As he, Poulidor, had won in front of own fans the day before, it seemed logical that Anquetil be the one who made the bigger effort today. We would see....

It was Easter Monday, a national holiday in Europe, and there was a real holiday atmosphere in St. Claud as the crowds rolled up by the thousands to pay 8 francs ($2) to get on the circuit, or 12 francs ($3) for the scaffolding-and-plank grandstands. Whole families arrived, with Maman carrying a vast canvas bag containing sliced ham and cheese, peaches and endless loaves; Papa with an equally large hold-all of bottles of wine, beer and lemonade; little Pascal with his Poulidor *casquette* and staggering along with the canvas chairs; and, of course, his sister Arlette whimsying along behind in her Sunday best that was sure to get stained as soon as Papa bought her that first chocolate *glace*.

The criterium at St. Claud is completely different from that at Châteauneuf-la-Forêt. For a start, this one is longer established, having been organized 15 times previously. The mountains of Haute Vienne have been left far behind and a rolling

**CRITERIUMS FOR THE STARS**

5.1-kilometer (3.2-mile) circuit is employed that runs down either side of a small valley, with a sharp dip and a climb to be made each half-lap, to get from one side to the other. There were 25 laps to cover for a total distance of 128 kilometers (79 miles), but it would be an easier race than the day before, with a bigger field, a bigger circuit...and an even bigger crowd.

All these factors led to a more evenly contested race, with no rider gaining much of a lead. Another reason was the field's incentive to stay together to sprint for the big lap primes donated by a happy crowd, in response to the inspired pleadings of the speaker. With the riders taking a "long" eight minutes a lap, his job was doubly difficult, yet he never seemed to run out of ideas to entertain the massed crowds at the finish area. The speaker kept things going by raising seemingly exorbitant sums of money for primes. He would say: "I have announced a 2000-franc prime for two laps' time. There is 200 francs in the kitty." (That's like announcing a $500 lap prize when there is only $50 collected). Then he would make the people fork out their change by giving a running commentary on how the prize pool was going. He always reached his target! The master stroke was when he was becoming hoarse and ready to conserve his vocal chords, so he had the two factions of the crowd contesting with each other over which group could chant "Poulee-dor!" the louder. It was a deafening sound.

In fact, Poulidor was again one of the stars of the afternoon, but only in a support role. Also in the cast were several hot riders of the moment: Italy's Franco Bitossi, France's Cyrille Guimard, England's Derek Harrison, Belgium's Ward Sels ... and, the designated star of the day's show, Anquetil. In the first half of the race, there had been some unscripted, prime-hunting attacks by Anatole Novak, Raymond Riotte and Jacques Cadiou (all Frenchmen); but with seven laps still to go, the entire cast remained tightly bunched togeth-

*Châteauneuf-la-Forêt and St. Claud • France • 1968*

John Wilcockson's **WORLD OF CYCLING**

· · · · · · · · · · · · · · · · · · · · · · · · · · · · · · · · · · · · · · · · · · · · · · · · · · · · · · · · · · · · · ·

**96**

er. At that point, Frenchman Robini and Englishman Webb went off the back with punctures, and Anquetil and Bitossi went off the front with ambitions.

The pair soon started to gain on the tiring bunch: They were 30 seconds up with six laps to go; a minute, a lap later; 1:30 with four laps (and 13 miles) left…. Then Guimard and Harrison came into the picture, and one lap later, an interesting situation had evolved: Anquetil and Bitossi together in the lead; Guimard and Harrison at 1:20; Poulidor alone at 1:56; and the rest at 2:25. Through the finishing zone, the crowds were thrilled to see Anquetil drop the Italian, while Poulidor, after an incredibly vigorous sprint up the main climb, latched on to the Anglo-French chase duo.

I had been walking around the circuit in the reverse direction, and was now at the bottom of the drop from the village that led over a narrow, hump-backed, stone bridge. There, I was privileged to see the full fury of Jacques Anquetil, time trialist extraordinaire, as he thundered toward me, negotiated the bridge and then swished past in his inimitable, relentless style. He was already 50 seconds clear of Bitossi, 1:30 ahead of the chasing trio, and three minutes in front of the rest. Those last five miles would be a formality; and indeed, there were two long minutes between the time the great Jacques crossed the line in triumph, and the sprint for second spot won by Guimard from Poulidor, Harrison and Bitossi.

So the metaphorical battle was over for another day. This time, Anquetil had pleased the fans to answer the opening salvo by Poulidor the day before. Their criterium clash would continue for the rest of the season, and the crowds would continue to flock to see their idols maintaining the struggle. Anquetil versus Poulidor is a well-worn epic that still has many more theaters of battle to play in before it becomes "gone with the wind."

**CRITERIUMS FOR THE STARS**

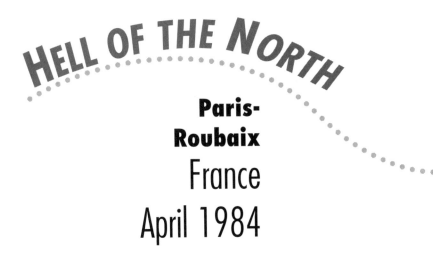

# HELL OF THE NORTH

**Paris-
Roubaix**

France
April 1984

In terms of prestige, few events in the cycling world can come close to Paris-Roubaix. The race, first held in 1896, built its tough reputation because of the cobblestone roads it encountered in the Nord (or North) region of France, on a course between Paris and the velodrome in Roubaix, a blue-collar city close to the Belgian border. By the 1960s, many of the cobblestone highways had been paved with asphalt, so the organizers switched the latter part of the race to small farm roads and forest tracks that date from the Napoleonic era. These "roads" are narrow and potholed, some paved with cobblestones, some just dirt. That's how the event gained its infamous moniker: *L'Enfer du Nord,* the Hell of the North.

# France

Roubaix

Brussels

Lille

Orchies

BELGIUM

Wallers

Valenciennes

Amiens

Neuvilly

Saint-Quentin

Compiègne

Paris

FRANCE

A PASSER-BY wandering into the Victorian era velodrome at Roubaix at 5:33 p.m. on Sunday, April 8, 1984, would have gained a curious view of the toughest classic in the world of cycling. Two zombie-like figures, caked from helmet to cleats in dried, grey clay, pedaled mechanically around the broad concrete bowl, the younger man in front. The shorter, slimmer rider followed, trance-like, until 150 meters from home he stamped briefly on the pedals. In 50 meters, he gained 30. And he did it as nonchalantly as a category-four racer outwitting his kid sister in a sprint down to the ice cream parlor. Sean Kelly had just won Paris-Roubaix.

After a race in which each of the 158 starters had a different story to tell, in which there was so much contradictory information emanating from radio commentators up and down the course that one really needed a computer with a very long memory to analyze it, one sentence spoken by one man cut like a laser through the muddied confusion that is Paris-Roubaix.

"At Wallers, half of my riders were on their backs, and the other half were flat on their faces," reported Cyrille Guimard, the leading French coach of the most powerful French team, Renault-Elf. None of his men arrived at Roubaix on their bikes. They had been beaten, not so much by lack of athletic ability as by their inability to get through the Forest of Wallers-Arenberg unscathed.

To the men who have survived this far on the road to Roubaix, the forest is the darkest, deepest jungle. One can almost feel the presence of Cerberus, the three-headed dog that guards the entrance to hell, lurking among the tall, sinister trees, waiting to draw innocent cyclists into his black, boggy clutches.

*Paris-Roubaix • France • 1984*

The forest is criss-crossed with every conceivable form of roadway, from narrow, dirt footpaths to a six-lane autoroute. In the distant past, the tracks were used for dragging felled trees to the nascent iron-making region of Valenciennes. But the ground was too soft, so chunky granite blocks were imported from some unknown quarry to build something more substantial.

The 3 kilometers of pavé (as these cobblestoned tracks are known in France) that links Arenberg with the hamlet of Grand Bray, remains the same (if a little more battered) as it was perhaps 200 years ago. Some of that pinkish-colored granite has sunk further into the clay than elsewhere, and these dips soon fill with water after rainfall. The sun rarely filters between the trees to evaporate it.

That was the situation in the Wallers-Arenberg "alleyway," the day of this Paris-Roubaix. The heavy rain through the week had cleared, but the puddles remained; and when a few vehicles had come this way, bringing rubber-necked crowds to see the chaos, there were few dry spots for thin rubber treads to grip.

Arenberg village lies just eight kilometers beyond the first feed zone of Paris-Roubaix, 158 kilometers from the start, and 108 kilometers from the finish. By this stage, more than 100 of the starters had been jettisoned from the leading group, beaten by the nine previous sections of pavé, between Neuvilly (105 kilometers) and Valenciennes.

Riding ahead of the 50-strong pack were just two men, the Teutonic twosome of Czeslaw Lang, Poland's only pro, and Ralf Hofeditz, an ungainly West German. They were part of a break that had a 12-minute lead before reaching Neuvilly, but as they approached the forest, they had retained only two of these minutes. The speed in the peloton was almost twice theirs....

**HELL OF THE NORTH**

"I was at the front," said reigning world champion Greg LeMond, "alongside Sean Kelly. He was riding within himself, looking around, whereas I was going flat out."

The previous evening, at the Ibis Hotel in Compiègne, where the race now starts, LeMond had judged that "Kelly is 20-percent better than everyone at the moment."

Since finishing a disgruntled second to Panasonic's Johan Lammerts in the previous Sunday's Tour of Flanders—"It's not sporting what the Panasonic team did. Anyone can follow like they did, and then jump away at the end. But that's not the way to race," said the Irishman—Kelly had flown to northern Spain for a race he hadn't really wanted to ride: the five-day Tour of the Basque Country.

His instinct was to stay in Belgium and compete in—and perhaps win—the Ghent-Wevelgem classic. But good start money for Kelly's Skil team in Spain depended on the Irish star's participation. Fortunately, things worked out well: He won two of the first three road stages, came in second in two others, and went on to take the closing time trial for a seemingly effortless overall victory.

"The weather was wet and cold in Spain," said Kelly before Paris-Roubaix. "So I'll be quite happy if it rains today. And it was quiet there, away from all the crowds and phone calls."

LeMond's week had been somewhat different. He had ridden over the Roubaix route—including "the forest" road—on Tuesday, and raced in Ghent-Wevelgem the next day. "I'm glad I didn't do the cobbles ride on Friday, as was scheduled. I'd have been wiped, man," LeMond sighed. "I wasn't going well in Wevelgem, and I was passed by two or three others in the last 150 meters of the sprint." (He finished ninth).

"I was so tired, I spent two days in bed, Thursday and Friday. I had to do four hours training Saturday, but I nor-

*Paris-Roubaix • France • 1984*

mally like to do a long ride two days before a race." It is small things like this that prey on a rider's mind when he is in a man-to-man situation. So as he raced toward the ungated rail crossing that is the entrance to Arenberg's little hell, LeMond was already a psychological victim of Kelly's strength.

Like every other rider, they knew the importance of reaching the crossing in front. And the leaders of the pack formed a solid, fast-moving phalanx, shoulder-to-shoulder, wheel-to-wheel as they hurtled between the brick row houses of Arenberg. Awaiting them, beyond the rail tracks and before the pavé, was a 20-meter stretch of red shale, made muddy by the week's rainfall. In the front line, along with Kelly and LeMond were two Frenchman on the Peugeot team, Francis Castaing and Dominique Lecrocq.

"I made an error," said Castaing, "by wanting to accelerate too strongly. The result was a crash, a deep cut on my knee, and I was out of the race."

Lecrocq fared little better. "I was in third place entering Arenberg," he reported. "But within 10 meters, I had a flat." He went on to finish the race, but arrived almost half-an-hour behind the leaders.

Another few, frenzied pedal strokes into the forest and LeMond came tumbling down. In trying to avoid him, Kelly was forced off the cobbles into the trees. "I didn't fall," recounted Kelly, "but I lost lots of time. I had to put my bike back on the road, and then get my feet back in the toe clips before starting to chase."

In front of him, Kelly could see other crashes, and riders picking themselves out of the mud after falling to the side of the "road." Much in evidence were the striped yellow shirts of the Guimard men—covered in the black slime deposited on the pavé from an overhead bridge that links a coal mine with its slag heaps.

 **HELL OF THE NORTH**

One of the Renault-Elf men, Pascal Jules, tumbled on the left, injuring his ankle. Another, Laurent Fignon, also came down, while their teammate Marc Madiot (who was fifth in 1983) was experiencing the second of *four* crashes that littered his progress along this three-kilometer section of cobblestones.

As Kelly began to start moving again, he saw Eric Vanderaerden (another prerace favorite) and Ronny Van Holen (winner of the Flèche Brabançonne two weeks earlier) tangle wheels and fall. They were straightening handlebars and saddles as Kelly, grim-faced, rode by, picking his way carefully between the puddles and the potholes.

Clear of the carnage, and racing toward the end of the "tunnel" were three riders: two from the La Redoute team, Gregor Braun, the big German, and French hopeful Alain Bondue; and the redoubtable Flemish roadman, Rudy Matthys. All three were prerace favorites. Maybe this was the winning move.

It could have been, but Matthys punctured his rear tire, and it was left to the two La Redoute teammates—both of them former world track champions in the individual pursuit—to blaze a trail. They soon passed the already forgotten Hofeditz and Lang, and a first time check placed them one minute ahead of 14 riders who had regrouped, but were yet to organize a chase.

"Joyeux anniversaire" (Happy birthday) read the many banners prepared by fans of local hero Bondue, who was born within shouting distance of the Roubaix velodrome. It was the incentive of success in his hometown that had fired up his imagination. And winning would be a perfect birthday present....

After another nasty stretch of cobbles, 1.7 kilometers long, Braun punctured. Bondue waited, and their lead was

*Paris-Roubaix • France • 1984*

cut to 35 seconds. But there was no question of waiting for the chasing group, which contained Kelly and the 1983 winner, Dutchman Hennie Kuiper, who was accompanied by three of his Kwantum team riders: Ludo Peeters, Adri Van Houwelingen and Leo Van Vliet. By continuing their attack, Bondue and Braun were making their opponents work hard, which in turn was taking the pressure off Jean-Luc Vandenbroucke and Ferdi Van den Haute, two other La Redoute men who were in the chase group.

This "peloton" had grown to 25 riders by Orchies (194 kilometers), where the leading pair was 1:48 ahead. Behind, Matthys had caught up with the chase group after a 20-kilometer pursuit, while seven others latched on to the end of the line as the Kwantum men pulled the chasers into another broken section of pavé across open fields. Four of these unfortunates were delayed immediately by a crash that involved Kelly's countryman, Stephen Roche, another La Redoute rider.

While Roche was destined to make another long and vain chasing effort, Kelly was wondering how he could extricate himself from another Tour of Flanders "situation." He was the only Skil rider in the two-dozen strong group, imprisoned by the tactics of Kwantum and La Redoute. Ahead, on either side of the town of Bersée, were two three-kilometers slices of "cottage-loaf"-sized cobbles. It was still too early to make a break for home, especially as the Kwantum riders—with the help of another Dutchman, Johan Van der Velde of the Italian team, Metauro—were still pegging the two leaders back to a two-minute advantage.

Perhaps Kelly should have let the situation take care of itself, as riders would be dropped from the group by natural attrition: fatigue, falls and flats. Matthys, for example, dropped back again with a puncture before the feed zone at Mons-en-Pévèle, where Braun also was halted to change a wheel.

The Skil team manager, a French aristocrat who owns a chain of furniture stores, Jean De Gribaldy, was urging Kelly to be patient, but the Irishman decided to test out the opposition with a short acceleration. Van der Velde followed him, as did Vandenbroucke and two other Belgians, Patrick Versluys (Splendor) and Jan Wynants (Tönissteiner). As the group exploded behind, Kuiper led up his Dutch colleague, Jacques Hanegraaf, and a third Belgian, Rudy Rogiers (Splendor).

The suddenness of this split, on a flat, concrete road without a cobblestone in sight, must have pleased Kelly. The gap was down to 1:30. And there were still 55 kilometers—and 15 more sections of pavé—for him to overcome his handicap.

The leaders were now in the Forest of Phalempin, riding on narrow, well-surfaced roads, which were drying out after earlier rain. It was almost pleasant there, between lines of mature trees, which bore a hint of spring greenery. But it was still cold enough for the arm-warmers that most riders were still wearing.

There is no pavé in this forest, and Bondue and Braun maintained their 1:30 lead as they topped a bridge crossing over the A-1 autoroute. In front of them was an atrociously potholed road. It had a broken tarmac surface, with loose stones lurking in its water-filled holes.

A large crowd had gathered beside this diabolical track to see first Braun, still riding hard in front of Bondue—their breakaway had already lasted more than 50 kilometers—and then Hanegraaf, slaloming between the potholes, ahead of Kuiper, Kelly and the other four. Wynants had been dropped.

*Paris-Roubaix • France • 1984*

Just beyond the bombed-out surface, the route turned sharply to the right, onto another jarring section of pavé. Kelly came through to the front in the paceline, with Van der Velde on his wheel. At that moment, he decided that his moment had come.

Those spectators fortunate enough to be there saw Kelly make the move that 47 kilometers later would see him win Paris-Roubaix for the first time—for there will surely be other victories.

As soon as the Irishman attacked, Hennie Kuiper came through to take up the chase. The defending champion had been training alone for up to eight hours a day for the previous week, in his native Netherlands. This formula of no racing worked for him last year, but this time he admitted that something was lacking.

"I was badly placed when Kelly attacked, and nobody else was willing to chase. Really, there is nothing to add: Kelly was the strongest. And he has been from the start of the season."

While Kuiper was defending hard, the two Splendor team men, Rogiers and Versluys, were talking together. The result was a sudden strong surge from Rogiers.

"I was at the back when Kelly went," Rogiers described. "He was the last one we should have let go, so I went flat out and didn't ease until I was with him."

It sounds simple, but it took considerable class to achieve. Rogiers, aged 23, is in his second year as a professional: His first season was wrecked by a crash and a broken collarbone in April's Ghent-Wevelgem classic. As an amateur, he finished second in the 1981 world championship road race at Prague, Czechoslovakia, where he was outsprinted by the Russian Andrei Vedernikov after a last-lap break. That same year, Rogiers finished second in the ama-

**HELL OF THE NORTH**

teurs' Paris-Roubaix, although he was only declared the winner after a positive doping result on the Frenchman first across the line.

Rogiers's move took Kuiper by surprise, his second surprise in 400 meters. "I lacked a little something to go with Rogiers," he agreed. "It was a pity, because I think Kelly had made a mistake in breaking away so soon. He was really afraid that he would not get up to Braun and Bondue."

It was not to prove an easy chase, because once the two leaders had been told what was happening behind, they once again stepped on the gas. It took eight kilometers for Kelly—with Rogiers giving only limited support—to halve the deficit to 45 seconds. And the next 45 seconds took a great deal longer....

The frequent sections of bad pavé, particularly before Templeuve (232 kilometers), complicated the Irishman's chore. On perhaps the vilest section of cobblestones on the whole route, at Ennevelin, where a car would gouge away its sump if it straddled the crown of the "road," there was a jam of slow-moving photographers' motorcycles in front of the two chasers. Rogiers wormed his way between them, but Kelly waited until the logjam had cleared, losing 50 meters in the process.

Not once did Kelly panic, and the junction between the two pairs of front-runners eventually took place on a wide main road before Wannahein. Now, just over 20 kilometers separated the four leaders from Roubaix.

Kelly went straight to the front on the next section of pavé, and Braun went straight out of the back. It was now left to Bondue to salvage something from his team's death-or-glory bid—but it was not to be. Bondue skidded into the mud at a place called La Vache Bleue (the blue cow), and his chance had gone, too.

*Paris-Roubaix • France • 1984*

Over the last half-hour, Bondue used his famed pursuiting skills in a valiant attempt to get back to the leaders, churning a huge gear, summoning up all his strength. In contrast, a frustrating 30 seconds ahead, Kelly was using a much lower gear ratio to maintain the same speed.

"I wasn't worried about Bondue," said a confident Kelly after the finish. "And I was strong enough to leave Rogiers whenever I wanted. But he had ridden hard to get there, and I knew that he wouldn't give me any trouble in the sprint."

If that final sprint was an anti-climax, the style of Kelly's victory was not. Only great champions win Paris-Roubaix, and the 27-year-old former block layer from County Waterford can now be numbered among the sport's elite. He had also won a victory over his own hesitation.

Kelly's first classic win, in the Tour of Lombardy at the end of last season, was achieved by a tire's width, with Stephen Roche's undenied complicity. In March of this year, he had come second at Milan-San Remo, after hesitating to follow Francesco Moser's attack; and he had finished second again at the Tour of Flanders, when a bolder approach may have brought him victory. At Paris-Roubaix, he finally showed that boldness.

Kelly is Irish, but he has also achieved immense popularity in his adopted Belgium. And there were a lot of happy Belgians in Roubaix's velodrome on April 8. As Kelly was mobbed at the trackside by pursuing cameramen, radio reporters, journalists, and the rest, two rather elderly Belgians caught my eye. They stood together on the grass, away from the hoi polloi, too emotional to speak. They simply hugged each other tightly, as tears streamed down their faces. "Their" Sean had won his most famous victory. Kelly was king. King of the cobblestones. King of the classics.

 **HELL OF THE NORTH**

# RAGE IN SPAIN

## Vuelta a España
## Spain
## May 1985

Everyone who had followed the tension-filled 40th Tour of Spain agreed: The race was all but over. Only two of the 19 stages remained when, for the eighth successive day, Robert Millar of Scotland pulled on the pale yellow jersey of leadership. History was on the verge of being made. After placing third in the race's longest individual time trial, and so overcoming his most difficult hurdle, Millar was about to become the first non-continental cyclist to win one of the three European grand tours. It appeared that his only remaining rival was Francisco "Pacho" Rodriguez, a Colombian on the Spanish team, Zor. After the time trial, Millar led Rodriguez by only 10 seconds. But with 3110 kilometers of racing behind them, the slim Scot was not going to let the South American professional out of his sight in the remaining two days....

# Spain

SATURDAY, May 11, 1985, dawned cool and clear. The only clouds in the opaque blue sky over the Castillian Plain were white puffballs lining the distant mountain rim. The first half of the Vuelta a España's 200-kilometer stage 18, from Alcalá de Henares to Segovia, was as calm as the weather. There was an initial burst of activity—"the Spaniards start attacking every day as soon as the flag drops," noted Sean Yates, race leader Robert Millar's English teammate— and then a solo break was made by Alexander Osipov, who was on the first Soviet Union team to participate in a major pro tour. Osipov had a lead of six minutes when light snow began falling on the first slopes of the 5900-foot Puerto de la Morcuera climb. This sudden change in the weather would also signal unimaginable changes in the race....

Although eight of the 10-strong Peugeot-Shell team were still in the race to support Millar, only two of the race leader's teammates had the ability to stay with him in the mountains: Pascal Simon, the unlucky yellow jersey of the 1983 Tour de France, and new pro Ronan Pensec. The other five riders had raced magnificently for Millar on the flatter stages, but they survived the hilly days on courage alone.

"This Tour of Spain has been harder than the Tour de France," said Sean Kelly, who started as the race favorite, but took a battering in the first mountain stages. The Irishman's form was improving as the Vuelta continued, while Millar's domestiques were close to their breaking point.

Yates, who had acted as Millar's guardian angel for most of the race, abandoned on this penultimate stage. "I was completely shattered," he said. "I was dropped on the first mountain and got back on after the descent, but I couldn't hold the pace on the second climb. I had nothing left."

*Vuelta a España • Spain • 1985*

In front, the Peugeot forces were being stretched by repeated counterattacks. "Rodriguez tried to get away several times," said Millar, "but I had no trouble countering him." The most dangerous move on the Morcuera—a long, evenly graded ascent to a cold, barren, rocky summit—was by a group of 12 that included Rodriguez and fifth-placed West German Raimund Dietzen, who rides on the Spanish team, Teka. Their attack was neutralized just beyond the feed zone of Raseafria, following a rapid descent that cut Osipov's lead to 4:30.

The race was now in a deep, pine-covered valley in the Sierra de Guadarrama mountains. And, unusually, the road leading toward the day's second climb, Los Cotos, was paved with cobblestones for almost 10 kilometers. It is a bumpy road that neither Osipov nor Millar will forget.

The tall, blond-haired Soviet visibly wilted, as he pushed an overlarge gear on the uneven surface. He was caught shortly after the cobble section gave way to smooth asphalt, still eight kilometers from the mist-shrouded summit of Los Cotos. The first to pass Osipov was talented Spanish rider José Recio of Kelme, a stage winner at Benidorm four days earlier. He had left the peloton with two other Spaniards, José Navarro (Zor) and Angel de las Heras (Hueso), and Frenchman Dominique Garde (Skil).

While these four were chasing Osipov across the cobbles, yellow-jerseyed Millar had a flat tire. Before stopping, Millar "tried to drift to the back (of the group) without anyone seeing. But the Spaniards saw and attacked." Despite receiving a quick change of bikes from his team car, Millar had to chase hard, assisted by Simon and Pensec. The other Peugeot men all fell back, as the peloton exploded on the climb.

The deterioration in the weather caused most of the riders to don rain jackets, and so it was difficult to identify

**RAGE IN SPAIN**

the composition of the various groups scattered up the winding mountain road. Millar jumped from group to group with his two teammates, before bridging the gap to the main race favorites on his own. "When I got back, I thought I was with the front group," said Millar. "I didn't know anyone was away."

On the climb, Recio dropped the others in the break and passed a hotel and ski lift at Los Cotos summit 37 seconds ahead of de las Heras. Next came the group that Millar had caught. The others in it were second-placed Rodriguez, third-placed Spaniard Pello Ruiz Cabestany of MG-Orbea, Spaniard Vicente Belda (a teammate of Recio), Frenchman Eric Caritoux of Skil, the 1984 Vuelta winner, and a third Spaniard, Pedro Delgado, a teammate of Ruiz Cabestany.

The immediate danger seemed over.

The attacks continued on an almost flat highway beyond the summit, before the true descent began 10 kilometers later. Millar comfortably countered moves by his immediate rivals, Rodriguez and Ruiz Cabestany, but he was not too concerned when the less dangerous Caritoux went clear with Navarro, Frenchman Pierre Bazzo (Fagor), and another caped-up rider, who proved to be Delgado.

On overall time, Rodriguez and Ruiz Cabestany were the only men within five minutes of Millar, so the Scot had eyes for only them. Delgado, who was sixth on general classification, 6:13 behind Millar, later said that the motivation for his attack was a stage win at his hometown of Segovia; and if he were caught, his teammate Ruiz Cabestany would have the chance to counterattack and maybe wipe out his 1:15 deficit on Millar.

Riding strongly, Delgado soon jumped across the 30-second gap to join Recio before the descent. Together, they had a chance to stay clear until the finish, 69 kilometers

*Vuelta a España • Spain • 1985*

away. Kelly was also keen to win another stage. He attacked from Millar's group on the damp descent with teammate Garde, and Spanish riders Celestino Prieto (Reynolds) and Alvaro Piño (Zor). "We were taking off our capes, freewheeling, when Kelly attacked from the back of the group with the other three. They came past so fast that there was no way we could have gone with them," said Millar. "But I wasn't worried about Kelly. He was no danger...."

The race leader was more concerned about the whereabouts of teammates Simon and Pensec, who were chasing in a 20-strong group that also contained fourth-placed Julian Gorospe of Reynolds, two Soviets, and three of the four Colombians left on the Varta team. They were less than a minute behind Millar's group at the foot of the descent, when the barriers of a railroad crossing closed in front of them. "We were stopped for two minutes," said Pensec, "but no train went by before the barriers were raised."

Meanwhile, Millar was casting anxious backward glances as he approached the third mountain climb, another first-category pass, the Alto do los Leones. It was shorter and steeper than the previous two climbs. At its foot, on leaving a crowd-packed Guadarrama, Recio and Delgado were 56 seconds ahead of Caritoux, Navarro and Bazzo, 2:17 up on Kelly's group, and 2:56 ahead of Millar's small peloton.

With Delgado, Kelly and Millar doing most of the work in their respective groups up the climb, the time differences were almost identical at the 5000-foot summit, where 10-deep crowds roared Delgado through, realizing that there was a possibility he could win the stage ... or even the Vuelta itself. His and Recio's lead was now 3:15 on Millar. Could they gain another three minutes in the remaining 43 kilometers?

**RAGE IN SPAIN**

That question almost came academic when, on one of the sweeping bends down the fast, main road descent to San Rafel, Delgado almost crashed as he followed the more adroit Recio. It was a moment somewhat reminiscent of the 1984 Tour de France, in which Delgado crashed on the descent of the Col de Joux-Plane and broke his collarbone. This time, he survived ... but he and Recio were not gaining anymore.

A brief spell of sunshine had given way to more rain, with hail adding to the riders' discomfort. Then, on the next climb, where black bulls dotted a bleak grey-green hillside, we stopped to make some time checks. The two leaders were 1:55 ahead of Caritoux and Navarro, who were on the point of being joined by Kelly's group. Millar and six others appeared 3:20 after Delgado and Recio. Only 30 kilometers remained.

Millar still had not been informed by his Peugeot team manager, Roland Berland, that Delgado was in front. "The first time I knew he was away, he had four minutes," said Millar. "Even then, I wasn't too worried." That time check of 3:58 was taken 26 kilometers from the finish, but just after Berland drove alongside Millar to give him this information, the 23-kilometer-to-go check showed 4:54.

The sudden increase in the leaders' advantage coincided with a sudden lack of action in Millar's group. Of the 10 men with the yellow jersey, seven were on Spanish teams; the others were Frenchmen Jean-Claude Bagot (Fagor) and Eric Guyot (Skil), and Dutch rider Gerard Veldscholten, one of only two Panasonic riders left in the race. Guyot and Veldscholten had been pulling with Millar, but not Bagot, whose Spanish-sponsored Fagor team had been working against the Peugeots for the whole race. Of the other riders in the group, two were teammates of Recio

*Vuelta a España • Spain • 1985*

(Belda and Arsenio Gonzalez), one was a teammate of Delgado (Ruiz Cabestany), two were on the Teka team (Dietzen and Antonio Coll), and the last two were the modest Juan Martinez of Hueso and second-placed Rodriguez.

"I spoke to Rodriguez," said Millar, "but he said he wasn't working because he would rather see Delgado win. There was also a danger that if I chased too hard, Rodriguez would have jumped me at the end to take his 10 seconds."

With his mind in this quandary and no teammates to help him, the Scot had nowhere to turn except to his own legs. Guyot had weakened and was no help in the chase. And Veldscholten had stopped working. "Nobody else was pulling, so why should I?" Veldscholten later explained innocently. Others saw a connection between the Dutchman's change in attitude and a visit to the Millar group of the second MG-Orbea team car. MG is one of the best-selling gins in Spain and a benevolent sponsor for Delgado and Ruiz Cabestany.

The two MG-Orbea cars had a CB radio link between them; and so its boss, Domingo Perurena, was one of the few directeurs sportifs who knew the exact time gap between Delgado and Millar. This was a considerable advantage, because the official time checks were few, and barely discernible on the poor-quality race radio. There was also an official motorcycle-borne blackboard for showing riders the time gaps, but this was seen only once during this vital final hour of the stage.

All these factors were building up Delgado's chances of taking over the yellow jersey. Spanish commentators on radio and TV were virtually screaming into their microphones, sending the roadside crowds into a frenzy of excitement. The two leaders were being carried on a tidal wave of enthusiasm toward Segovia.

**RAGE IN SPAIN**

It was an unequal struggle, as Kelly partly explained: "When we caught Caritoux, we started riding hard to try to catch the two in front, because we wanted to win the stage. We rode really hard, but we never made any impression on them. It's unbelievable how the Spaniards ride when they are at the front. I was riding really well at the end, riding hard with Garde and Caritoux, and we still lost time to Delgado and Recio. It's unbelievable...."

A time check 17 kilometers from the finish showed Kelly's group 2:27 down, with Millar's at 5:12. Unaided, the race leader was now losing three or four seconds every kilometer. He could afford to lose only one more minute. It was clearly going to be a dramatic finish. Unfortunately for Millar, the stage end was not in Segovia itself. Five kilometers had been tacked on to the route at the request of the stage sponsor, DYC whisky, which wanted the stage to finish outside its distillery.

Later, an analysis of the times showed that Millar averaged a fine 41 kilometers-per-hour for the final 10 kilometers, despite his effort being disrupted by the Spaniards, who were sprinting past Millar and then freewheeling as soon as the yellow jersey took their wheel. On the same section—a main road into town, a descent on a cobbled street, a climb past a ruined bull ring, and a dipping highway to the distillery entrance—Kelly's group averaged 42 kph, and Delgado-Recio, 45 kph.

Delgado allowed Recio to win the stage as reward for his efforts, but Recio had ridden so hard that he retired from the race early the next morning, complaining of damaged knee ligaments. Three-and-a-half minutes after Recio won the stage, Kelly outsprinted Prieto and Navarro for third place. By now, the crowd was chanting Delgado's nickname: "Perico, Perico...." Then, as the six-minute mark

*Vuelta a España • Spain • 1985*

approached, they began counting off the seconds, and when 6:13 arrived, a huge roar erupted—just as police whistles blew to signal the arrival of the yellow jersey's group around the final turn, 400 meters from the finish line. That was the margin of Millar's defeat in the 1985 Vuelta a España.

Sprinting across the finish line at the head of his group outside the DYC distillery, Millar did not know that he had lost the race leader's yellow jersey he was wearing. He stopped among a melée of spectators, straddled over his bike, exhausted after his long chase. When told that Delgado had taken the overall lead, Millar swore loudly with shock and anger. "I didn't know there was a risk of losing the jersey," he said. He then silently reported to the trailer that housed the anti-doping control, emerged 15 minutes later, and rode straight to his team car for a 30-kilometer drive to that night's hotel.

Four hours later we visited his hotel, the Club Nautico Nayade, a residential and sports complex occupying a site by the wide Moros River, on a private estate. Millar was in the bathroom washing his shorts. His eyes were red, almost certainly from crying. He was depressed. "I haven't said more than three words since we arrived here," he said. "I will try to sleep tonight, but I guess I won't be able to."

After bearing all the physical and mental pressure as leader of the world's third most important stage race for more than a week, Millar was understandably disillusioned. "I am disgusted with it all," he continued, after several moments of silence. "The crowds throw things at you and spit at you because they want a Spaniard to win. But I don't let them affect me; I still get on and race. The other night at the hotel [in Albacete], I blew my top. We had been waiting an hour for dinner, and when it came it was food you wouldn't give your dog. The others couldn't

**RAGE IN SPAIN**

believe it when I stormed out. I went down to the cake shop and stuffed myself.

"The next day, the Fagors attacked with Delgado at the first feed, because they thought I was hungry. I had planned for our team to ride through both feeds to make the others hungry, but the guys said they were hot and wanted their feeds."

"I haven't lost this race because I cracked up," Millar pointed out. "You can't compete against the whole peloton."

Proof of his arrival among the world's elite was Millar's performance in the 43-kilometer time trial at Alcalá de Henares the day before the fatal Segovia stage. With a 10-second lead overall on Rodriguez, he gambled on using two bikes: a carbon-fiber-framed machine for the opening 20 kilometers that included a steep hill, and one fitted with a rear disc wheel for the return journey on smoother, mainly descending roads.

Millar began well, taking 25 seconds from Rodriguez in the opening 14 kilometers. He was still 21 seconds ahead of the Colombian after the planned change of bikes. "But four kilometers later, just as I was feeling the benefit of the wheel, I rode down a hole," said Millar. The Scot had to change back to his original bike, which possibly cost him the stage lead. He did not panic. Millar steadily regained his rhythm, and a time check six kilometers from the finish showed him to be one second ahead of Rodriguez and 23 seconds behind Cabestany.

The rider in the yellow jersey entered the new concrete velodrome at Alcalá to a chorus of derisive whistles from the partisan crowd. But they couldn't take away a wonderful ride by Millar, who freewheeled for an extra lap before stopping beside his directeur sportif, Berland. "You've done it, Robert," said the bespectacled Frenchman. Millar was

*Vuelta a España • Spain • 1985*

ecstatic. Tears of joy were welling behind his smiling eyes…. Twenty-four hours later, he would be crying for a different reason.

There were few observers who did not agree that Millar was the race's moral victor. But there are few morals in professional sports. The 18th stage of the Vuelta had seen an obvious coalition between teams that are meant to be rivals. Other factors completed Millar's unhappy fate: the rain, snow and fog in the mountains; the lack of information over the race radio; and the bizarre incident of the closed rail crossing, which prevented Millar's two teammates from catching up with his group. With them, his Vuelta would surely have been saved.

In the end, a Spaniard won. Delgado indeed raced hard to achieve his stunning victory, but his sporting achievement was not reflected in the words he used on the winner's rostrum. Asked to comment on his yellow jersey, the home-town champion had the audacity to say: "I must thank the directeurs sportifs of the other Spanish teams. Without their support, this win would have been impossible."

His sad words emphasized the day's dark deeds, which prevented a brave-hearted Scot from winning the Vuelta and making history.

**RAGE IN SPAIN**

# A RACE OF PASSION

## Giro d'Italia
## Italy
## June 1988

First held in 1909, the Giro d'Italia has a history almost as glorious as that of the Tour de France. The distance, about 4000 kilometers in 21 stages, is the same. And it boasts many of the same names on its list of winners, including Italians Gino Bartali, Fausto Coppi and Felice Gimondi; Frenchmen Jacques Anquetil, Bernard Hinault and Laurent Fignon; Swiss Hugo Koblet; Luxembourger Charly Gaul; Belgian Eddy Merckx; and Spaniard Miguel Induráin. In 1988, a 26-year-old American was aiming to join that line of champions....

# Italy

AUSTRIA

SWITZERLAND

Chiesa Valmalenco
• Merano
• Bormio
Sondrio • • Aprica
FRANCE • Bergamo    Vittorio Veneto
Milan •         •
Venice •

Urbino
•
ITALY

• Rome

• Naples

Mediterranean Sea

ON THE OUTSIDE, the stucco-walled Bar Augusto in Villa d'Alme near Bergamo, Italy, is an austere modern building. Inside, its cavernous reception room is brought to life by hundreds of framed, historic bike-racing jerseys that decorate the walls in glass cases. There's even a *maglia rosa,* now slightly faded, worn by the legendary Fausto Coppi at the 1940 Giro d'Italia.

The Bar Augusto has a strong connection with American cycling, as this is where U.S. national teams would stay when they were racing in northern Italy in the early-1980s. When most of those national team players turned pro in 1985 for 7-Eleven, the Bergamo hostelry became the team's adopted home. Naturally, this is where the team would gather after important races: either to celebrate a new victory or commiserate with each other after less successful results.

There was one such get-together on the rainy night of June 12, 1988. Many of the 7-Eleven team members were inside, having come straight from the 71st Giro d'Italia that finished that afternoon in Vittorio Veneto. Along with the riders were most of the team personnel, including team founder and general manager Jim Ochowicz, directeur sportif Mike Neel, team doctor Massimo Testa, and Erminio Dell'Oglio, a rotund, balding industrialist whose Hoonved washing machine company co-sponsors the team. The tall, loquacious Neel—who speaks fluent Italian learned during his own pro racing days in Italy—had become something of a personality in the previous three weeks, answering questions and translating for his riders on daily television shows. People were saying that it was Neel's presence that helped the 7-Eleven team earn respect so quickly in its quest for glory in Europe.

*Giro d'Italia • Italy • 1988*

Besides the team, dozens of local team supporters came to the Bar Augusto that night, to relive the three weeks and 21 stages of the race that had just ended....

IT ALL STARTED in the medieval streets of Urbino, where 7-Eleven's Andy Hampsten was among the long list of prerace favorites that also included Frenchman Jean-François Bernard, who placed third at the 1987 Tour de France; Swiss climber Urs Zimmermann, third at the 1986 Tour; Spaniard Pedro Delgado, runner-up in the 1987 Tour; and Dutch hope Erik Breukink, who was third at the 1987 Giro. The main Italian chances lay with 1986 Giro winner Roberto Visentini, climber Franco Chioccioli—nicknamed "Little Coppi" for his likeness to the late Fausto Coppi—and Flavio Giupponi.

Hampsten was only 13th in the opening time trial at Urbino—won by Bernard from Switzerland's Tony Rominger—and he was down to 37th place after 7-Eleven came in ninth at the fourth day team time trial. That same day, second-year Italian pro Massimo Podenzana of the Atala team took over the leader's pink jersey by winning the morning stage by five minutes.

He still had that advantage when the race reached its sixth leg: the only mountain stage of the first 11 days of the race. This relatively short, 137km stage in the central Apennines crossed two intermediate passes, the Miralgo and Serra de Perrone, before reaching the steep, 10-kilometer-long uphill finish to Campitello Matese. Before the stage, Hampsten had said he would attack about three kilometers from the finish. He went through with his plan, but he couldn't catch Del Tongo's Chioccioli, who broke clear at the foot of the mountain. Hampsten took second on the stage, only 12 seconds behind Chioccioli, picked up a valu-

**A RACE OF PASSION**

able 34 seconds (including time bonus) on men like Breukink, Bernard and Visentini, and moved into eighth place overall.

The American was now 2:38 behind the plucky Pondenzana, who managed to hang on to the overall lead by 45 seconds over Chioccioli. Zimmermann, who finished the stage on Hampsten's wheel, was up to third overall, with Visentini in fourth. Those positions didn't change much until the race reached the Lombardy region for the first of several days in the mountains of northern Italy.

On the 12th stage, Podenzana finally lost his lead. He was dropped on the third of four climbs, and had no chance of chasing back when Chioccioli's Del Tongo team set a furious pace before the final climb. It was here that Hampsten made three attacks in the final three kilometers of the uphill finish to Selvino, to take a magnificent stage win by 11 seconds over Delgado. That put Hampsten into fourth place overall, 1:18 behind new leader Chioccioli, while Zimmermann moved up to second, 33 seconds back.

For Hampsten, the 10-kilometer-long Selvino climb was a great dress rehearsal for the more serious move he was already planning on the stage over the Gavia Pass, two days later....

MIKE NEEL AWOKE early on the morning of the 14th stage in Chiesa Valmalenco, heard rain pouring on the roof of the team's hotel, and instinctively thought: "cold weather gear." Before leaving the hotel, he made all the 7-Eleven riders grease up with Vaseline. Neel and team manager Jim Ochowicz then developed a system for getting hot drinks and dry clothes to the racers on the main obstacle of the day, the 8600-foot-high Gavia Pass, where reports indicated a foot of fresh snow had fallen.

*Giro d'Italia • Italy • 1988*

This epic stage, only 120 kilometers long, started in freezing rain. On the opening descent to Sondrio, riders were unidentifiable in their rain jackets, goggles, ski hats and overshoes. Understandably, the peloton rode in close formation until they reached the day's first climb, a steady 14-kilometer ascent to Aprica, 44 kilometers from the start. Here, a break was made by Swiss Stephan Joho and Italian Roberto Pagnin, and by the 78-kilometer point—after a long, skin-numbing descent—they were 43 seconds ahead of the chasing Pondenzana, and 2:09 ahead of the first pack.

Ahead now was the much-feared Gavia, an old mountain pass that still has a dirt road, which the day's rain was quickly turning to mud. As the narrow mountain road began to steepen, with two switchback turns, Dutchman Johan Van der Velde made a sudden attack with the Italian rookie Stefano Tomasini. Van der Velde, wearing only an undervest, bib shorts, and his short-sleeved purple jersey as the Giro's points leader, quickly passed the lead pair and pulled away as the tarmac gave way to dirt.

At the same point, Hampsten raced clear from the diminishing peloton. He was chased by Breukink and Chioccioli, while behind them formed a group containing Delgado, Zimmermann, Tomasini, Dutchman Peter Winnen, Swiss Beat Breu and Italian Marco Giovannetti. Hampsten—who said he prepared for this climb on the dirt roads climbing out of his Boulder home into the Colorado Rockies—looked comfortable on the muddy surface, calmly spinning his bottom gear of 39x25. Breukink and, further back, Bernard seemed to be struggling with a 39x23.

As Hampsten overtook all those in front of him, except for the inspired but seemingly foolhardy Van der Velde, it looked as though history could be in the making. In front, Van der Velde was frequently out of the saddle, battling

**A RACE OF PASSION**

against the heavy rain that turned to snow about six kilometers from the summit. Within two kilometers of his attack, Hampsten was 44 seconds behind Van der Velde, but already 16 seconds ahead of Breukink, 44 seconds ahead of race leader Chioccioli (riding with only Pagnin and Zimmermann), and 1:06 ahead of a group led by Bernard and Delgado.

The now heavy snow was being blown into the riders' faces by a fierce crosswind as they struggled on the frequent sections of 16-percent grade. It was impossible to keep warm. The bare-armed Van der Velde, however, still rode strongly in the final, paved kilometers. He emerged through the horizontal snow at the mountain top, a minute ahead of Breukink, who had caught Hampsten when the American stopped to put on extra clothing: a rain jacket, balaclava, and neoprene gloves.

The positions at the summit were: Van der Velde alone; Breukink and Hampsten, at 1:00; Zimmermann, at 2:12; Giovannetti and Chioccioli, at 2:20; Delgado, Hernandez, and Winnen, at 3:00; Bernard, Madiot, Breu, and Vandelli, at 4:00; Visentini, at 5:40.

On the long descent to Bormio, back on dirt roads, Hampsten quickly took command. "I knew the descent would be the race," he said. Within a kilometer, he had passed Van der Velde, who had come to a slow-motion halt, unable to move. The tall, gaunt Dutchman was stripped of his ice-stiffened clothing by team helpers, who carried him into his team car. After being revived with hot drinks and the car heater, and donning dry apparel, Van der Velde eventually continued ... and finished the stage almost 47 minutes behind the leaders!

Plowing a lone furrow through the snow-covered mud, Hampsten was concentrating on survival, not the race, while Breukink gamely followed 20 seconds or so behind—

*Giro d'Italia • Italy • 1988*

although no one was quite sure of where anyone was in the white-out conditions.

Words are not enough to express the desperate, frightening conditions on the Gavia descent. So devastating was it that hardened competitors such as Visentini, Giuseppe Saronni and Zimmermann were reduced to tears of pain from the freezing weather. Visentini was like a rag doll, freewheeling at less than 15 mph down a pass he could ordinarily have raced at three or four times that speed. He stopped three times, once to put on a padded ski jacket, another to drink hot tea, and then to have his frozen muscles rubbed back to life.

In front, Hampsten raced alone through the snow as if in a trance, ahead of all the race vehicles, guiding himself by the *tornante* ("sharp bend") signs that appeared through the mist. It was unbearably cold, and later, recalling the descent, Hampsten said, "On one of the hairpins in the snow ... I looked down at my legs. I knew they were going around, and that they stung a bit, which I knew was good. They weren't totally numb, I made sure I kept spinning. But they were bright red and they had chunks of ice everywhere. Just that one glance terrified me. I'd never seen my body look like that, and I refused to look down after that."

When the snow changed back to rain in the valley, Hampsten was brought back to reality by the arrival of the police motorcycles and the race director's car. He had another shock when Breukink burst past him about five kilometers from the finish. The blond Dutchman hung on strongly to win the stage by a slim seven seconds. But behind them, the next to arrive in Bormio was Tomasini, 4:39 back. Zimmermann (in sixth) lost five minutes, 10th finisher Delgado seven, Bernard nine, and the distressed Visentini more than 30 minutes.

**A RACE OF PASSION**

The well prepared 7-Eleven team had placed their team cars at regular intervals up the climb, with Ochowicz handing up dry clothing to all the team members just before the summit. It paid off. Besides Hampsten in second, Bob Roll was 24th, Raúl Alcalá 26th, Dag-Otto Lauritzen 41st, and Jeff Pierce 43rd out of the 143 finishers, all of them heroes.

Despite the dry clothing, Roll was suffering from hypothermia when he finished, his body temperature way below normal, and his heart rate a dangerous 27 beats per minute. He was carried into the team car, with an ambulance standing by in case of an emergency. In a similar state to Roll were Pagnin and the leader of the young riders' competition, Franco Vona. But on reaching the warmth of their hotels, Roll's and the other riders' temperature gradually came back to normal. Hampsten, too, was shivering with cold at the finish line—where he received the pink jersey as the new race leader. The emotion was all too much, and after becoming the first American to be awarded the maglia rosa, Hampsten returned to his team car and sobbed uncontrollably.

ALTHOUGH MOST of the race favorites were now minutes behind, the Giro was still far from over. There were still eight days remaining, and Hampsten was separated from second-place Breukink by just 15 seconds.

The bad weather continued, and stage 15 was shortened because the 9035-foot Stelvio Pass was closed by snow. With a rearranged start at Spondigna, most of the 83-kilometer stage was all downhill or flat, except for a final 15-kilometer climb to the Merano 2000 ski station. Neel said he "ordered the team to ride tempo to make sure everyone arrived at Merano together before the climb. We may have ridden too fast, but it made sure that Andy would not get attacked before the climb."

*Giro d'Italia • Italy • 1988*

*John Wilcockson's* **WORLD OF CYCLING**
● ● ● ● ● ● ● ● ● ● ● ● ● ● ● ● ● ● ● ● ● ● ● ● ● ● ● ● ● ● ● ● ● ● ● ● ● ● ● ● ● ● ● ● ● ● ● ● ● ● ● ● ● ● ● ● ●

**130**

As soon as the road began to climb, Bernard accelerated. Zimmermann and Chioccioli followed him, while Hampsten remained with Breukink and Giupponi 200 meters behind. Chioccioli soon dropped back to the Hampsten group, while Zimmermann was dropped by Bernard four kilometers from the finish. In the battle for the pink jersey, Breukink managed to stay with Hampsten until nine kilometers from the top, when the American's relentless pace proved too much and he dropped steadily behind, doing well to limit his loss to 27 seconds.

"It was a real tough climb," noted Hampsten. "I was in my 23 sprocket at times, and (Breukink) rode very well. It was a hard battle between us, and I think we were both tired from yesterday." Commenting on the battle after winning his third stage of the race, Bernard said, "Hampsten is the clear favorite now. He is stronger than Breukink on the climbs and he'll be able to match him in the last time trial."

Memories of the snowy Gavia Pass were still haunting the peloton at the start of the 16th stage, which was due to take the 143 survivors over the giant 8232-foot Rombo Pass into Austria. In fact, some riders wanted the race neutralized, when persistent rain turned to snow as the race climbed into the clouds. The riders stopped in a tunnel.

While officials argued with the leaders of the "strike," Hampsten sat calmly in his warm team car. Then the officials suddenly decided that the race was on. The bizarre ascent of the Rombo took two hours because of two halts, and lulled many into a false sense of security. While some riders stopped to don extra clothing, Urs Freuler and Winnen led an attack for the Panasonic team. Suddenly there was a group of 15 zooming down past the ski slopes into Austria. Hampsten and teammate Lauritzen were safely in the lead group, but not Zimmermann, Giupponi, Chioccioli,

**A RACE OF PASSION**

Bernard or Tomasini. Breukink was in the front with no less than six teammates to help him.

The confusing situation became much clearer in the valley, where the snow and rain gave way to warmer, brighter conditions. The break gained two minutes before a chase was started by Zimmermann, Bernard, Chioccioli and nine others, who caught the leaders in the final kilometer. Such was the intensity of the chase that the 126 kilometers from the Rombo summit to the finish in Innsbruck were covered at an average speed of 49.4 kph.

IF THERE WERE any doubts that Hampsten was entitled to the pink jersey they would be exposed on the crucial 18th stage: an 18-kilometer uphill time trial from Levico Terme to Vetriolo. With Bernard out of the race because of a crash the previous day, Hampsten, Breukink, Zimmermann and Visentini were the logical favorites for the stage win. There was enormous pressure on both Hampsten and Breukink, who were separated by only 42 seconds overall. Whoever gained time on this stage would almost certainly win the Giro.

The battle of nerves between the two was accentuated because they were sharing the same hotel in Levico, seeing each other at dinner and breakfast, knowing what each other was thinking and doing. "The pressure even got to me," said coach Neel. "I started freaking out, and I had to go and lie down in my bedroom at one in the afternoon. I was shaking, as if I was on drugs.

"But Andy was very calm. After riding up the hill in the morning he went to his room, reading a book and listening to music. And when we reached the start we parked in a shady back street and Andy warmed up on the rollers. He was super calm—but as soon as the race started he came alive."

*Giro d'Italia • Italy • 1988*

The 7-Eleven team had prepared things to perfection. After inspecting the course, Hampsten chose chainrings of 53 and 42 (instead of the usual 53 and 39), and an eight-speed freewheel of 13-14-15-16-17-18-19-21. Hampsten also followed team doctor Testa's advice to perfection, keeping his heart rate at 180 bpm during the climb, and riding with a calm intensity that he has rarely displayed before.

From a four-second advantage on Breukink after five kilometers, Hampsten gradually pulled farther and farther ahead. The American was 16 seconds faster halfway up the 3300 foot climb ... and when he sprinted in a 53x16 gear to the finish, the time gap over Breukink was 64 seconds.

After crossing the line with the winning time, Hampsten quickly braked to a halt and sat down on the side of the road, leaning against a metal barrier, surrounded by photographers, TV cameras and journalists. His eyes were still glazed from the effort. "I hurt so bad it was like a meditation," said Hampsten. "I knew I was winning because Mike was telling me, but I wasn't conscious of the fact."

It was a magnificent effort by Hampsten, probably the hardest of his life, and he was now 2:06 ahead of Breukink on overall time, with Zimmermann in third, at 5:10. Breukink said after the stage, "The Giro is now over for me. Hampsten is too strong."

But it still wasn't over. Despite his resounding stage victory, Hampsten made some big mistakes the next day, when he let Zimmermann break clear on the first of the day's three climbs,. "My first mistake," Hampsten later admitted, "was to underestimate the climbs. They were both much harder than I thought. I could have followed Zimmi when he attacked, but I didn't think there was a big danger with so far to go."

Zimmermann's attack came on a warm, sunny day in the Dolomites, at the foot of the deceptive Duran Pass, 140

**A RACE OF PASSION**

kilometers from the finish. The Duran climbs 3300 feet in 13 kilometers on a narrow, winding road, much of which was unsurfaced because of road construction. It proved ideal for Zimmermann's smooth climbing style.

At the 5000-foot summit, the tall, blond Swiss was 45 seconds ahead of Hampsten, who was riding with teammate Pierce, Tomasini and Giuliani. Breukink was just behind, and caught the Hampsten group on the descent. At the same time, Giuliani broke away to catch Zimmermann, and the pair began to eat up the terrain. They passed through Pieve 4:10 ahead of Hampsten's group—which now consisted of six riders with the addition of Italian Roberto Conti and Frenchman Dominique Arnaud. Another group, which contained 7-Eleven men Roll, Ron Kiefel and Alcalá, was 6:45 back.

The situation was critical when Pierce led the six chasers onto the first slopes of the Mauria Pass, still 73km from the finish. The gaps were now 5:30 and 7:30, making Zimmermann the virtual race leader. It was then that Hampsten and Neel made a big decision.

"I spoke with Mike," said Hampsten, "and we decided that we might lose two minutes by waiting for the [second chase] group, but we would gain much more later." It proved a crucial decision, one made without panic, when the pressure was at its most intense. This is how big tours are won or lost. By the Mauria summit, the group with Alcalá, Roll and Kiefel was only 30 seconds behind the awaiting Hampsten group, and they merged midway down the long descent.

The narrow, winding roads, sheltered from the wind by tall pine trees, gave an advantage to Zimmermann's escape, and Giuliani was having to race flat out just to stay on the Swiss rider's wheel. For another 30 kilometers, Zimmermann clung to his lead, and with only 20 kilometers to go he was still 5:35 ahead of the now 50-strong chase group.

*Giro d'Italia • Italy • 1988*

Fortunately, Breukink's Panasonic team agreed to help the hard-working 7-Eleven riders. And though the four Carrera men in the group were doing their best to slow down the chase for teammate Zimmermann, the gap started to close. Hampsten himself took charge in the final, slightly uphill kilometers, and after Giuliani led in Zimmermann for the victory in Arta Terme, the final margin was just over three minutes. Hampsten had saved his pink jersey, but Zimmermann was up to second place, 1:49 down, and his specialty, a flat time trial, still remained....

Everything seemed under control before the last-stage time trial. Hampsten had enjoyed a spaghetti lunch in Vittorio Veneto, after a morning road stage. He then rested in his room, and warmed up over the first part of the rolling 43-kilometer time-trial course. Neel had made a full inspection of the circuit the night before, declaring it fast and fair except for a dangerous corner after 18 kilometers. However, the real danger came from another source: the big black clouds that were gathering over the Venetian vineyards that hot, humid afternoon.

With only two minutes covering the first three riders on general classification, a slight mistake could be costly. After 10 kilometers, nearing the top of the third of three short hills, Hampsten—who was the final starter—was a few seconds up on Zimmermann and almost level with Breukink. Just then the skies opened and torrential rain began to fall amid lightning and thunder as loud as cannons.

Breukink had made it down the winding descent at 18 kilometers before the rain began. Next came Giuponni. His front disc wheel slid out and he careened onto the slick asphalt and skidded head first into the ditch, his bike still locked to his feet. Three minutes later Zimmermann appeared, anxiously freewheeling around the turn. He, too,

**A RACE OF PASSION**

went crashing off the pavement and onto the grass. His team mechanic helped him back up and pushed him back into action.

"I heard on the race radio that Zimmermann had crashed," stated Neel. "So I screamed at Andy, 'Slow down! Slippery!'" Hampsten heeded the warning. "I went real slow, but I still slid out," Hampsten said. "It was like being on ice." Hampsten made it around the long curve without falling, but only just. One factor that probably helped was the fact that he didn't use a front disc. It seemed that the two who crashed couldn't control their machines in the gusty wind.

Five kilometers later, Hampsten was 19 seconds behind Breukink, and 25 seconds ahead of Zimmermann. With the rain still falling, there were some anxious looks on the faces of Hampsten's support crew as the rider in the pink skinsuit headed home, and raced under the ancient, narrow stone archway into town. Hampsten had conceded two minutes to stage winner Lech Piasecki of Poland, who had enjoyed perfect conditions almost two hours before the race leaders went into action. But despite his self-imposed slowdown, Hampsten conceded only 23 seconds to Breukink, who took back second overall from Zimmermann. Andy Hampsten, 26, had become the first American to win the Giro d'Italia.

Following the Giro's dramatic finale, the 7-Eleven team drove to Bergamo for dinner at the Bar Augusto. There, the riders celebrated until 1 a.m. They talked about Hampsten's triumph in the Gavia Pass snowstorm, emerging with the maglia rosa. "Terribile, ma bella," (terrifying, but beautiful) said Hoonved's Dell'Oglio. They discussed Hampsten's brilliant win in the Vetriolo hill climb. "At the finish of that time trial, I was apologizing to my body and thanking it at the same time," Hampsten recalled. They also spoke of the nailbiting three-hour chase when Zim-

*Giro d'Italia • Italy • 1988*

mermann threatened to grab the maglia rosa on the final stage in the Dolomites.

Amid the popping of champagne corks and the flashes of the photographers, Hampsten moved from group to group in the Bar Augusto, thanking them for their efforts and support. He seemed overcome. "I'm in a daze," he admitted. "I set out from the start wanting to be in there, fighting for the win. But I didn't know whether I could win. Now that I have won the Giro, I've proved that my methods have been right. I don't mean to sound self-centered because (the win) has also proved the 7-Eleven team's methods to be right. I couldn't have done this without the team. Everyone worked so amazingly hard."

By the end of the evening, not far from the maglia rosa worn by Fausto Coppi a half-century before, a new pink jersey was suspended on a hanger from the ceiling. The signature hastily scribbled on it was that of Andy Hampsten.

**A RACE OF PASSION**

# THE MILLION DOLLAR WALL

## USPRO
## Championship
## United States
## June 1993

Before the 1984 Olympic Games in Los Angeles, there were no professional road cyclists in the United States. The following year, two separate actions gave American pro cycling a jump start: the 7-Eleven team turned professional and joined the European peloton; and Philadelphia's CoreStates Financial Corp (now owned by First Union of Charlotte) agreed to sponsor the first U.S. professional road championship, over a distance of 156 miles, with a prize list of more than $100,000—the richest in the world. The race was an instant success, when its first champion was 7-Eleven rider Eric Heiden, the former Olympic speedskating champion. A decade later, another star was about to emerge....

# United States

NEW YORK

New York

PENNSYLVANIA

Philadelphia

Wilmington

NEW JERSEY

MARYLAND

Baltimore

DELAWARE

VIRGINIA

Atlantic Ocean

AT A PRESS CONFERENCE in a Philadelphia hotel, the day before he raced for a million-dollar prize at the 9th CoreStates USPRO Championship, Lance Armstrong, 21, was asked what his next sport would be—after being a national champion in triathlon, then cycling. His first, facetious, reply was: "Indy car racing." Then, reflecting on the question, he added, "I'm gonna stick to cycling for a bit." Phew!

In that same press conference, a journalist asked the Motorola team rider what he thought of the contention that he was the "next Greg LeMond." Armstrong replied, "I'm flattered by the description, but I'm on the Lance Armstrong agenda."

It's perhaps inevitable that the brash young neo-pro from Austin, Texas, will continue to be compared with LeMond. But already, Armstrong is showing that he is indeed on his own agenda. He has already achieved attention in the national media because of his exploits in this country—including the two races he had won in the preceding two weeks: the Thrift Drug Classic at Pittsburgh and the Kmart Classic of West Virginia. Of course, when LeMond turned pro in 1981, events like the CoreStates Championship didn't even exist, and the only race that commanded any sort of national publicity was the Coors Classic in Colorado. LeMond won that, but to achieve real fame he had to start winning races in Europe....

Armstrong still has to prove himself in the European arena, and by already being a well-known personality in the United States, he may have a hard time doing that. After all, LeMond had two-and-a-half years in which to develop his pro racing skills, before he entered his first Tour de France; Armstrong will be on the Tour start line in his first season.

*USPRO Championship • USA • 1993*

However, the two Americans do have some things in common: They can both smooth-talk the media and cope with pressure—although Armstrong still has nightmares about his disappointing performance at last year's Olympic Games, when he was still an amateur, and at the 1991 world championships. Both times, he failed to live up to his role of prerace favorite. Now, as the center of media hoopla in Philadelphia, he needed to prove to himself that he could come through when it mattered. Those thoughts were on Armstrong's mind when he was called to the line the next day, June 6. "I've been in races before when everyone has been looking at me to win," he confided at the start. "This time, I'm gonna do it." That's the type of brash statement that has sometimes gotten Armstrong into trouble ... but if he can come through and win, then such talk will only make him more popular with his fans.

After winning in Pittsburgh and West Virginia, Armstrong was on target to do the "impossible"—to win in Philadelphia, the third event of the Thrift Drug Triple Crown. So confident were the race promoters that such a feat was unlikely, even impossible, they had taken out a million-dollar insurance policy with Lloyd's of London. It was the biggest prize ever offered in cycling.

To be on the best form for this challenge, Armstrong—with advice from his former U.S. Cycling Federation coach, Chris Carmichael, and the Motorola team's sports doctor, Massimo Testa—made adjustments to his training routine. After finishing second at the Tour DuPont in May, he returned home for five days, before going back East for the Thrift Drug Classic in Pittsburgh. His main training ride that week was on the Thursday, three days before the race: about 200 kilometers, on the plains east of Austin. "That was a mistake," admitted Armstrong. "I should have

**THE MILLION DOLLAR WALL**

gone west, for a hard, hilly ride. I came into the Thrift Drug Classic flat."

Despite being flat, the Motorola rider won that ultra-hilly event—although his eventual two-man sprint victory over Polish strongman Andrzej Mierzejewski was a little too close for Armstrong's comfort. Then, after breezing through the five-day West Virginia stage race, he again returned to Texas. Describing this second week at home, Armstrong said, "I looked at it the same as after DuPont—I was coming off a stage race, with a big race the following Sunday. I flew home Monday, and did a short, one-hour ride. Tuesday, I did 160 kilometers motorpacing, which included four three-minute efforts, coming off the motor, at a heart rate of 180. Wednesday, I did a shorter ride of one-and-a-half hours—not easy, hilly. Then, on Thursday, I did my long, 200-kilometer ride, which was very hilly, going to the west this time, not the east. Friday was basically the same as Wednesday, one-and-a-half hours, hilly. Then I flew here."

Concluding his week's preparation for the CoreStates Championship, Armstrong went for a 60-kilometer ride Saturday morning, riding part of the race circuit, and including two climbs of the main climb, the Manayunk Wall. That night, he watched the third game of the Stanley Cup finals on TV, and then had "a good sleep." Sunday morning dawned early for Armstrong and his Motorola teammates, who had breakfast at 6:30 a.m. "I had my usual prerace breakfast of pasta, with eggs mixed in," Armstrong reported. By 8:30, he was in the staging area on Benjamin Franklin Parkway. At 8:55, he was the last rider to be introduced to the already huge crowd, as the man who might win the million dollars.

Armstrong was relaxed, his chin on his arms, resting on the handlebars, as he listened to some words from Philadel-

*USPRO Championship • USA • 1993*

phia mayor Ed Rendell, and then "The Star Spangled Ban-ner," sung by a seven-year-old. A minute later, the CoreStates Championship began, with Armstrong riding comfortably in the field of 125 pro racers.

The organizers of the USPRO Championship always hoped that the Manayunk Wall—a half-mile-long hill, with a short section of 17-percent grade—could fulfill its role as a springboard to victory. It comes at the northern end of Philadelphia's 14.4-mile circuit, which is lapped 10 times during the race. But even though The Wall has always been a spectacular viewing point for the fans who jam six-deep between Manayunk's Victorian stone, row houses and the metal crowd barriers, it had not been a significant factor in the previous eight editions of the race.

Armstrong, not a great sprinter, knew that The Wall offered him the best chance of success—if his highly moti-vated Motorola squad could control the 156-mile race and set him into orbit at the right time. Under the command of its veteran riders Phil Anderson of Australia and Sean Yates of England, Motorola soon showed that its plans were on target. The team dispatched two men—former East German national team rider Jan Schur and Dane Thomas Bay—in the day's early break. The move, powered by riders from the rival Coors Light team, lasted for almost 100 miles, and at one time held a nine-minute lead. Meanwhile, Motorola's other five riders gave Armstrong an armchair ride in the peloton, and when they decided to close down the break, they did so with immense confidence. Yates, Anderson, Andy Bishop and Frankie Andreu rode a team-time-trial for-mation at the head of the peloton, and once the break was caught, they were joined by Bay and Schur in maintaining a high tempo. This is a classic tactic in discouraging other rid-ers from attacking.

**THE MILLION DOLLAR WALL**

A half-lap later, with 46 miles left in the race, Armstrong made his first move.

At that point, Coors Light's English rider Dave Mann was 30 seconds ahead of the pack. Mann had made a solo attack, going north on the wide, flat Kelly Drive, fighting a head wind that was whipping the waters of the adjacent Schuylkill into whitecaps. Pursuing Mann, the Motorola team led the 80-strong pack into the cobbled streets of Manayunk, and around the three 90-degree turns that precede The Wall. There, on the climb's first slopes, Anderson accelerated to open up some gaps in the long line of riders.

With the grade steepening and the concrete road narrowing between the barriers, Armstrong moved to the front. Once there, he responded immediately to a surprise counterattack by another Coors Light rider, and former race winner, Roberto Gaggioli of Italy, and sprinted ferociously up the hill. There was panic behind them, as rivals scrambled forward in response to Armstrong's attack. In fact, in the rush to the front, a few riders fell when they touched wheels, while others were forced to stop.

However, four riders were alert and adept enough to go with Armstrong and Gaggioli—two Americans, Bobby Julich, riding for Portuguese team Pacos de Ferreira, and Jim Copeland of Chevrolet-L.A. Sheriff; and two Italians with the Mercatone Uno squad, Angelo Canzonieri and Simone Biasci. These six riders caught Mann by The Wall's summit—where belated chases were started by Saturn's Brian Walton, and then Darren Baker of Subaru-Montgomery and German Markus Schleicher of Varta-Elk.

After dropping back to the valley road, alongside the Schuylkill, the Armstrong break was already 42 seconds ahead of Walton, 55 seconds up on the next two chasers, and 1:07 ahead of the pack. Under Armstrong's inspiration,

*USPRO Championship • USA • 1993*

the break continued to eat up the terrain, setting a pace that proved too fast for Mann. The tall Brit dropped off the break before the end of the lap, saying "I'm bollixed. Armstrong was going much too hard for me."

But Armstrong didn't ease the pressure: He went to the front whenever he sensed that the break was losing its momentum, and by the time the six leaders tackled The Wall the next time, they were 1:44 ahead of Walton, 2:00 up on Baker and Schleicher, and 3:13 ahead of the pack…. The first decisive move had been made.

The situation was almost perfect for Armstrong, whose one remaining problem was how to rid himself of the three Italian sprinters, Biasci, Canzonieri and Gaggioli. In the meantime, however, they were his allies, making strong pulls, and knowing that the only way they could win the race was to keep this breakaway alive. In contrast, Armstrong was planning how to get away from them.

The Texan had thought about this possibility beforehand. Talking on the start line, Armstrong said, "The wind makes it hard for a solo rider up by the river. But if you get away (on The Wall), you have a tail wind blowing you back to the start-finish." With those thoughts in mind, he didn't attack on this ninth lap, not wanting to tackle the seven-mile head-wind stretch on his own. Instead, he rode steadily up The Wall, topping it ahead of Julich, Copeland and the three Italians, 1:48 ahead of Walton, and 2:30 before the pack. Then, riding with the wind back to the start-finish area outside Philadelphia's Art Museum, Armstrong continued to cajole his companions. They began the last of the big loops (which would be followed by three laps of a three-mile circuit) with a 2:43 advantage on the peloton—which had absorbed Walton. Back into Manayunk, the gap was still a healthy 2:20, as the six leaders emerged from the cool shade of the rusting iron viaduct that supports an elevated railway, and raced into the furnace-like heat bouncing from the steep city street.

Julich and Copeland were at the front as the leaders began climbing The Wall for the 10th and final time. And, as they completed the first part of the hill, the two Americans were still in front. But then, as the climb curved left to begin the steepest pitch, Armstrong literally exploded out of the group. The roar of the fans was deafening, as they urged on their new favorite, in his spectacular attack.

In a press conference the previous day, the rock-and-roll-loving Texan had declared the race a "crap shoot." Now, the dice were loaded in his favor: The other five leaders were already riding at their limit, and as Armstrong sprinted away, all they could do was stare up The Wall, and hope that he would blow. By the top, however, 17 miles from the finish, Armstrong was already 26 seconds ahead of them.

"I looked back to see I'd gotten the gap. I checked again at the top. Then, I just put my head down and went for it," he later described. This was a dream unfolding for the Motorola prodigy. He hurtled down the straight, roller-coaster descent of Manayunk Avenue, as if a carload of hoodlums were in pursuit; and, blown by the wind, continued his rampage alongside the river (now 45 seconds ahead), through Fairmount Park's Mount Pleasant (with the gap up to 1:07), and over the short, switchback climb of Lemon Hill (1:20 before the five chasers).

Armstrong was 1:42 ahead by the end of this final loop, with a fast-moving pack at 2:30. He still had nine miles to ride, but the Texan already knew that the race—and the million dollars—were in his pocket. After one lap of the finishing circuit—where the five chasers were about to be absorbed by the pack—he spotted his mother Linda Walling in the crowd. After two laps—when a pursuit was underway

*USPRO Championship • USA • 1993*

from Italian Gianluca Pierobon of Mecair-Ballan and New Zealander Graeme Miller of Duck Head—Armstrong blew his mother a kiss. And as he returned from his final loop over Lemon Hill, he responded to the waves of his teammates in the pack, heading in the opposite direction, still more than two minutes behind him.

Then, on entering the final straightaway, he straightened his blue-and-red Motorola jersey, adjusted his blue-tinted Oakleys, and cruised down Benjamin Franklin Parkway, punching the air and waving to the 100,000 crowd, all the way to the checkered flag. "This was the loudest crowd I've heard in my life," exclaimed the exultant Armstrong, the new U.S. champion, who'd won the CoreStates Championship more decisively and spectacularly than anyone in the race's history. The Motorola rider crossed the line 1:30 ahead of Pierobon, who had dropped Miller on the last climb; while the joyous New Zealander just held on to third place ahead of Armstrong's English teammate Yates—who won the sprint for fourth place, at 1:48, from a late, eight-strong counterattack.

After finishing, the Motorola riders wove their way back through the crowds to the finish line, to celebrate with Armstrong, who was already hugging his mom. In two dramatic thrusts, Armstrong had used The Wall to shape a memorable victory, and scoop that "impossible" million-dollar Triple Crown. It took character and exceptional ability to overcome the pressure and ride a perfect race ... and earned him a whole new set of fans. Typical, perhaps, was a spectator named Jennifer Miller—who was watching a bike race for the very first time. When asked by a reporter from the *Philadelphia Daily News* whom she was rooting for, Miller replied, "That guy named Lance."

**THE MILLION DOLLAR WALL**

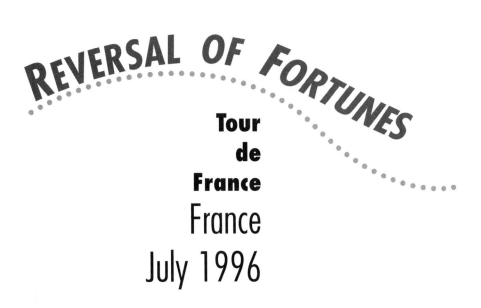

# REVERSAL OF FORTUNES

**Tour
de
France**

France
July 1996

**Nobody knew** what the result would be on that November day in 1902, when a group of Paris newspaper editors and executives gathered in the Zimmer restaurant on the Boulevard Montmartre. They were there to discuss ways of boosting the waning circulation of their daily sports paper, *L'Auto*. One of them suggested promoting a "Tour de France," by linking together a half-dozen marathon cycling races around the country's perimeter. The race happened the following summer ... and every July since, except through the two World Wars. It is now the biggest annual sports event in the world. The 83rd edition took place in 1996.

# France

SHEETS OF HEAVY RAIN blown in their faces by a boisterous southwest wind. Vivid bolts of lightning. Ominous rumbles of thunder. Roads awash with rivers of mud-filled storm water. Clouds swirling around the giant limestone cliffs of the pine-clad Jura mountains. A sky that was nighttime black by mid-afternoon. Riders in plastic rain jackets racing at insane speeds, focused on the spraying wheels in front of them. This was the sixth stage of the 1996 Tour de France, the day, according to several team directors, that would see the Tour really start. Indeed, the racing was brilliantly aggressive, averaging more than 40 kph on the hilliest stage yet—and 45 kph for the final two hours, which included three of the days five climbs. No wonder 17 men quit the race on this apocalyptic journey.

Amazingly, at the end of a day marked by some of the worst weather conditions of any stage in Tour history, more than 70 riders were still together to contest the stage victory in the final kilometers. And, appropriately, the slick conditions eventually decided the outcome....

On a complicated run-in to Aix-les-Bains, during another torrential downpour, Dutch buccaneer Michaël Boogerd sprinted around and through a roundabout as if he were on dry roads. But instead of falling, the Rabobank team rider went clear by 50 meters. The chase came from Spaniard Melchor Mauri, whose ONCE team had been pulling the peloton for the past hour. Mauri overtook Boogerd, with the aim of controlling the Dutchman's attack and opening the way for his team leader Laurent Jalabert to win the stage. Then, on a sharp left turn, 1100 meters from the line, Mauri slid out and came to a humiliating halt, leaving the way clear for Boogerd to dash away to the first victory in his career as a professional cyclist.

*Tour de France • France • 1996*

Five hours earlier, the 207-kilometer stage had opened quietly, as the pack rode for 40 minutes in the dry, before the race burst into life at Pont d'Hèry, a kilometer from the top of the day's first climb. As the pace increased, the weather turned nasty, and the peloton split into two groups. After a partial regrouping, a series of attacks came, before Dutchman Leo Van Bon of Rabobank went away with the Italian Marco Saligari of MG-Technogym at the 63-kilometer point.

With their lead at 40 seconds, the chase was taken up by Djamolidin Abdujaparov—the Italian-based rider from Tashkent, Uzbekistan, who has three times won the sprinters' green jersey at the Tour. Abdu's a solid-thighed sprinter, but was having no luck in this race, and so was seeking to add to his career total of eight Tour stage wins in a different way. But he's no climber, and after closing to within seven seconds of the two leaders, the seven-kilometer-long Chatel-de-Joux climb relegated him to 35 seconds. Abdu' didn't give up. After dropping almost two minutes behind the two leaders at the day's feed zone, he was caught and dropped by Italian Andrea Ferrigato of BresciaLat on the 12-kilometer-long Croix de la Serra climb (118 kilometers) ... yet finally caught up with the leaders descending through the rain into Bellegarde, 37 kilometers later.

With four men together at the front, 60 kilometers to go, and the peloton 3:20 back, the breakaway riders appeared to have a good chance of success. However, their lead was cut to 1:40 on reaching the foot of the last and steepest of the day's climbs, the 4.5-kilometer-long Senoy hill. With the rain again lashing down from black thunderheads, and the wind against them, Van Bon rode away from his three companions. By the top, however, a strong surge by ONCE riders Neil Stephens and Alex Zülle pulled the first

**REVERSAL OF FORTUNES**

part of the pack to within 10 seconds of the Dutchman. Van Bon sat up soon after.

With most of defending champion Miguel Induráin's Banesto teammates left behind on the hill, the ONCE riders decided to ride hard all the way to the finish. They led Jalabert to a six-second bonus sprint win at Rumilly, and then closed down all the attacks—until Mauri slipped up on the second-to-last corner, allowing Boogerd to claim the stage. It was a memorable day for Rabobank, but a miserable one for most of the other 21 teams.

Bad weather had been with the Tour since it started in the Netherlands, where a rainy prologue victory went to Jalabert's Swiss teammate Zülle. The ONCE rider kept the yellow jersey for a couple of days as the Tour headed south into France, but the constant head winds kept the race together, and mass sprint finishes marked the first three stages, won by Frenchman Frédéric Moncassin of GAN, Italian Mario Cipollini of Saeco, and German Erik Zabel of Telekom. Moncassin's consistent high finishes and time-bonus haul earned him the yellow jersey, the day the Tour entered France.

The next day, Moncassin would give up the lead to his young GAN teammate Stéphane Heulot—who was still in the yellow jersey after that debilitating sixth stage into Aix. Neighboring Chambéry was the starting point of stage seven, which headed into the French Alps for one of the most spectacular days in the race's history. By stage end in Les Arcs, a modern ski resort high above the Upper Isère Valley, huge changes had taken place in the Tour's hierarchy. And at the center of everyone's attention was Induráin, the winner of the previous five Tours, who was fully expected to make this win number six.

_Tour de France • France • 1996_

THERE WAS NO EXPRESSION on Miguel Induráin's face when he reached the stage finish at Les Arcs in 16th place—after suddenly cracking on the final climb and losing three-and-a-half minutes in three-and-a-half kilometers to his perennial rival, Tony Rominger of Switzerland. The Spaniard didn't even notice a fly settle on his cheek as he was whisked through the awaiting melée of media hounds. But nobody got a word out of the Tour maestro ... except perhaps the fly.

Induráin—who later said he didn't even remember crossing the line—was chaperoned straight to an awaiting Mercedes-Benz minivan, whose smoked-glass windows soon screened him from the world. Inside, he ravenously stuffed a packet of fruit tarts into his mouth, before being driven away to his hotel.

Not since 1990 had we seen Induráin in as much trouble as he was in the finale of this epic alpine stage. That year, he was the first lieutenant for 1988 Tour winner Pedro Delgado, and after riding hard for his leader on the road to L'Alpe d'Huez, Induráin blew up on the final climb, finishing almost 10 minutes down.

The difference between then and now is the matter of his five Tour victories. In each of those Tours, Induráin had frustrated his challengers by grinding them down in the mountains after dominating them in the time trials. But this Tour was proving very different. Induráin's Banesto team was not functioning as efficiently as in the past; the defending champion himself was showing the strain of being the super-favorite; and his rivals were displaying more strength and aggression than ever before.

But no one could have forecast the astounding turnaround at Les Arcs—a 14.5-kilometer-long climb on which Induráin said he was even thinking of attacking moments

**REVERSAL OF FORTUNES**

before he "bonked," as they say in cycling circles. The defending champion didn't have an explanation for his blowing up. He said he had eaten correctly during the stage, and in fact had refused a water bottle offered him by rival Zülle, five kilometers before he cracked. If explanations are in order, then they have to be taken in the context of the previous week's cold, wet weather, and the developments of this particular stage—one which provided more drama than the previous six stages combined....

Besides the Induráin shock, the day saw the overnight yellow jersey (Heulot) and King of the Mountains leader (Van Bon) both pull out; the demise of several team leaders (including Jalabert, Chris Boardman of GAN, Laurent Madouas of Motorola and Claudio Chiappucci of Carrera); the spectacular crashes of leading contenders Rominger, Zülle and Johan Bruyneel; and the emergence of exciting new riders (including Telekom's German Jan Ullrich and Carrera's Austrian Peter Luttenberger). In the end, the stage was won by Frenchman Luc Leblanc of Polti, and the overall lead went to the enigmatic Eugeni Berzin of Gewiss—the first-ever Russian to wear the yellow jersey. But behind these headlines were a host of subplots that scripted this memorable stage ... and Induráin's downfall.

***Act One (0-60km)*** After leaving Chambéry in a thunderstorm, the race headed east on a series of rolling back roads, with a strong tail wind encouraging attacks. No less than 43.4 kilometers were covered in the first hour. The most significant move was made by Frenchman Laurent Roux of TVM, who was joined by Chazal's Frenchman Jacky Durand, Motorola's American George Hincapie and Banesto's Portuguese Orlando Rodrigues ... and then Festina's Frenchman Pascal Hervé. They were caught after 24 kilometers, but that early action meant that within 90 minutes—half an hour

*Tour de France • France • 1996*

ahead of schedule—the race was at the foot of the Col de la Madeleine, the first of the day's three giant climbs.

**Act Two (60km-80km)** Riding into the clouds and a steady rain, the peloton was almost immediately split by ONCE—which set a rapid tempo, hoping to put Zülle and Jalabert into leading roles—and by Leblanc, who made a short, but significant attack. The ONCE plan backfired when Jalabert, who hadn't realized he had an oncoming virus, was dropped from the front group of 50 riders only three kilometers into the 20-kilometer, eight-percent climb.

Then, the surprisingly strong Telekom squad took over, with team leader Bjarne Riis of Denmark tucked in behind pacesetters Udo Bölts, Brian Holm and Ullrich. After only eight kilometers of climbing, zigzagging across a pine-wooded mountainside, the Telekom-led pack was down to 32 riders—including five from Banesto, and three each from ONCE, Mapei and Telekom. Behind came a group led by a riding-at-his-own-pace Boardman at 20 seconds, and another with Jalabert at 45 seconds.

Within a further four kilometers, when race leader Heulot dropped back, those gaps were 50 seconds and 1:25. And by the 6560-foot summit, high on a grassy crest, the leaders were 1:35 ahead of Heulot, three minutes up on Boardman, and 4:35 clear of Jalabert. These were huge gaps for the Tour's first significant climb. Richard Virenque of Festina sprinted away to take the maximum KoM points, ahead of Induráin, Zülle, Rominger, Berzin, Luttenberger and Leblanc.

**Act Three (80km-116km)** It was expected that many of the dropped riders, perhaps even Jalabert's group, would catch back on the fast, twisting downhill. But Riis had other ideas. Just after the Italian Valentino Fois of Panaria had crashed out of the lead group, and while Heulot was rejoin-

**REVERSAL OF FORTUNES**

ing, the Telekom team leader dashed away into the mist. Taking massive risks on the narrow, wet roads, Riis was 1:15 clear by the end of the long Madeleine descent, and he continued to force the pace as the race remained in hilly back roads for another eight kilometers. His acceleration, and a steady chase by Banesto, meant that Boardman and Jalabert were still no closer to the front than they were at the summit.

After a chat with his Telekom team director, Belgian Walter Godefroot, and in view of the 90 kilometers still to race, Riis now slowed his pace, and allowed himself to be caught as the race headed down a last steep drop before flatter valley roads were reached. It was on this downhill that Mapei's Rominger tumbled spectacularly into a pasture. After clambering back to the road, he was checked by the race doctor for injuries, and then his Spanish teammate Manuel Fernandez Gines helped pace him back to the pack.

*Act Four (116km-144km)* Right after Rominger's fall, Telekom sent another rider on the attack, Bölts, who was quickly joined by ONCE's Australian Patrick Jonker and MG-Technogym's Italian Alberto Elli. Through the feed zone at Albertville, the three new leaders were two minutes clear of the pack, while Boardman's group was just behind. The Brit finally caught back after a 50-kilometer chase, just as the race headed back into the mountains; but he was then dropped once more, this time for good. Boardman later said his heart rate wouldn't go over 150 beats per minute, compared with his normal 180. Jalabert was having similar problems, and he never got closer to the main group than two minutes, before steadily drifting back, to finish the stage almost 13 minutes in arrears.

*Act Five (144km to 164km)* The lead trio was 2:45 ahead by the foot of the second big climb, the Cormet de Roseland. On its steep early slopes, which climbs relentlessly across a

*Tour de France • France • 1996*

steep, craggy mountainside, Bölts soon dropped Jonker and Elli, while in the group behind Induráin saw all his teammates drop back, except for José Maria Jimenez. While this was happening, Festina's Swiss climber Laurent Dufaux blasted out of the pack and started to close on the leaders.

Midway up the 20-kilometer ascent, Dufaux's French teammate Virenque, followed by Leblanc, then by Kelme's Fernando Escartin each made probing attacks. This staccato action didn't please Induráin, who prefers a steady climbing pace. So the Spanish superstar stepped in, with his strong tempo stopping the attacks and splitting the group. Unfortunately, his last teammate, Jimenez, fell back, leaving Induráin on his own for the stage's remaining 44 kilometers.

This looked like the Induráin we knew, as he rhythmically pounded the pedals, asserting his control once more. Was he ascending through the clouds toward that unprecedented sixth Tour?

Ahead, at the Roseland's rocky peak, Bölts was in the lead by 1:15 over Dufaux, while 40 seconds later came Virenque, sprinting for third place, ahead of Riis, Induráin, Zülle and Rominger.

Many minutes behind, race leader Heulot had stopped by the side of the road, holding his right knee. He was suffering from tendinitis, a fact kept secret by his team for several days. Even though he was hurting badly, his team director Roger Legeay encouraged Heulot to start riding again, "to see how things go when you get over the climb." Heulot tried, but the pain was so great, he was pedaling with one leg, moving at walking pace. He again stopped, tears in his eyes, and once more Legeay persuaded him to carry on—but within a few meters he stopped for the last time. A commissaire came up and removed race number 92 from his yellow jersey. His dream was over.

**REVERSAL OF FORTUNES**

**Act Six (164km to 185km)** The twisting, steep, often narrow descent of the Roseland has often seen crashes on its irregular corners, such as the one four years ago when Spaniard Iñaki Gaston collided with a stone wall and fractured a leg. There were three crashes this year. First, on a sharp right turn, the accident-prone Zülle went straight on, and flew 15 meters into the branches of a tree, his bike landing beyond him. Next, on the bend that claimed Gaston in 1992, Bruyneel mis-read the line, braked hard, skidded between a rock face and parapet wall, dropped over the edge of the canyon—and, like Zülle, landed in some tree branches. As the Belgian was being pulled back to the road, Zülle came flying by on the wheel of Spanish teammate Aitor Garmendia; but just as they caught back to Induráin's group, Zülle touched another rider's wheel and landed in the middle of the road on his back, ripping his shorts. Again, Garmendia had to play the Good Samaritan.

Ahead, the first two riders had descended faultlessly, and on reaching the Isère valley at Bourg-St. Maurice, Bölts was 43 seconds in front of Dufaux, and 2:30 up on the 14-strong group of race favorites.

**Act Seven (185km to 200km)** The rain clouds were now clearing, and sunshine was shyly making an appearance, causing riders to roll down their arm warmers, and remove rain jackets and shoe covers. The business ahead was a smooth, engineered road, climbing 2838 vertical feet in 14.5 kilometers at a steady six-percent grade. Although not particularly difficult on its own, this climb to the Olympic ski resort of Les Arc proved otherwise at the end of this aggressive stage. And the aggression continued....

After Zülle and Garmendia recaught the group, Mapei's Fernandez Gines attacked—and was chased down by the remarkable Ullrich. But no one went after an immediate

*Tour de France • France • 1996*

counterattack from TVM's tiny Dane Bo Hamburger. Up ahead, Dufaux closed on Bölts and shot straight past him. The Swiss rider passed below the 10 kilometers-to-go banner 12 seconds clear of Bölts, 1:20 ahead of Hamburger, and 1:40 up on the group—which was now being led by Garmendia, with Zülle and Induráin just behind.

Garmendia continued to set the tempo, and it was fast enough to see Fernandez Gines get dropped, and Hamburger and Bölts be overtaken. This left Dufaux alone with a 1:47 lead when, with seven kilometers to go, Leblanc blasted away from the group, hauling a huge gear. The 1994 world road champion, only now finding his best form after an injury-ridden 18 months, soon had the valiant Dufaux in his sights, and bounded by him just inside three kilometers to go.

While the stage win was being played out in front, Garmendia continued to lead the group, before peeling off, his team duties seemingly over for the day. As the ONCE rider dropped back, Luttenberger (marked by Virenque) made a sharp acceleration at the five-kilometer mark. Induráin was still sitting comfortably in second or third slot when, suddenly, he drifted to the back of the now 10-strong group. At the same time, Rominger and Mapei teammate Abraham Olano went to the front. and set a pace that Induráin simply couldn't follow. With 3.5 kilometers left, the Tour super-favorite lost contact—followed a few minutes later by Zülle. No one could quite believe what was happening.

Now there were three battles taking place: At the front, Luttenberger was chasing Leblanc; in the middle, Olano and Rominger were climbing the fastest of all, with Riis, Escartin, Ullrich, Piotr Ugrumov and Berzin on their wheels; and behind, Induráin and Zülle were battling for their cycling lives.

 **REVERSAL OF FORTUNES**

Induráin was also fighting hunger and possible dehydration; he seemed to be in a trance, and gladly took a Coke from Gewiss directeur sportif Emanuele Bombini, who was driving past on his way to the Berzin group. Despite his zombie-like state, Induráin still managed to chase back to Zülle with two kilometers to go—but he didn't stay on the Swiss rider's wheel for long. Zülle moved away again, and then a resurgent Garmendia, seeing what was happening, came charging past Induráin and up to help his team leader.

Ahead, Rominger dropped the others in the group, and raced past Dufaux, Virenque and Luttenberger, to finish second, only 47 seconds behind stage winner Leblanc. Garmendia helped Zülle limit his losses on new race leader Berzin to 2:33. Induráin arrived a further 50 seconds behind; later, he had another 20 seconds added to his losses, when he was assessed a penalty for taking that drink from a team car in the final climb. "But without that drink I may have lost another minute," he said, his sixth Tour win now in severe jeopardy.

IN THE EXCITEMENT of the final climb to Les Arcs, the fact that Berzin and Olano were tied for first place was almost overlooked. It was only thanks to a 16-hundredths-of-a-second difference in their prologue times that Berzin earned the right to wear the yellow jersey. Nonetheless, the 26-year-old Russian proved the next day, in a 30.5-kilometer uphill time trial to Val d'Isère, that he deserved to be the race leader.

With a swashbuckling ride, particularly on the flatter opening and closing sections, Berzin blazed to a 35-second victory over runner-up Riis—who was actually the fastest on the steep middle section that contained most of the course's 3200 feet of climbing. Behind these two came the Mapei

*Tour de France • France • 1996*

pair, Olano and Rominger, respectively 45 seconds and 1:01 slower than Berzin.

As for the previous day's two main victims, Induráin recovered enough to take a solid fifth place, level with Rominger, while Zülle finished a disappointing ninth, 2:36 down. Their performances might have reflected their different attitudes to their recent setbacks. Induráin said, "Lost? Are you joking? I haven't lost the Tour;" while Zülle commented, "You have to be realistic, the Tour is played out for me."

The biggest news to emerge from the time trial, however, was that 11 men were still within five minutes of the yellow jersey—and, in this topsy-turvy Tour, that meant all 11 had a chance of making the podium in Paris—while the four front-runners were closely packed, within 68 seconds of each other.

Besides the main players, newcomers Ullrich and Luttenberger put in outstanding rides, although both faded on the final stretch, which went through nine tunnels and contained enough downhill for Berzin to average more than 64 kph (about 40 mph) for the final 7.5 kilometers! It was in the style of a Greg LeMond or Bernard Hinault that the 5-foot-7, 141-pound Russian, gripping the hooks of his handlebars, the wind parting his straight blond hair in the middle, blazed the last 500 meters to the line. This was Berzin at his best. But would his time-trial strength be enough to win the Tour?

STAGE NINE was the one that should have played a huge part in the outcome of the 83rd Tour de France. Instead, the weather intervened once more, and we were given only a brief taste of what this stage might have provided. Not since the 1920s had a stage of the Tour been

**REVERSAL OF FORTUNES**

shortened because of bad weather—winter is not expected in France in July.

After the day's planned start at Val d'Isère was abandoned, the riders were driven in their team cars to the other side of the Col de l'Iseran, at Lanslebourg, where a stage of 144 kilometers was planned to start. It was very cold, in the 30s Fahrenheit, but the riders made themselves ready, knowing they would have 40 kilometers to warm up before the start of the Tour's hardest climb, the Col du Galibier. Then came the news of 100-kph winds and blowing snow on the mountain's 8661-foot summit, forcing everyone to get back in their vehicles to drive over the Galibier, too.

It was a tough decision for race director Jean-Marie Leblanc, but a correct one. However, not only did it remove the longest, toughest climb from the Tour, it was also a huge disappointment for the thousands of fans who lined the 35-kilometer-long ascent, many of whom had camped on the cold mountainside overnight. Certainly, those fans would have seen one of the high points of the race, one in which Rominger and Induráin were expected to test the mettle of Berzin and Riis. Instead, the eventual start at Monetier-les-Bains offered only a 46-kilometer mini-stage with two shorter climbs: the Montgenèvre and Sestriere. Even so, they were sufficient to expose Berzin's limitations....

It was still cold, and the roads were dry when the starter's flag was dropped at 3:12 p.m. This shortened stage started down a valley with a strong tail wind, and the peloton covered the 17 kilometers to Briançon in just 14 minutes (that's 85 kph!). The race now turned left and began the 12-kilometer climb to Montgenèvre, and the attacks began.

Festina's Hervé was the first to try, followed by Polti's Italian Giuseppe Guerini, Jimenez and Elli. Neither attack worked. Then the ambitious Riis entered the picture, and

*Tour de France • France • 1996*

was marked immediately by Berzin. Guerini attacked again, and Riis went with him; the response again came from the yellow jersey. Riis went for a third time, still without success. But seeing that Berzin was finding it a little harder to chase him down each time, Riis asked Ullrich and Bölts to make the pace even faster. This split the group and gave the Telekom leader the opening to make a decisive attack about four kilometers from the top, where the grade increases to 12 percent on a series of switchbacks. The Dane was sprinting out of the saddle, perhaps releasing his frustrations from sitting in a car most of the day. About 100 meters behind, Berzin already looked beaten, heading a group that was now down to 11 riders.

In the climb's last two kilometers, Leblanc and then Virenque charged after Riis; and at the 6200-foot summit, the Danish champion was 19 seconds ahead of Leblanc, 27 seconds ahead of Virenque, and 31 seconds clear of the group led by Rominger, Berzin, Induráin and Ullrich.

Riis continued his push on the fast, steep descent into Italy, and as he started the 11-kilometer climb to the Sestriere finish, he was 38 seconds ahead of a partially regrouped pack. For about a kilometer, Berzin's Italian teammate Francesco Frattini led the chase—but he soon dropped back, leaving the race leader on his own to set the group's tempo.

With 10 kilometers to go, the gap was down to 32 seconds, but Berzin was now weakening, while Riis was pushing a huge gear in a do-or-die effort. The gap started to open again, to 40, 41, 45 seconds—which made Riis the overall race leader. For a while, Mapei's Olano, then teammate Fernandez Gines, helped with the pace-setting, but Riis continued to gain. His lead was 51 seconds with four kilometers to go, the moment chosen by Luttenberger to counterattack.

 **REVERSAL OF FORTUNES**

The Austrian's effort was neutralized, but then he went again, following another burst from Guerini—an acceleration that caused Berzin to be dropped from the group.

Luttenberger tried a third acceleration, but then with two-and-a-half kilometers to go, Induráin surged through, and only Luttenberger, Virenque, Rominger and Leblanc could catch his wheel. With two kilometers remaining, these five were 32 seconds behind Riis, while Berzin had dropped to 1:07 back. The yellow jersey was going to change hands once again.

Into the streets of Sestriere, a chic ski resort on a grassy saddle in the Italian Alps, Leblanc and Virenque repeated their acceleration of the first climb, to take second and third places on the stage behind Riis, while Rominger "outsprinted" Induráin for fourth place at 28 seconds—perhaps showing the Spaniard that he could match him in strength. But the 35-year-old Swiss, who finished with blood on his right leg, later told the press: "I wasn't capable of riding harder, as I had crashed, and my knee was hurting."

Berzin came in all alone in 13th place, 1:23 behind the gasping, open-mouthed Riis, who had literally ridden himself to a standstill on his solo 24-kilometer break, giving an upbeat ending to a downbeat day.

SPAIN WAS STILL A FEW HOURS AWAY by bike, but on the climb to Hautacam, Riis performed like a *matador del toro,* toying with his opponents before delivering a body blow to their aspirations. Not since Laurent Fignon at the 1984 Tour had anyone oozed such confidence as this balding, pencil-slim Dane. And not since that same Fignon in 1989 had a rider in the yellow jersey won a road stage of the Tour.

For a whole week, ever since his other mountaintop win on the truncated stage to Sestriere, Riis had been looking for

*Tour de France • France • 1996*

terrain that would favor his bolt-from-the-blue style. He had held himself in check on the Superbesse and Tulle stages … but had no intention of holding anything back on the savage stage 16 finish. After all, he knew that another Sestriere-type performance could virtually seal his overall victory.

Almost as confident as Riis before the stage were the Banesto, Festina and Mapei teams. They, too, knew that a strong ride on the Hautacam was needed by their respective leaders—Induráin, Virenque, Olano and Rominger—if they were going to stand a chance of overtaking Riis before Paris. Others, such as Leblanc, Luttenberger and maybe Ugrumov, were hoping for a stage win.

All these disparate ambitions came together on the 13.5 kilometers of erratically climbing road that separates the richly cultivated valley of the Gave de Pau and the bleak, windswept grasslands of Hautacam, 3300 feet above.

Before reaching the stage terminus, the peloton had rolled for more than four hours at a steady 43-kph tempo, passing fields of sunflowers and wheat along the rolling roads of Gascony, and coming ever closer to the mist-covered line of mountains on the horizon: the Pyrénées. For most of the day, the pack was chasing the irrepressible Laurent Roux of France, Pascal Richard of Switzerland and Mariano Piccoli of Italy—all of whom had figured in previous long-distance raids. They escaped at 29 kilometers, reached a maximum lead of 7:30, and were still 3:40 clear when Roux sprinted away from the other two on a short hill, 50 kilometers before reaching the Hautacam.

Roux's escape gave impetus to the eventual chase by the pack, when Festina (for Virenque), Carrera (for Luttenberger), Mapei (for Rominger) and Roslotto (for Ugrumov) rode hard to get their leaders to the front. And after passing through pilgrim-packed Lourdes, Telekom also came for-

**REVERSAL OF FORTUNES**

ward, on the narrow, hedge-lined valley road that took the strung-out pack to its day's destination—and its destiny.

Two years ago, most of the same players reached the Hautacam when it was the first big climb of the Tour. Then, Induráin's only challenger after the preceding time trial, Rominger, cracked, and the Spaniard raced into the clouds (with Leblanc on his wheel) to his fourth Tour de France victory. This time, Riis (who finished alongside a sick Rominger in 1994) was in the driving seat; Rominger and Induráin were the challengers.

At the start of the climb, after Zülle made a token attack, Induráin and Riis rode alongside each other until, after three kilometers, Dufaux increased the already elevated tempo—and Rominger dropped back (was he sick again?). Already the front group numbered fewer than 12. As he had in the Alps, the bull-like Ullrich now took over the pacemaking, with Riis, Induráin, Dufaux, Virenque and Italian climber Leonardo Piepoli following. Then, suddenly, on a steep left curve, Riis pulled wide to his right, looked across at the line of riders, dropped back and slotted in behind the front five and ahead of five others, including Berzin and Olano. Was Riis struggling? Or was he just checking out the opposition?

Two minutes later, we got the answer: On one of the steepest pitches of the unevenly rising road, Riis launched a devastating attack—in his 13-tooth sprocket, out of the saddle, and racing with the same raw ambition he exhibited at Sestriere. At first, Induráin led the chase, with Dufaux and Virenque on his wheel. But Induráin's defense lasted less than a kilometer. The five-time champion, who was climbing in a fairly hefty 39x17 gear, later said, "I don't know what happened. It was impossible to climb faster."

*Tour de France • France • 1996*

Berzin already had dropped back when Induráin eventually had to slow down (along with Olano and Luttenberger). Meanwhile, Leblanc and Dufaux momentarily closed on Riis, before the Dane accelerated a second time, to go definitively clear about seven kilometers from the top.

Within two kilometers, Riis was 28 seconds ahead of the Virenque-Dufaux-Leblanc-Piepoli quartet—whose cause wasn't helped by Piepoli and Leblanc making unsuccessful counterattacks. Still, as Dufaux later said, "We were all riding at the limit ... and we couldn't get any closer to Riis."

Behind, Rominger was riding the strongest of the other favorites. With five kilometers remaining, the compact Swiss veteran raced smoothly past the struggling Induráin, who was riding alone. Within another 1500 meters, which included a back-breaking left turn that rose like a wall, Rominger came up to Olano, Ullrich, Luttenberger, Escartin, Ugrumov and Brochard. It was an impressive comeback. Rominger went on to take sixth on the stage, although his bandaged right knee confirmed that he was still below the 100-percent that a challenger had to be on this relentlessly steep ascent.

Riis, of course, was again at his very best, even though the race leader started to struggle with two kilometers to go, when he was 54 seconds ahead of the Virenque group. But just as he did at Sestriere, Riis battled through his pain, gasping for air, and yet still riding in the big ring. A combination of relief and fatigue showed in his gaunt, flushed face as he crossed the line, 49 seconds ahead of runners-up Virenque and Dufaux ... 1:33 on Rominger ... 1:45 on Olano ... 2:28 on Induráin ... and 2:50 on Berzin.

Remarkably, Riis had climbed the Hautacam's 13.5 kilometers under a blazing sun in just 34 minutes—that's 90 seconds faster than the Induráin-Leblanc tandem rode in the

**REVERSAL OF FORTUNES**

misty conditions of '94! The Tour wasn't over, because the next day's daunting stage had the potential to disrupt even Riis. But, supported by hordes of red-flag-waving fans, the Danish matador looked ready for the kill.

"HOT . . . HARD . . . " Those were the only two words an exhausted Neil Stephens of Australia could think of to describe the gigantic 17th stage he had just completed across the Pyrénées into Pamplona, Spain. Stephens was one of the day's heroes. He took off in a break after 17 kilometers; was first over the Aubisque, Marie-Blanque and Soudet passes; and finished the stage in 11th place, in the same group as Rominger, Olano and Induráin.

That was great for Stephens, but a disaster for the big three favorites, because their group arrived in Pamplona more than eight minutes behind the leaders—eight riders who now occupied the top eight places on overall time: Riis, Ullrich, Virenque, Dufaux, Luttenberger, Escartin, Ugrumov and Leblanc.

The day was particularly distressing for Induráin, who couldn't follow the pace set by the Festina and Telekom riders on the hugely difficult Col de Soudet; was dropped by the chase group on the even tougher Port de Larrau; and rode into his hometown after enduring his worst Tour stage in six years.

This was intended to be a day of triumph for Induráin. The race organizers had routed the stage into Pamplona, expecting the Spanish superstar to be wearing the yellow jersey at the end of the Tour's toughest day. They even staged a prime sprint outside the Induráin family home in Villava, five kilometers before the finish. Celebrations had been planned. Thousands of special flags were handed out to the roadside masses to salute their Miguel. And Pamplona was

*Tour de France • France • 1996*

jam-packed with hundreds of thousands of adoring fans, many of whom had paid $30 a head to stand on balconies of the massive apartment blocks overlooking the finish area.

To prepare for this stage, Induráin had ridden over most of the 262-kilometer course during the spring. And Campagnolo had custom-made him a triple chainring for the stage—though he didn't use it. Induráin knew that his Tour was already over. He had arrived at Hautacam the day before almost in tears. And for him, this day was destined to be a matter of survival rather than spectacle.

The motives of the Festina racers were quite different. They, too, had reconnoitered the course in training, and now vowed to make the race as hard as they could, in a bid to put Virenque on the podium in Paris. That's why, despite knowing they had at least seven hours of racing ahead of them, the seven Festina riders climbed on their bikes 10 kilometers before the stage start in Argelès-Gazost, to warm up.

The first of seven categorized climbs, the 16-kilometer-long Col du Soulor, began right from the 9:34 a.m. start. And the first attack came in the very first kilometer: Motorola's Jésus Montoya made a solo bid, and was joined by Telekom's Bölts. Virenque himself closed the gap. On the second part of the climb, after a flat section along the high valley of Arrens, Montoya attacked a second time, this time covered by Festina's Hervé. The Frenchman soon dropped the Spaniard, and topped the Soulor alone, 18 seconds in front of a group led by Virenque, Brochard, Riis and Dufaux.

It was on the subsequent two-kilometer drop, down a narrow, cliffside road, that ONCE's Stephens launched his counterattack with the ever-enterprising Italian, Fabio Baldato of MG-Technogym. Like Hervé—whom they joined very quickly—they knew that $6000 in primes awaited at the Souvenir Henri Desgrange (in memory of the Tour's

**REVERSAL OF FORTUNES**

founder) on the 5607-foot summit of the Col d'Aubisque, now six kilometers away. Stephens dashed clear to take the main prize, 10 seconds ahead of Hervé and Bartoli, with Virenque and Riis still heading the peloton 2:15 behind.

The two-part Soulor-Aubisque ascent took just over an hour, while the downhill to the next valley took the three leaders just 18 minutes. They reached the valley 1:40 ahead of pursuing Italian Maurizio Fondriest—a former world champion—and 3:45 on the peloton. Ten kilometers later, after the pack had raced hard in single file along the valley floor, those gaps were cut to 1:25 and 2:20. Now began the day's third climb, the eight-kilometer-long Marie-Blanque. By the top, two hours into the stage, the three leaders were still 1:20 ahead of Fondriest, while the pack had eased back to a four-minute deficit.

That gap increased to six minutes before the village of Issor, where seven more riders left the peloton: Abdujaparov, Durand, Sørensen and Frattini, along with Banesto's Arrieta, Telekom's Bölts and Mapei's Federico Echave. Like Hervé in front, Arrieta, Bölts and Echave had been sent forward to be of help to their leaders, on or after the upcoming Soudet and Larrau climbs.

On reaching the foot of the Col du Soudet, just after noon, Stephens-Hervé-Bartoli were two minutes in front of Fondriest, four minutes ahead of the seven chasers, and still six minutes ahead of the field. By the summit, an hour later, the race had exploded.

On a bumpy road that first climbed alongside a cascading creek, with shade from overhanging oak, beech and hazelnut trees, Stephens and his companions rode at a steady 20 kph, dropping to 10 kph on the steepest pitches of 11 percent. These early slopes found the peloton riding even slower, dropping 6:40 back 15 kilometers from the summit.

*Tour de France • France • 1996*

Then the action began. Dufaux was the first to raise the tempo, splitting a group of 15 or so off the front, and momentarily causing Olano to lose contact. Telekom's Christian Henn was the next to increase the pace, forcing Berzin, then Rominger to drop back. When Virenque took over, overall runner-up Olano fell back at first, but then rejoined.

At a check 10 kilometers from the top, the lead trio was 2:05 ahead of Fondriest; 2:55 up on Bölts, Echave, Arrieta and Sörensen; 3:15 on Abdujaparov; and 4:05 on the Virenque-Riis group that still included Induráin and Olano.

Right after this, where the road climbs in wide switchbacks up a partially wooded mountainside, Ugrumov made two attacks. And then Dufaux unveiled the next part of Festina's game plan: a surge that, initially, only Ullrich, Riis and Virenque could follow, while Induráin, Olano and Fernandez Gines were left behind. Leblanc, Ugrumov, Luttenberger and Escartin were also unseated, but they managed to rejoin in the next two kilometers.

All these accelerations—on the steepest part of the 18-kilometer-long climb—were bringing the yellow jersey group closer and closer to the front. With 4 kilometers left to climb, the Stephens trio led a pursuing Bölts by 1:25; Fondriest and Sørensen had been caught by the Riis group, at 1:45; while Induráin and Olano were at 2:30.

Stephens again sprinted to be first to the summit, 12 seconds ahead of Virenque, Riis and his now 11-strong group; 48 seconds ahead of Sørensen and Fondriest (who would catch back on the long descent); and 2:05 up on the Induráin-Olano group, which Rominger had now joined. Berzin was in a group almost seven minutes behind, a gap that would become more than half-an-hour by Pamplona.

With team riders Bölts and Hervé doing most of the driving on the very fast, technical 22-kilometer descent on

**REVERSAL OF FORTUNES**

narrow roads, the front 14 steadily gained on the 15-strong Rominger-Olano-Induráin group, and reached the foot of the much-feared Port de Larrau—which climbs at almost 10 percent on a zig-zag course for its first 10 kilometers—2:40 in front.

It was now 1:38 p.m., four hours into the stage, with the sun at its hottest, melting the tar on the narrow road. One by one, Fondriest, Stephens, Sørensen, Hervé, Bölts and Bartoli were dropped by the leaders, leaving only the eight strongest in front.

There were thousands of Basques on this climb, waving their red-white-and-green flags, and most of them waiting for Induráin. All they could do was encourage their hero, who was suffering as never before, unable to stay with the Rominger-Olano group on the steepest part. Perhaps he could have done with that third chainring, right now. But Induráin battled through his pain and ignominy, and managed to catch back to his group on a short descent, three kilometers before the final summit—which could be seen ahead at the top of a cliff-like rock wall, reached by a giant staircase of hairpin turns.

Climbing to this savagely beautiful peak, where the crowds were thicker than ever, Escartin and Virenque both collided with some spectators, with the Frenchman pulling his rear wheel over. But he was soon back on his bike, and easily took the KoM sprint from Riis and Ugrumov. The eight were 2:45 ahead of the dropped Bölts and Bartoli, and 4:50 ahead of the now 12-strong group of chasers.

It was almost 2:30 p.m., the stage was in Spain, and there were still 107 kilometers to race, mostly on smoother, descending roads. At first, the chasers were closing. Led by five Mapei men—Rominger, Olano, Fernandez Gines, Lanfranchi and Echave—they cut the five-minute gap to three

*Tour de France • France • 1996*

minutes by the end of the 20-kilometer descent. At this point, it looked like Induráin still had a chance of getting a stage win in his hometown....

Then Riis entered the picture. On waking up that morning, he had said to Danish roommate Brian Holm, "My legs feel so strong today!" Now, after almost six hours in the saddle, he showed just how strong they were. Leading all the way up the five-kilometer-long, 4.4-percent Alto de Garralda hill, under a fierce sun, Riis pulled the leading eightsome to a four-minute lead by the top. That news broke the spirit of the chasers, and in the remaining 56 kilometers to Pamplona, the lead doubled.

The Tour had been definitively played, so all that remained was the prestige of winning this stamina-sapping stage, with its 262-kilometer course and its 15,000 feet of climbing. After Virenque took the Villava sprint, Ugrumov, then Riis tried to get away on the short climb into Pamplona. Ugrumov tried again inside three kilometers, only to be brought back by Ullrich and Luttenberger. Then, inside two kilometers, Riis jumped again, followed by Dufaux. They went clear, and after following the yellow jersey through the final 600 meters, Dufaux matched Riis's desperate sprint and came home a clear winner.

It was appropriate that a support rider came first on this grueling day, when the Tour de France showed its harshest, cruelest face. It was almost 6:30 p.m. by the time the last group of 32 riders arrived in Pamplona. Hot, yes. Hard, yes. But also magnificent.

MIGUEL INDURÁIN crossed the finish line in Pamplona in 19th place, 8:30 behind the stage winner. It was a humiliating result for the reclusive rider whose home is on the city's outskirts. But the crowd cheered anyway, especial-

**REVERSAL OF FORTUNES**

ly when Bjarne Riis invited Induráin onto the stage where the day's prize presentations were being made. There was a shy smile on the Spaniard's handsome face, as he shook hands with his vanquisher. The sixth Tour victory dream was over, and so probably was Induráin's Tour de France career. He did somewhat redeem himself two days later, placing second in the Tour's final time trial at St. Emilion— a minute behind upstart stage winner Ullrich, and more than a minute ahead of fifth-placed Riis—but finishing 11th overall in Paris was not what he had in mind.

In the end, Riis's nearest challenger was his own Telekom teammate, 22-year-old Jan Ullrich, who was hailed as the new *wunderkind* of German cycling when he won the world amateur road championship three years ago; and, after starting his first Tour as a last-minute entry, he is now being hailed as the man most likely to give Germany its first Tour victory in the years ahead—especially after his final time-trial win through the Bordeaux vineyards. Ullrich finished the Tour in second place, only 1:41 behind Riis, while third-time-running King of the Mountains Richard Virenque of Festina claimed the first French step on the Paris podium since Laurent Fignon came second to Greg LeMond in 1989. Ironically, Riis used to be a domestique for Fignon back then, in the years before the now 32-year-old Dane realized he had the makings of a Tour de France challenger.

Riis was the toast of the Danish fans, who, wrapped in huge red-with-the-white-cross national flags, their faces painted like the Vikings of centuries past, and carrying banners proclaiming "Bjarne No. 1," came in the thousands to Paris on July 21, to celebrate the first-ever Tour de France victory by one of their countrymen. And make no mistake, the six-foot, 156-pound Riis was a worthy winner of what had been yet another dramatic, destructive Tour.

*Tour de France • France • 1996*

## ON A MISSION

**Olympic
Games
Road Race**

United States
August 1984

The cycling road race was one of the original events in the first modern Olympic Games at Athens, Greece, in 1896. For most of the 20th century, it was the ultimate challenge in their sport for amateur racers from around the globe. Such was the case when the Games came to Los Angeles in 1984—three Olympiads before the race was opened up to professionals. In L.A., North Americans were challenging to win an event in which they had medaled only once, back in 1912. And for the first time, there was an Olympic road race for women, and U.S. riders were the gold-medal favorites.

# United States

Sacramento

San Francisco

CALLIFORNIA

NEVADA

Santa Barbara

Los Angeles

San Bernardino

Mission Viejo

San Diego

Pacific Ocean

UP ON VISTA DEL LAGO HILL, in Mission Viejo, where houses cost $150,000 and the view is free, a cosmopolitan crowd produced a huge cheer for an even more cosmopolitan group of cyclists, who were struggling up the 12-percent grade in the burning heat of a 90-degree Southern Californian afternoon. There were Spanish voices mingling with the American, Italian *forza's* with the French *allez's*. There was a group from Colombia waving their striking red-yellow-and-blue national flag; and another from New Zealand giving encouragement to the all-black-clad Kiwis.

The men the crowd was cheering were from Korea and Cameroon, from Malawi and Zambia. It was only the fourth lap of the 1984 Olympic road race, but these enthusiastic cyclists from distant parts of the globe were already 15 minutes or more behind a lead group of 10 that included a tall, lean rider wearing big, dark glasses and a red-white-and-blue American racing jersey. He had originated this break two 16-kilometer laps earlier, and here he was gliding up the circuit's toughest climb as if he would be quite happy to stay in front all day.

His dream, like those of the men with him, was an Olympic gold medal. It was a dream that had been a nightmare less than two weeks earlier, when he, Alexi Grewal, had been disqualified from the lead position in the Coors International Bicycle Classic for a positive doping control.

The news of his disqualification reached me when I was on the phone to my London newspaper, during the Tour de France. "Is it worth putting a paragraph in the paper?" the sports editor had asked. "Well, yes," was my reply. "Grewal would have been one of the favorites for the Olympic road race. He's a great climber, and he doesn't mind the heat. He

*Olympic Games Road Race • USA • 1984*

rode the Tour of Britain Milk Race last year, but he wasn't on form. He helped Matt Eaton win the race."

Grewal shared a room with Eaton during that race, and I remember his cutting humor during an interview with Eaton on the morning after Eaton had won the yellow jersey. Three months later, after the 1983 world amateur road race championship—in which he finished a fine 14th, and best American—I congratulated Grewal on a good ride. "Bullshit!" was his one word reply. "I have to improve my sprint if I'm ever going to win anything."

Another 11 months later, the scene was the finish of this Olympic road race. Grewal was still at the front. His only companion was Steve Bauer, the Canadian who seemed destined for greatness. One of them would win that gold medal. And Bauer was virtually unbeatable in a sprint, except perhaps by Davis Phinney, who was more than a minute back down the road.

As the two riders appeared in the distance, emerging between the shadows cast by roadside trees in the evening sunlight, the crowd that was massed on a scrub-covered hillside began to chant the familiar "U-S-A! "U-S-A!" Bauer was gradually quickening the pace at the front, with Grewal following closely. Only 300 meters to go.

The Canadian probably thought back to other important sprints he has contested: the 1982 Commonwealth Games road race at Brisbane, Australia, where he was edged out of the title by England's Malcolm Elliott; the 1983 USPRO Championship at Baltimore, where Phinney beat him for the $25,000 prize. Would the 1984 Olympic gold medal prove just as elusive?

The finish was approaching, only 200 meters left, and still Bauer held the front position. This was going to be a sprint of character, as much as a sprint of speed. They had

**ON A MISSION**

been out under the penetrating sun for five hours, racing hard. Brian Fowler of New Zealand, who was still out on the road, said he got through 14 bottles of water ... and still lost nine pounds in body weight!

Grewal didn't have nine pounds to lose from his spare, 6-foot 2-inch, 150-pound frame. He has been a cyclist for half of his 23 years, and the hundreds of miles he has pounded out in the mountains around Aspen, Colorado, have honed the American's body into a finely tuned pedaling machine. In 1983, his climbing ability took him to stage wins in the Coors Classic (on the Morgul-Bismarck circuit), France's Tour de l'Avenir (in the Vercors section of the Alps) and Switzerland's William Tell Grand Prix (over the formidable Soviet Victor Demidenko). Then came that 14th place at the world's ... and he'd had a year to improve his sprint.

The American still followed the Canadian, who was beginning to accelerate, as they neared the 150-meters-to-go board. Here, the level road began to rise and curved to the right. As Bauer went wide, Grewal cleverly took the inside line, sprinting out of the saddle for all he was worth. The light breeze was from the left, so Bauer had to attempt to pass his rival on the right—but he was beaten by the combination of surprise, fatigue and the gradient that continued to steepen through the finish. Grewal, the improbable champion, had won!

The American fans whooped with astonishment. They waved their stars-and-stripes more vigorously than ever. They were on top of world road racing, not only through Grewal, but also with the gold-silver double of Connie Carpenter and Rebecca Twigg in the women's Olympic debut six hours earlier. It had proved quite a day for the estimated 200,000 who had traveled by bike, bus and car to Mission

*Olympic Games Road Race • USA • 1984*

Viejo, to be part of what can only be termed the modern American revolution.

Some of those estimated 200,000 spectators arrived the previous day to set up camps and reserve their spots around the 15.85-kilometer circuit for Sunday's races. There were overnight barbecue parties, both in the camps and in those well-appointed hillside homes. It had been quite a decision by these Mission Viejo residents to close down their whole community for a day. What they received were 12 hours they will remember for the rest of their lives.

Outside those houses that overlooked the circuit, dozens of banners proclaimed such messages as "Go, go, go USA!"... "Americans are the Biking Champions" (a message for the ABC TV cameras) ... and even "God bless America!" In contrast to Europe, where nearly all the fans gather on the actual climbs, the great California public positioned their picnic tables and chairs at any available spot—even if it were alongside a fast downhill. The important thing was to be present at this Olympic happening—and be able to cheer on the racers.

It was perhaps unfortunate that no provision had been made for the public to watch the race in the finish area, which was sealed off for exclusive use of Olympic dignitaries, guests and the press. As a result, spectators climbed trees and street lights to get a better view. It may have been a so-called free show, but people had been paying upwards of $10 to park their cars, and there were thousands who would have doubtless been willing to pay for a seat beside the finish line.

Another serious omission was the lack of information for the crowds outside the immediate range of the public-address system near the finish. Riders were cheered on their way without the fans knowing who was passing. There were

**ON A MISSION**

no start lists distributed, as would happen in the smallest of amateur races in Europe. Still, the stars-and-stripes jerseys of the Americans were always prominent—and that's what the people came to see.

One wonders what the crowd's reaction would have been if the circuit had been easier and both races had ended in field sprints. Happily, it was a far tougher circuit than most team managers had thought, resulting in two of the best races seen at top international level. The former British road race champion Mark Bell said unequivocally, "I've ridden three previous world championships, and this was the hardest circuit of them all."

The women's event was a race of attrition. The steep slopes of the Vista del Lago hill, combined with the shadeless heat of this humid day, saw the peloton reduced to just 21 riders after two laps. Already, such favored starters as 1983 world champion Marianne Berglund of Sweden, the Canadian Karen Strong-Hearth and Maria Blower of Britain were floundering off the back, destined to finish nine or more minutes behind the leaders.

The third of the five laps saw the logical conclusion to the previous activity, with the strongest climbers making a clean break on the hill. Maria Canins has been known to drop male riders on the Italian national squad in training, so it was no surprise to see her drawing clear with the inseparable home favorites, Connie Carpenter and Rebecca Twigg, and the powerful French champion, Jeannie Longo. But it was a slight surprise to see them accompanied by a 17-year-old West German, Sandra Schumacher, and Unni Larsen of Norway.

Carpenter said she was quite happy to see which riders had come with her and Twigg. "We were pretty certain it would finish the way it did," Carpenter added. Even

*Olympic Games Road Race • USA • 1984*

when Canins crashed shortly after the break formed, the other five were pleased to see the rugged Italian chase back. They knew that her continual forcing on the climbs would preclude any chance of a comeback by the riders behind. In the 15-strong pack, the other two Americans, Janelle Parks and Inga Thompson, were able to cover any moves that looked dangerous.

The American's only valid opponent in an eventual sprint was Longo, and she was effectively removed from the confrontation in a clash of wheels with Canins, 800 meters before the line. Longo's rear derailleur was broken and the chain came off, leaving her helpless.

"I was sure I could have beaten Twigg," commented the 27-year-old from Grenoble, "only Carpenter can go faster."

While Longo limped down to the finish, lamenting her ill fortune, the other five were speeding toward the sprint that would decide who would enter the Olympic history books as the first female cyclist to win a gold medal. Canins was at the front, but knew that her chances had already disappeared, while both Larsen and Schumacher were simply pleased to be still in the company of the world's top women riders.

Entering the final 200 meters, just before the right-hand curve, Twigg went to the front with confidence. As the grade steepened, she seemed to have victory within her grasp ... but Carpenter was coming up quickly on the right. Perhaps Twigg had gone too early, or was feeling the effects of a solo break attempt less than two laps earlier.

Carpenter's effort was more about pride and ambition. "I've ridden deliberately this year to make this the best race of my career," she told ABC viewers after the finish. It is a career that goes back to 1972, when as a Madison, Wisconsin 15-year-old speedskater, she went to the Winter

**ON A MISSION**

Olympics. Since then had come two separate cycling careers—before and after she met Davis Phinney, now her husband—and only last year her first world championship, the individual 3000-meter pursuit title.

This background, added to the knowledge that "this is probably the last race of my career," pushed Carpenter to her limit. She was still behind Twigg as they entered the final three meters; then she was level; and then Carpenter threw her bike at the line in true Phinney style. She closed her eyes with the effort, then looked across to Twigg and kissed her on the cheek. They had won gold and silver, all right, but it wasn't until the photo-finish confirmed it that Carpenter knew the gold was hers.

The crowd, many of them on touring bikes that will never go as fast as Carpenter's, erupted with joy. Not only at the finish line, but all around the circuit, where the spectators had gathered in knots around portable TVs and transistor radios. And the chanting began: "U!S!A! U!S!A!" After the presentation ceremony, the two Americans showed their male counterparts what an Olympic medal was like. "Now it's your turn," they said.

Whatever was true for the women's race was doubly true for the men. They had to cover 12 laps instead of five, in heat that peaked at close to a 100 degrees, and they had to cope with much higher speeds. No doubt, the east Europeans—who boycotted the Games—would have made the going even tougher, but it was tough enough as it was. Before halfway, the Belgians had no riders left in the race, while another strong European team, France, would finish just two riders, 12 minutes behind the winner.

The heat was the X-factor in this memorable race that would find a successor to Hennie Kuiper of the Netherlands, Bernt Johansson of Sweden and Sergei Soukhoroutchenkov

*Olympic Games Road Race • USA • 1984*

of Russia. It was hot in Moscow when the Soviet superman destroyed the 1980 field and rode away to a predicted solo success. There was no such clear favorite at Mission Viejo; but it soon became obvious that the riders who could withstand the high temperature as well as the hills would come out on top. Before the Olympics, there had been a lot of ink wasted on the "inhuman" schedule for the marathon runners, starting at 5 p.m. in the heat of the day. Yet they would be competing for only two-and-a bit hours. Few commentators had thought to publicize the plight of cyclists who would be racing for five hours through the whole length of a July afternoon.

The humidity and the heat were taking their toll as the early break group toiled up Vista del Lago for the fourth time. The nine men with Grewal were soon to be joined by a chasing group of 14 that included the other three Americans: Phinney, Thurlow Rogers and Ron Kiefel. Another, larger group was close behind, but new accelerations in front prevented them from joining the leaders. An enterprising attack was made by one of the race favorites, Dag Otto Lauritzen, the Norwegian who wowed his French club ACBB with a string of victories early this year. With him went an equally powerful Austrian, Helmut Wechselberger, who works in a bank when he's not bike racing.

A lead approaching one minute was too much to concede to such well-heeled customers, and the chasers split during a lap six pursuit. In the front line, Grewal, Phinney and Bauer were in a group of seven that went clear on the hill. The two aggressors were caught by the lap end, resulting in a temporary truce and a lead group of 25 that would contest the second half of this fine race.

It was so hot that even the franchise booths were running out of Coke. That parched-throat feeling was clearly

**ON A MISSION**

more critical among the racers, who were now more content to wait for developments rather than sparking things themselves. It was on the eighth climb of the circuit's second hill, up La Paz Road, that the decision was made for them. The line stretched, and on the subsequent rise along O'Neill Road, six men found themselves with daylight behind them. Grewal, Phinney and Bauer were again together, along with Lauritzen, his Norwegian colleague Morten Saether, and the unconsidered Nestor Mora of Colombia.

As they topped the final crest before descending to the finish of the lap, Rogers and Kiefel were carefully controlling the 20-strong chase group that followed at less than 10 seconds. There was a resigned air about the chasers, though, and Rogers cleverly jumped across the gap before it grew too large. In a lap, the seven-up break gained more than a minute. The race was effectively over, even though there were still three never-ending laps to go.

Along O'Neill Road on lap 10, Grewal briefly went clear with Lauritzen and Rogers. And the lead was back to 1:10 at the lap end, over a chasing group of seven in which Kiefel was playing his policeman's role.

On the La Paz climb, more attacks stretched the resources of the seven leaders. Grewal, Lauritzen and Bauer tried to escape, and then Bauer on his own. Grewal immediately counterattacked, but was neutralized. And then, along the O'Neill crests, the 23-year-old from Aspen again chanced his arm. This time, he was clear.

There were still 20 kilometers left, the toughest 20 kilometers of the race, but Grewal was confident that he had the necessary reserves to succeed. He heard the bell ringing 25 seconds before the other six, but one wondered if he had made his move too soon. That doubt became a reality when he started to zigzag up Vista del Lago, searching for air and

*Olympic Games Road Race • USA • 1984*

the right gear. It seemed like a heaven-sent opportunity for the blond Bauer, who whipped past the desperate American across the summit.

It took the greatest of efforts for Grewal to compose his thoughts and rejoin the Canadian after the steep, straight descent, and it took great tenacity to stick to his rival over the remaining 11 kilometers. The conclusion we know, but the consequences of Grewal's and Carpenter's great golds will be felt in cycling for years to come. The world's road racing fraternity and an enthusiastic crowd came to Mission Viejo with expectancy; they returned home as converts to the exciting American way of cycling.

 **ON A MISSION**

# BEHIND THE IRON CURTAIN

## World Amateur Championships
## Czechoslovakia
## August 1969

World championships for amateur riders began in 1893 for track racing, and 1921 for road. The two branches came together in 1923. Some of those championships have been more significant than others. In 1969, the world's best amateur cyclists came to Brno, a city that is now part of the Czech Republic, for competition at a new velodrome and on a road circuit high in the Moravian hills. Twenty years before the fall of the Iron Curtain, communism reigned in eastern Europe. And, during a memorable week of racing, it was hard to separate the politics from the pedaling....

# Czechoslovakia

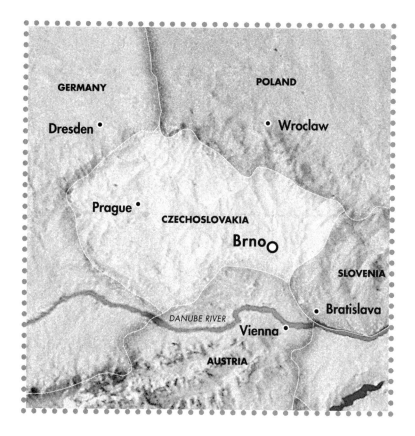

TWO NOTABLE ANNIVERSARIES were celebrated in Czechoslovakia in August 1969—and in vastly contrasting manners. The first was August 15, the centennial of the first bicycle race held in eastern Europe, in 1869, at Brno's Luzanky Park. This historic date was commemorated by the opening of the world amateur cycling championships, organized in Czechoslovakia for the first time. The championships continued to August 24 ... but one day was free of any events, because that day, August 21, was the other historic date—the first anniversary of the Russian invasion of Czechoslovakia. The people had planned to remember it with a day of silence, but it turned into one of violence, especially in Brno.

This mixture of celebration and mourning was the sad background to one of the most moving world championship series of recent years. Through it all, though, the cycling events were enthusiastically received by the big crowds, both at the track and for the road races.

Brno is the second city of Czechoslovakia with a population of about 330,000, and has been the capital of Moravia since 1642, having been granted its charter in 1243. Up until World War II, Brno was a bustling, free city, on a par with such cities as Paris and Madrid.

However, there is relatively little traffic in modern Brno, which has a predominance of pre-war cars and more modern motorcycles. There is also a vast number of cyclists, who can be seen everywhere, riding in their dull crimson tracksuit tops. The cycling section of the Favorit Brno club has 1200 members alone, and along with rival club Dukla, the city can boast of current national champions on road, track and in cyclo-cross.

*World Amateur Championships • Czechoslovakia • 1969*

Cycling being such a part of the local culture helps explain why the racing was received so enthusiastically by the Czech and Slovak crowds, and why the organizers could overcome the despair and anger caused by the dangerous incidents marking the invasion anniversary that took place in the city center.

My journey to Brno was made via Switzerland, from where I took a train that snaked its way through a night of torrential rain among the wooded mountains of Austria to reach Vienna 17 hours later.

From Vienna, I rode my bike along the ambitiously named E7 highway to Brno. After a long stretch of wide, improved pavement, the Austrian length deteriorated into a rudimentary affair with a succession of long, cobbled climbs. There was also a strong head wind that tempered the warmth of a hazy sun.

The state of the road was only one of the unknowns that lay ahead, as I rode slowly across the no-man's land that marks the boundary between West and East. There were two barriers on the Communist side of the Iron Curtain while a look-out tower pointed skyward among the distant trees. Soldiers lounged at the first barrier, scanning the barren horizon with binoculars. At the actual border post, another 300 yards on, I joined a short queue of French, German, Austrian and Italian cars, and then waited in the sun for 40 minutes as papers were checked and stamped. With a salute from the soldier on the gate, I was finally on the road to Brno.

It was a rough road. At one little cobblestoned village, I stopped at a pump for some water, and nearing the city, I was even forced to walk up one of the hills. Struggling into Brno, it was a pleasure to meet friendly people, who understood my rudimentary German and were only too willing to show me the way to my lodgings.

**BEHIND THE IRON CURTAIN**

The austere modern concrete building I was guided to was a student hostel that was being used as an overflow from the hotels for foreign visitors. I was assigned a small room, sharing with a Czech graduate student, who told me he planned to take part in illegal demonstrations against the Soviet Army, which had taken over the downtown area. There was a strict nighttime curfew, but my roommate ventured out each evening, and returned around midnight, telling me of his escapades: throwing rocks at the Soviet tanks and then running away down dark alleys. He managed to escape each time, but a Scottish woman student, also staying at the hostel, didn't know about the curfew; she was arrested and taken to a police station, where she was beaten on the legs while walking up a spiral staircase.

The championship cycling teams didn't experience such danger because their hotels were some way distant from the center, and the only disturbances they encountered were the tanks and army trucks rumbling past on a couple of occasions. Still, the curfew, which was in operation for three nights, kept everyone in after 8 p.m., and thick clouds of tear gas remaining through the daytime were a real reminder of the hazards—as were the barricades, broken windows and the tank tracks that had gouged holes in the streets.

This, then, was the passionate background to Brno '69, an electric atmosphere that was nowhere more pronounced than at the first cycling events I saw—the final night at the track.

THE USUAL WAY of reaching the Brno velodrome was by a rickety bus that did a half-hour tour of the town and its hotels to reach a destination that took five minutes by bicycle—so I went by bike. Others had the same idea, and I encountered some of them at the end of the night, on my way back to town. Riding up a long hill, I was overtaken in

*World Amateur Championships • Czechoslovakia • 1969*

the dark by a whirring of gears and panting breath. It was a small group of riders who had also been down to the track. The last man in the line dropped off, and when I caught up with him, he turned out to be an English cyclist from Yorkshire. He said the rider who was leading our group was American Jackie Simes (who had reached the semi-finals of the tandem sprint the previous night with Tim Mountford). The Englishman had been in Brno since the weekend, following a two-week touring holiday in Austria.

"It was fabulous on Sunday night," he told me. "It was the first big track meeting we'd ever been to, and the racing and the crowd were just fantastic. We'll always remember the standstills in the sprints and the way in which the crowd rose to Morelon after beating Phakadze in the final. And it was just superb to watch Kürmann winning the pursuit: Nothing could match up to that night again."

I could well understand his enthusiasm, after experiencing the explosive atmosphere around that brand-new 400-meter concrete bowl. The white track had colorful advertising painted on it all around its 35-degree banking and along its 24-foot-wide straights. But the real making of the place was the roof—which covered the whole of the 10,000-spectator section, and cantilevered beyond the inside curve of the track. Because of this, none of the enthusiasm of the crowd was lost, and the riders appeared to respond to this encouragement by putting on a superlative show. The track was lit by lights fixed to the underneath side of the "roof" and there was a battery of lamps focused on the finishing area. The actual track center was an impressive pattern of white concrete, emerald green grass and masses of red, yellow and blue flowers.

When I arrived at the track, the unmistakable crackle of the pacing motors was echoing out into the night sky. It was

**BEHIND THE IRON CURTAIN**

the eight-up final, with three Swiss, two Dutch, two Italians and a Belgian having just set off on their 40-mph race of one hour's duration. The crowd seemed strangely quiet, which was explained when I was told that Russia had just beaten the Czechs in the semi-final of the team pursuit. My informer was London newspaper colleague David Saunders, who welcomed me to "the world whistling championships," as he put it.

His comment referred to the hostile, deafening reception the partisan crowd was giving to the Russians any time they were on the track. That crowd had encouraged Czechoslovakia to a fastest time of 4:33.9 in the qualifying round of the 4000-meter team pursuit, but the fans' cheers had been to no avail in the semi-final against the more experienced U.S.S.R. quartet, whose veteran campaigner, Stanislav Moskvin, had pushed the Soviets to a superb 4:30.6, almost seven seconds too good for the home team. In the other semi-final, the Italian *squadra* of coach Guido Costa had reached the final for the sixth year in succession ... their victims being a largely untried French combination.

That motorpaced final was a disappointment as a highlight of the last night, mainly due to the rather unreliable motors. All the same, winner Albertus Boom of the Netherlands received an incredible ovation from the fans. He had to do lap after lap of honor, and was finally lifted high, bike and all, by the ecstatic melée of people on the finishing line. After that came the official medal presentation, which resembled a military operation. The winners' rostrum stood in the very center of the arena, with a vast roped-off area surrounding it.

With the world championships theme tune blaring from the loudspeakers, an army of people marched on. There were the three medalists, followed by three young girls carrying

*World Amateur Championships • Czechoslovakia • 1969*

the medals—one dressed in white, one in blue and one in red; then came those carrying the multitude of prizes for the winners, and finally, "archbishop" Adriano Rodoni—the plump, balding president of the Union Cycliste Internationale—arrived with his delegation of blazered disciples. Behind them swarmed a mob of photographers and rubber-neckers.

The rainbow-hooped world champion's jersey was slipped over the slim shoulders of the gaunt, nervous Boom; the medals and prizes were handed over; the cameras clicked in a firework display of flashbulbs; and the Dutch national anthem was played as the three national flags were hauled slowly to the top of their tall masts ... with the second one catching up with the other two in a late flourish.

And then everyone trooped off again—and Boom did another lap of honor.

The cheers continued for the Czech pursuit squad in its ride-off for the bronze medals against France; but the semi-final defeat had demoralized the team's spirit and the French led throughout to record a fine time of 4:33.3.

That over, the ten-thousand Czechs started their whistling cat-calls again, as the Russian team pursuit quartet came out to warm up. They and the Italians had been passing the time sitting in their trackside pits, with blankets around them. One of the Italians had been nervously riding up and down on his road machine, while others made use of the rollers in the track center. The tension in the air on this eve of the Twenty-First of August anniversary could be sensed, as silence dropped onto the velodrome like a heavy blanket. The two teams were ready to go.

The tension of the occasion was even communicated onto the track: As the starter's gun exploded into the still air, there was an obviously false start. The Italians realized it

**BEHIND THE IRON CURTAIN**

immediately and eased up; but the red-jerseyed Russians increased the animosity of the crowd by continuing their starting effort until halfway around the first banking.

Finally away, with the crowd at fever pitch, the two teams presented a memorable finale to a fine series. The Italians went immediately into the lead, smoothly stretching their advantage to 1.2 seconds (about 25 yards at this speed) by the halfway mark. They were being encouraged even more than the home team had been, and a chanting cry of "Vasy, vasy, vasy. . . ." was taken up as they passed each different section of the fans. In contrast, the Russians were racing around to the accompaniment of a thunderous trail of derisive whistles. Rarely has a sporting event been marked by such a display of unified patriotism.

But the crowd's reaction had little effect on the outcome, and it was difficult not to admire the fighting qualities of Moskvin, Bykov, Kuskov and Kuznetsov, who pulled back the Italians yard by yard to take the lead on the very last lap. It was a superb display as the two teams, each down to three men, sprinted for their respective finish lines on opposite sides of the track: 1st. USSR 4:33.13; 2nd. Italy 4:33.65. The crowd went silent . . . and the arena was almost completely emptied in less than five minutes! The crowd had no wish to see the medal presentation to the arch enemy. It was a dramatic demonstration of their feelings, a demonstration that would not be so peaceful the next day.

WHILE TEAR GAS quelled the crowds downtown, I spent the day writing at the press center. Others reported the August 21 incidents to their newspapers. We were all glad when the championships continued. In the women's road race, there were major shocks. First, British sprint champion Bernadette Swinnerton, just 18, took second place on

*World Amateur Championships • Czechoslovakia • 1969*

hilly Masaryk circuit. If this was something of a surprise, the solo victory of American Audrey McElmury was nothing short of sensational. It was the first world championship win for the USA in more than 50 years!

These were not fluke performances. It was one of the hardest world championship races the women have had for years. The circuit's two-mile climb had to be raced up five times; the distance was 43.3 miles (70 kilometers); and the race ended in heavy rain. McElmury's and Swinnerton's medals were a just reward for dedication, training and the correct preparation. They were also the result of the excellent team spirit existing in both the British and American camps.

The day before, the morning of the team time trial, I had gone out for a training ride with the three British women and the men who were not in the team trial. It was only a 30-mile loosener, but it was long enough to discover that Ann Horswell, Swinnerton and Pat Pepper were all in good form. Swinnerton's policy of riding as many track events and road races as possible had certainly worked out well.

In contrast, Horswell's cycling education has been mainly in time trialing, and her way of riding reflects this. As she says, "I'm no *pedaleur de charme.* I'm more of a thrust-and-clutcher." And she thrusts and clutches very well indeed, as I found out when I "broke away" on the latter, hilly part of the training circuit. I found that Horswell could go up hills as hard as most men, and she admitted that she couldn't find anyone to train with: "Last year, I went training with Pete Harris [a top British road racer], which was great, as we used to try to roar each other off all the time. But Pete's not going so well this season and I've been mainly training alone." It is a pity that such a talented rider does not have much of a chance to improve. For this race, she was as fit as could be expected. Before coming to Brno, Hor-

**BEHIND THE IRON CURTAIN**

swell was in the hilly Roanne area of France, where she convincingly won the international 10-day stage race contested by women from a dozen countries.

Horswell said that the English team had come out on top in the heat of France because of their frequent time trialing. It is the durability they learn from racing alone that helped them dominate a stage race; but bike-handling and sprinting are at a greater premium in a one-day race. These, however, are just the qualities that Swinnerton possesses, and earlier in the week, I was told, she had clearly outsprinted Britain's top man, Doug Dailey, while out training. Everyone hoped that she could show such speed the next day at the end of those five hilly laps.

The day was cool and overcast, with a slight drift of breeze blowing up the hill. The circuit was 8.66 miles round, with not one section of flat. And the finishing straight was very wide and slightly uphill; but after a short dip, there was a long, exposed drag up to the first corner overlooking the city of Brno. Then came a long swoop down and up through the red-tiled village of Liskovec, before another drop through pine trees to the tricky left-handed sweep two miles from the start. This was the beginning of the hill, curving up a green valley, with stretches of 10 percent as the dusty village of Kohoutovice was reached. The trickiest section was a series of near hairpins just before the final straight stretch to the exposed summit, now four miles around the circuit. The descent was a smooth, wide asphalt ribbon, tumbling down through the woods for a mile. As for the rest of the course, it pleasantly undulated past open fields, a sharp left-hander leading back into the home straight that led down through another village, before the final kilometer up to the line.

Of the 11 nations represented on the starting line, to provide the field of 44 women, there were seven Italians, six

Russians, six Dutch, five French, five Czechs, four Belgians, four Americans, three British, two Germans, an Austrian and one Luxembourger. Lining-up order was decided by drawing lots, and was it an omen that the U.S. was drawn out first?

The 10 a.m. start was given four minutes late, and it was clear that the riders were all tensed up as they began at an easy pace, probably apprehensive of climbing the big hill five times. The first time up, Ann Horswell showed how nervous she was by muffing a gear change, losing 20 yards before chasing back into the fold. Over the top, two or three riders had been dropped, and Italian Maria Pecuhenini crashed on the descent and was taken to the hospital. By the end of the lap, two more had retired—Barbara McQueeney (USA) and Jana Brink (USSR)—and three others were off the back. That left 38 in the bunch. Lap time was a slow 25:42 (20.25 mph).

The pace on the second lap was much livelier and another Italian, Maria Cressari, crashed on the bend before the climb. Up the hill, Bernadette Swinnerton was riding beautifully, calmly turning a small gear alongside the 1968 world champion, Katie Hage of the Netherlands. Their pace-setting soon took its toll, and another eight riders had been dropped by the top, including three from the French team. Pat Pepperova (as the Czech program named her) was riding comfortably enough in the middle of the group, but Horswellova was still not showing her form. The increased speed was reflected in the lap time: 24:20.

It would have been interesting to see how many-time champion Beryl Burton would have coped with this circuit; she would probably have done exactly the same as Katie Hage did now. Hage attacked on her own, as a fine drizzle started to make the roads slippery. She took a 200-yard lead, and the chase was taken up by Horswell on the third climb,

**BEHIND THE IRON CURTAIN**

splitting the bunch behind. Over the top, the positions were: Hage alone, Horswell alone at 10 seconds, a group of 14 (including Pepper, Swinnerton and McElmury) at 30 seconds, and a group of eight at 50 seconds.

We hoped that Horswell would catch Hage, and perhaps the two would stay away together; but the Dutchwoman was not interested in that idea, and she raced ahead on her own, despite seeing the Brit chasing hard just behind. The pursuit was also taken up by two Russians, Caune and Sergejev, and the attentive Swinnerton went with them!

And then, just as suddenly, everything changed. Hage punctured, having to wait for the service vehicle behind the group; Horswell was caught by the three chasers, and the four women were absorbed by the first bunch before the end of the lap. The time of 23:55 (35 kph: 21.8 mph) was the fastest lap.

The drizzle now became heavier, and it seemed to dampen the spirits of the bunch of 15 now in control, making the fourth lap two minutes slower than the previous one. On the hill, there was a break by McElmury, which finished when she fell off on the now treacherous descent. Horswell also came off—off the back—because of her fear of crashing. As team manager Eileen Gray said, "She even falls off in time trials."

As the bell sounded to start the final lap, McElmurey had fought back to the bunch, but Horswell was still behind, riding in the line of following cars. The unfortunate Hage had never rejoined after her puncture, and she was now plugging on through torrential rain 1:50 behind the leaders. Up in front, the decisive point of the race was being reached—the foot of the hill. As Horswell rejoined the pack, McElmurey went away on the attack again, while Pepper touched wheels, tumbled in a heap and never got back on.

McElmury was only a few seconds ahead all the way up

*World Amateur Championships • Czechoslovakia • 1969*

the climb, yet nobody was strong enough to take up the chase. Swinnerton was still riding well at the front but, echoing Horswell's words, later said: "We would rather see Audrey win than take up the Russians." Horswell, tired by her earlier efforts and that chase, also admitted that she did not have the strength to go any faster. Even so, the California mother was only 10 seconds up at the top. But this time she did not fall off on the slalom down through the trees, and she reached the bottom (three miles to go) with a 30-second advantage.

As the announcements came over the loudspeakers at the finish, the crowd, seeking shelter under the dripping canvas roofs of the pits and umbrellas, could hardly believe that an American was winning the world championship. But still, a new time check confirmed what was about to happen: "Number 10 now has a lead of 40 seconds." There seemed little doubt now, and every eye was focused down the road through the torrential rain looking for visual confirmation. By my side, a matronly American lady suddenly shouted: "Gee! It's really her!" Yes, there was Audrey McElmury storming toward us, and across the line she came: a transient flash of a blue-red-and-white jersey, an upraised arm and a nervous smile. The 26-year-old from San Diego was world champion.

McElmurey was engulfed by the joy-crazed members of the U.S. team, but there were still the silver and bronze medals to fight for. Now it was the Brits' turn to get excited, because fighting out the sprint in the middle of the road was young Swinnerton. "Come on Bernie!" we were shouting. And she more than responded by going away from the shocked Russians to take second place by a clear five lengths. Horswell was just behind in ninth place, while we had to wait another 1:20 for Pepper in a creditable 15th.

It was a memorable day for the English-speaking con-

 **BEHIND THE IRON CURTAIN**

tingent, and nobody minded standing in the rain for half an hour while a record of the "Star-spangled Banner" was found, and the medal ceremony could go ahead. Besides the silver medal and championship sash, Swinnerton also took home a beautiful cut-glass vase and a bone-china coffee set. Later, she could still not believe that she had finished second in the world's, but she had done it on sheer merit.

McElmury finished in fifth place last year, and back in California, she regularly races against the men … hence her fearless riding, especially on that tricky descent where she really won the championship of the world.

THE CLIMAX of the week was the men's amateur road race championship, and what a fine event it was! Fast, hilly, numerous attacks—and finally, a break created and sustained by a Yorkshireman … before the final solo attack by a 23-year-old Dane named Leif Mortensen, a young man who had gained a silver medal in the team time trial two days before, to add to the individual silver he had acquired in the 1968 Olympic road race in Mexico.

After the previous day's rain, the Sunday was hot and sunny, with barely a breath of wind. There were tens of thousands of spectators gathered around the hilly circuit, to be covered 13 times for a total of 112.6 miles. It was a daunting task for the 150 men who lined up at 10 a.m. The British team was drawn at the back of the starting grid, but Billy Bilsland and Dave Rollinson managed to creep through to the front before the flag was dropped. The other four in the team were Doug Dailey and Pete Smith (who had already ridden the team time trial), national champion Brian Jolly and Dutch-trained hope Phil Edwards. The American hopes lay with multi-national champion John Howard.

The first five laps (the distance of the women's race)

*World Amateur Championships • Czechoslovakia • 1969*

were largely a wearing-down process, with most of the weaker riders (including the Cubans, Libyans and Algerians) quickly finding themselves off the back. In fact, those "green" Libyans had five off the back on the first lap, and they were seen working well together ... about 50 yards apart from each other! There were a number of small attacks, but none gained more than 15 seconds, mainly because of the high average speed of more than 39 kph—a savage pace for such a course, the circuit giving over 12,000 feet of climbing by the end!

The pace was certainly beginning to tell by lap six, and among the riders struggling at the back was Swiss star Josef Fuchs, who soon dropped out. Of the British riders, Dailey had been most consistently near the front, and on lap seven, he got into a short-lived break with two race favorites, Fedor Den Hertog (Netherlands) and Ryszard Szurkowski (Poland). Meanwhile, Pete Smith had been calmly sitting in the middle of the bunch, riding out some of the stiffness left over from his team time trial efforts. Jolly, Bilsland and Rollinson were also looking comfortable, but big Phil Edwards was beginning to suffer a little on the climb, and an acceleration the eighth time up saw him lose contact, along with several others.

The acceleration was due to a dangerous-looking move by Joseph Bruyère (Belgium), Sorlini (Italy) and Régis Delepine, French winner of this year's Paris-Rouen centennial race. They had a lead of almost half a minute on the climb, but the reaction was furious, splitting the bunch in three. Smith and Bilsland were particularly active in the pursuit and consequent counterattack, and there was then a general regroupment of about 90 riders—still a big bunch.

The next lap, the ninth, there was another attack, this

 **BEHIND THE IRON CURTAIN**

time by Sanchez (Spain) accompanied by Smith, now really in the swing and in his "I-can-beat-anybody" mood. Through the finish, the pair was 25 seconds clear of a chasing group of five: Bilsland, Mortensen, Cumino (Italy), Grigore (Rumania) and Takacs (Hungary). They were another 200 yards clear of the bunch. The seven joined up on the hill, only to instigate another fierce reaction that again split the bunch into three groups. The break was caught by about 20 men, yet there was no let-up in the pace. The wind had got up now, and the sky was clouding over as the big pursuit match continued.

A momentary easing up gave the middle group the chance to latch on at the start of lap 11. I had been following the race in an open Jeep, and I will never forget the battle that took place this eleventh time up the two-mile Kohoutovice hill. The bunch of 50-or-so riders was snaking up the climb, the closely packed crowd enthusiastically applauding as they climbed at a frightful pace. Then it happened. On a long straight stretch, Smith put his head down and went steaming off on his own. In this mood he could beat the world, or so he thought. In an instant, the Italian Bergamo was up with him, and two more peeled away from the front: the restless Sanchez ... and Mortensen. This was the vital move, and they soon had 150 yards' advantage. Six more joined them before the top: Oosterhof (Netherlands), Saez (Spain), Labus (Czechoslovakia), Dmitruk (USSR) and the dangerous Belgians Monseré and Van Roosbroeck. Bilsland had also tried to get up, along with Den Hertog, but the bunch would not let them go, and Bilsland later admitted that he did not have the strength left anyway.

The lead of the 10 increased dramatically: 35 seconds after the descent and a minute through the packed stands. It was the decisive break at last, and an Englishman had started it. Would he have the strength to attack again, we wondered, as the hill came into view for the penultimate time. It would be no use for him to wait for the sprint against such dangerous riders. Also in the break, remember, were three of the big favorites: Jean-Pierre Monseré, Leif Mortensen and Popke Oosterhof.

This was no deterrent to Smith, though, and he was at the front all the way up the climb. He told me later: "When I'm in that mood, I just get carried away with myself and I think I can roar anyone off my wheel. I should know better by now, but I just can't control myself." It was agony sitting there watching him throw away a world title ... for that is what his attacking ride deserved. Toward those hairpin bends at the top he still led, then there was a sudden move by the white-and-red-clad figure of Mortensen. He dived for the inside of the curve, sprinting desperately out of the saddle. Nobody replied until Smith belatedly spotted the attack from his forward position. The Englishman even managed to increase his pace, dropping the others but getting no nearer than a desperate 10 yards from Mortensen's back wheel. It was a heart-breaking sight.

Seven other riders came up to the gallant Briton, but the Dane had a 100-yard lead at the top. And at the bottom, he was still the same distance ahead, and still the same three miles later, at the bell ... just eight seconds. It was a magnificent ride by Mortensen to hold off the best riders in the world by such a "catchable" margin. If they had worked together, they surely would have brought him back, but all of them were trying to chase on their own. Once again, Smith tried to drop the rest on the climb, but he had tired himself out by his remarkable efforts and would certainly have no chance in the sprint.

The two Belgians, Monseré and Van Roosbroeck, were

**BEHIND THE IRON CURTAIN**

also making determined solo efforts, but neither could match the superb performance of Mortensen, who doubled his lead in the last four miles to finish to a standing ovation a minute ahead of the remnants of the break. His time for that last lap was 20:53, the fastest of the day at 40.05 kph. There has not been a more convincing win since Eddy Merckx won the title at Sallanches in 1964.

The fight for second place started a long way out. After sitting in, the little Czech Labus attacked hard through the last village; again, Smith replied, but the Czech blew up and the others all came by, with the two Belgians sprinting irresistibly down the right-hand curb for a processional second and third. Even Oosterhof was no match, while Smith had to be content with eighth place. Labus was a few seconds adrift, but the Czech crowd gave him a rapturous welcome as he crossed the line with his arms aloft!

It was 2:43 before the main bunch arrived, with Bilsland, Rollinson and Dailey all well up, to end a convincing display by the Brits. Howard was the only American finisher, in 79th, almost 11 minutes back

The world championships were over for another year; and left behind were only memories of 10 days in August when the world came to Brno. They are mixed memories of triumph and tear gas; track racing excitement and rumbling tanks; winners' delight and losers' demonstrations. The world has left Brno, leaving behind a sad nation that the world should not forget about. There are no barriers between nations in sports. Perhaps some day the Iron Curtain will come down, too.

*World Amateur Championships • Czechoslovakia • 1969*

PIONEERS The 1985 Étoile de Bessèges (page 11) saw the very first participation of an American pro team in European racing. On the squad were (l to r) Jeff Bradley, Richard Scibird, [*Alexi Grewal rode for Panasonic*], Matt Eaton, Chris Carmichael, Davis Phinney, Ron Hayman and Ron Kiefel. Within 18 months, Phinney (below) won a stage of the Tour de France. English amateur racer Darryl Webster (below, right) won many British championships in road time trialing (page 47), a cycling discipline that was pioneered by the North Road Cycling Club in 1895.

THE GREAT RACE The opening race of the classics season in Europe is Milan-San Remo, first held in 1907. This near-300km Italian event heads south from Milan across the valley of the Po River, and then over the Turchino Pass (below), to the Mediterranean, where the race follows the corniche roads of the Italian Riviera (above) to San Remo. One of the best editions of the great race was in 1970 (page 57).

HELL OF THE NORTH Atrocious cobblestone roads define the French classic, Paris-Roubaix. In 1984, the event (page 97) saw a brilliant victory by Irishman Sean Kelly (above), who would dominate the European one-day classics scene for nearly a decade.

RENAISSANCE MEN Scotsman Robert Millar (opposite, bottom) rode a phenomenal race at the 1985 Tour of Spain, a race that climaxed with a dramatic last mountain stage near Madrid (page 109). Three years later, at the Tour of Italy, Andy Hampsten (opposite, top) became the event's first non-European winner. That 1988 Giro (as the Tour of Italy is known) included grueling mountain stages in the Dolomites (page 121), racing in snow and rain (above) and sunshine (opposite, far left). A new American talent to emerge in the 1990s was Lance Armstrong, who made a breakthrough in 1993 to take the U.S. Pro Championship in Philadelphia (page 137), a stage of the Tour de France (below), and the world championship in Norway.

LA GRANDE BOUCLE The Tour de France is without question the greatest bicycle race in the world. In 1996, the 4000-kilometer event (page 147) saw a memorable confrontation between Spain's five-time winner Miguel Induráin (left) and Denmark's Bjarne Riis (below). The monumental seventh stage in the French Alps proved decisive for Induráin and Switzerland's Alex Zülle (opposite, top), who struggled to keep in contention on the uphill finish at Les Arcs. Riis (opposite, below) emerged as the overall winner.

CONTRASTS It's all bike racing, but there is a world of difference between (left) the world professional road championship, won in a sprint finish in 1989 by Greg LeMond, from Russian Dmitri Konyshev and Irishman Sean Kelly (page 207); (right) the Grand Prix des Nations time trial won in 1984 by Frenchman Bernard Hinault (page 243); and (below) the Three Peaks Cyclo-cross in the Yorkshire Dales of England, an event where clambering over dry-stone walls and crossing peat bogs are among the required skills (page 221).

MOUNTAINS AND HILLS Juli Furtado (above) became the first official world champion in women's cross-country racing at the 1990 World Mountain Bike Championships near Durango, Colorado (page 255); and the hills of Ireland, particularly St. Patrick's Hill in Cork (opposite, below), provided a glorious setting for the inaugural Nissan International Classic in 1985 (page 265).

ETERNAL LOMBARDY There is timeless quality to the season's final one-day classic, the Tour of Lombardy, from the precipitous roads surrounding Lake Como (above), to the cyclists' chapel of the Madonna del Ghisallo (left), where a century of cycling memorabilia line the walls, and a bust of the legendary Fausto Coppi stands sentinel for today's racers. The 1968 Tour of Lombardy reflected all of the race's rich history and drama (page 279).

CONQUISTADOR In the last major effort of his glorious career, Spain's Miguel Induráin (left) made a much-publicized attempt on the world hour record in Bogotá, Colombia, in 1996 (page 301). Buckling on a space-age helmet, the five-time Tour de France winner warmed up (below) in front of a pre-dawn crowd at the world championship velodrome. The fans cheered (opposite, bottom), as Induráin powered his Espada IV Pinarello around the concrete bowl, while the great champion later spoke to the media (above) about the difficulties of racing at high altitude.

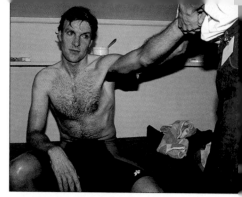

BACKSTAGE On the surface, six-day track racing is one big show. Indeed ace Australian track racer Danny Clark often grabbed the mike between events (right) to croon the crowd, while there were many victory celebrations for Clark and his excellent English racing partner, Tony Doyle (below). But beneath the glitter, there is a challenging under-belly to the discipline (page 313), as shown by Clark (above left), who had to sit out the 1986 Zürich Six with a stomach ulcer in a cramped trailer in the parking lot; and Doyle (top, right) as he takes a short break in a trackside cabin between two fast, sweat-inducing races.

# RAINBOW OVER THE ALPS

**World**
**Professional**
**Road**
**Championship**
France
August 1989

**There are no single-day races** quite as dramatic as the world road race championship. Normally held on a hilly circuit, the often-seven-hour contest has a slow build up, with tension increasing as, lap by lap, the finish gets closer, until one man crosses the line, often alone. The champion is awarded a white jersey, with rainbow stripes around the chest. The first world pro road title race took place in 1927, on the famous Nurburgring circuit in Germany. The winner was Alfredo Binda of Italy, who would win the title twice more in a glorious career. Since then, only one other rider has collected three rainbow jerseys: the Belgian legend Eddy Merckx. A young American was compared to Merckx when he won the title in 1983; six years later, he was after another victory....

# France

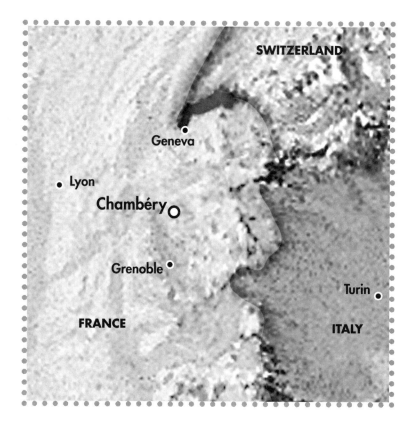

SWITZERLAND

Geneva

Lyon

Chambéry

Grenoble

Turin

FRANCE

ITALY

ALMOST ONE YEAR before the 1989 world championships, Greg LeMond paid a private visit to Chambéry, France, to scout out the road race course on the edge of the French Alps. He found terrain similar to the circuit at Altenrhein, Switzerland, where he won the rainbow jersey in 1983. "But the hill is a little bit longer and steeper," he reported. It was surprising that LeMond had designs on a second rainbow jersey, as since almost dying in a hunting accident in 1987, he hadn't won a single race. Injury followed illness, and some people were saying he would never rediscover the strength that took him to that 1983 world title and the 1986 Tour de France victory. But LeMond is a fighter....

What he discovered at Chambéry was a course that fit perfectly his capabilities. Maybe he wouldn't be strong enough to finish alone as he did in '83, but such a circuit had possibilities. After two kilometers riding along flat, shadowy city streets, the course turned left into the grassy foothills of the impressive limestone massif of the Chartreuse. A narrow byway then gradually climbed south between open fields, with a 300-meter long stretch of 10-percent grade before the road dipped momentarily, then swung left to tackle the course's main climb: the formidable Montagnole hill.

Looking up on race day, the racers saw a mass of humanity spread across the wide, green hillside, where most of the 150,000 crowd had gathered to watch the race—aided by a giant 800-square-foot television screen. Some had been camping here for a week, while most fans—from Italy, Belgium, the Netherlands, Britain and Switzerland—had filtered in through the night to claim the best spots. The course was patrolled by a security force of both paid and volunteer staff, while pay booths were manned 24 hours to collect the 200-franc ($33) admission price.

*World Professional Road Championship • France • 1989*

Already having climbed 300 feet from the town, the course now switchbacked up the final 400 feet in 1.5 kilometers. In terms of time, the racers were climbing for fully 50 percent of the day. After the Montagnole climb, they began a steep, fast downhill, which included part of the descent from the Col du Granier used in the recent Tour de France. Then, on reaching a hillside high above the finish line, the course curved to the right, and climbed another short hill, called Mont Carmel.

The next short, twisting descent took the race back to base level and the final kilometer on flat streets, past the team pits, to the 300-meter-long finishing straight. It was an ideal championship course: challenging, but not extreme; only the riders at the top of their form would stand a chance of winning.

As leader of a full-strength U.S. squad (the world championships are contested by national teams), LeMond was one of the men on hot form. A month before, after almost quitting the sport in May, he won a dramatic, come-from-behind Tour de France, by eight seconds from two-time Tour winner Laurent Fignon. These two had both prepared meticulously for the world's, with LeMond having based himself at nearby Grenoble, from where he took long training runs into the Alps.

Most experts agreed with the predictions of the respected French sports daily *L'Équipe*, which published the following list of favorites for the August 27 title race:

***** Fignon (France)

**** LeMond (USA), Charly Mottet (France), Steven Rooks (Netherlands)

*** Gianni Bugno (Italy), Marino Lejarreta (Spain), Robert Millar (GB), Gert-Jan Theunisse (Nl)

** Claude Criquielion (Belgium), Pedro Delgado

 **RAINBOW OVER THE ALPS**

(Spain), Federico Echave (Spain), Pascal Richard (Switzerland)
      \* Raúl Alcalá (Mexico), Eric Caritoux (France), Franco Chioccioli (Italy), Thierry Claveyrolat (France), Maurizio Fondriest (Italy), Martial Gayant (France), Andy Hampsten (USA), Miguel Induráin (Spain), Sean Kelly (Ireland), Marc Madiot (France), Tony Rominger (Switzerland), Abelardo Rondon (Colombia)

Surprisingly, *L'Équipe* didn't list Canadian Steve Bauer. The previous weekend, Bauer became the first North American to win a World Cup classic, when he made a late solo attack to take the Championship of Zürich in Switzerland. Also, a year ago, the 30-year-old from Ontario almost won the world title, when he crashed in the final sprint with Belgian Claude Criquielion of Belgium, allowing their breakaway companion Maurizio Fondriest of Italy to take the gold medal. After picking himself up and crossing the line, Bauer was consoled by a man standing behind the crowd barriers: a non-competing Greg LeMond. The two are good friends, but on this August Sunday in 1989 at Chambéry, in the shadow of the Alps, they would be rivals....

OVERNIGHT RAIN had cleared by the 10:30 a.m. start time, but more rain was forecast. The azure jerseys of Italy were the first of the 26 national teams to line up across the start-finish line, with Gianni Bugno its top man after he'd won a final preparation race four days before on a course similar to this one at Chambéry.
      With the Soviet Union presenting its very first pro team at the world's, there were a record 190 starters. It took the speakers much longer than usual to announce the complete list of riders, and the race began only 20 seconds after the last name echoed around the stands.

*World Professional Road Championship • France • 1989*

The race developed in three distinct seven-lap sections: a fast early pace by a compact peloton; followed by a nine-man break that gained a maximum of five minutes; and a finale that saw a war of attrition before the winning move developed on the last climb and descent of Montagnole hill.

The only riders to break (briefly) in the opening part were three Portuguese riders Carlos Moreira, José Santiago and Acacio Da Silva. Only Da Silva's attack on the seventh climb brought a reaction, with Bruno Cornillet of France jumping across to him, and the peloton rejoined on the descent.

The high early pace produced a steady string of retirements, including an out of form Adri Van der Poel of the Netherlands, who pulled into the pits after only one lap. The first American to lose contact was Thomas Craven of Wheaties-Schwinn, who dropped back on lap five, by which point the 7-Eleven riders John Brady of Ireland and Alex Stieda of Canada had already abandoned.

LeMond showed he was nervous as well as relaxed by nonchalantly stopping to pee near the end of lap three—but most of his American teammates waited to pace him back to the pack. He had worked his way back into the top dozen by the top of the next climb.

The rain first started to fall as the seventh lap ended. It was the signal for Denmark's Kim Andersen to attack through the finish area. He was joined by Peter Declercq of Belgium and Celio Rocancio of Colombia, while Maarten Ducrot of the Netherlands tagged on to them before the hill on lap eight. It was on this climb, 167 kilometers from the finish, that the little French climber Thierry Claveyrolat burst from the pack with Marco Vitali of Italy, Thomas Wegmüller of Switzerland and Jokin Mujika of Spain.

Claveyrolat wasn't content with towing the others up to the break, but, pounding on the big ring, he went straight by

**RAINBOW OVER THE ALPS**

to cross the summit 26 seconds clear of the other seven, with the peloton at 1:09. In between the leaders and the pack, a young red-jerseyed Russian, Dmitri Konyshev, was chasing alone, and he caught the lead group on the descent.

Some sunshine began to appear between the rain clouds, but it was too late to dry the road out for former champion Moreno Argentin, who crashed and quit. Meanwhile, Claveyrolat was caught by the eight chasers before the climb on lap nine, where the gap had already reached 2:31. Now the nine men, from nine different nations, were together. With all the major teams represented, except the United States, it was certain the break would stay clear for much of the remaining 150 kilometers.

After the fast start and the several laps of establishing the break, the pace noticeably slowed. Even the sun returned for an hour to add to the more relaxed air. In front, most of the pulling was being done by Andersen, Wegmüller, and Ducrot, the three most experienced racers in the break. Besides, Ducrot and Wegmüller are colleagues on the Domex-Weinmann trade team for the other 51 weeks of the year....

In contrast, Claveyrolat remained steadfastly at the back of the group, conserving his energy, while Konyshev did minimal pulls. Even so, the gap gradually increased: 3:02 at the end of lap nine, 3:41 a lap later, and 4:50 at the end of lap 11.

When the gap topped five minutes at the start of the 12th Montagnole climb, the French team director Bernard Hinault ordered his men to increase the tempo, resulting in a 45-second reduction by the summit. And the gap was down to 4:02 a lap later.

This acceleration proved too much for another 10 riders, including Americans Roy Knickman and Ron Kiefel, and Canadian Brian Walton. But the Americans had done

*World Professional Road Championship • France • 1989*

their job in pulling both Andy Hampsten (after a flat) and LeMond (after his rest stop) back to the peloton. In total, 53 men had already quit.

With the gap back to 4:56 as they hit the hill for the 14th time, Swiss strongman Wegmüller (whose nickname is "Thomas the Tank") suddenly attacked, trying to rid himself of the deadwood in the break; and only Ducrot, Konyshev and Claveyrolat could catch him. At that moment the big black clouds that had been rolling in from the west unleashed their repository of rain and lightning. A roof of umbrellas suddenly covered the Montagnole hillside, and the race started to split apart.

In the pack, the pace increased, too, with Scottish climber Robert Millar accelerating and pulling with him a sizable group that included many of *L'Équipe's* prerace favorites: Charly Mottet, LeMond, Steven Rooks, Kelly, Raúl Alcalá, Hampsten and Gert-Jan Theunisse. This push, coupled with Wegmuller's forcing at the front, caused the lap to be a minute faster than the previous one.

The combination of factors caused almost 50 riders to quit during the next two laps, including Americans Chris Bailey, Jeff Pierce and Mike Engleman, as well three sponsored by 7-Eleven Sean Yates of Britain, Phil Anderson of Australia and Dag-Otto Lauritzen of Norway.

The rain eased, but the pressure didn't. The Italians were now pulling the pack, having lost Vitali from the break, while the French helped, unwilling to put all their eggs in the Claveyrolat basket.

The accelerations saw the gap reduced to 2:27 when Pedro Delgado surged in lap 17. The 1988 Tour de France winner was followed by Italy's Emanuel Bombini, and they had closed to within 1:51 of the break by the Montagnole summit. But the Italian team closed them down on the

**RAINBOW OVER THE ALPS**

descent, and did the same to world championship specialist Criquielion when he attacked with Fignon on the short Mont Carmel climb.

Only four laps (49.4 kilometers) were left, and the four leaders were still almost two minutes ahead. Everyone was starting to get anxious. In front, the riders in the break were now starting to work against each other. Claveyrolat attacked on the hardest part of the hill; Ducrot followed, and Wegmüller was dropped, while Konyshev gamely inched his way back to the front two by the summit.

The thinned-out pack was also splitting apart, with Italy's Franco Chioccioli and Dirk De Wolf of Belgium pulling them over the crest, only 1:25 down. Still near the front were Hampsten, LeMond, Criquielion and Kelly ... and Kelly's top Irish teammate, Martin Earley.

The rain had stopped, but the roads were still slippery under the trees. It was here, near the foot of the 90-kph descent, where De Wolf suddenly lost control of his bike. The Belgian skidded across the road, his bike clattering away in front of him; while Chioccioli came careening after him. The crash forced Switzerland's Jörg Müller to the outside of the left turn and he thumped head-first into a stone wall that was thankfully covered with protective padding. All three abandoned, but were not seriously injured.

On the same descent, the remarkable Wegmüller recaught the leaders, and then attacked through the pits, starting the 19th lap with a 10-second lead. The leaders' spectacular infighting was keeping the pace high, and keeping the chasers at bay.

This time on the climb, where the crowds were again trying to shelter from a heavy rain, Wegmüller was caught; again, Claveyrolat attacked, and this time only Konyshev had the reserves to follow him.

*World Professional Road Championship • France • 1989*

Behind, Millar made another strong surge from the pack, marked by a Spaniard, Jesus Rodriguez-Magro. And then Hampsten moved impressively to the front, followed by Fignon, Earley, Kelly and Bauer. There were still 30 riders in the chase group, 1:28 behind the two leaders, as Ducrot was caught with two laps to go.

The gap was down to 1:06 starting the climb for the penultimate time, just as the heroic Wegmüller was caught and passed by the pack. Without him, the leaders would surely have been absorbed long before.

Miguel Induráin of Spain now moved his broad carcass to the front of the chase group, leading the pursuit ahead of Luc Roosen of Belgium and Spanish teammate Marino Lejarreta. With the gap down to just 39 seconds, Steven Rooks put the orange jersey of The Netherlands at the front. The tall Dutchman quickly opened a gap, turning a much smaller gear than any previous attacker. He was only seven seconds behind Konyshev and Claveyrolat at the top of the main climb, and 21 seconds ahead of the first part of the peloton.

Rooks caught the two leaders on the descent, while a tremendous pursuit from the bunch thrust forward nine riders: Bauer, Bugno, Criquielion, Earley, Fignon, Kelly, Lejarreta, LeMond and Rolf Sørensen of Denmark. When the bell rang, they were only 11 seconds behind the three leaders, but the nine were looking at each other on the flats, and had dropped back to 20 seconds as the final ascent began.

Up the climb, 1988 world's protagonists Bauer and Criquielion found themselves riding side by side, and they pulled for most of the climb, reducing the lead to 18 seconds. It was then, just about a kilometer from the summit, that Fignon, on his big ring, made the move that all France was awaiting. It was the same punching attack that won him

**RAINBOW OVER THE ALPS**

the past two editions of Milan-San Remo; and the same aggressive Fignon we saw at the recent Tour de France.

Then, just as the pony-tailed Parisian was taking a right-hand switchback, powering toward the three leaders, he turned to check what damage he had done. No one was yet in sight—and he turned back to focus on catching Rooks, Claveyrolat and Konyshev. Only moments later, however, Fignon had the shock of his life when he looked to his side and saw .... LeMond. "I was really astonished to see him," said Fignon.

And no sooner had his American nemesis arrived than LeMond stood on the pedals of his carbon-fiber bike one more time and projected himself toward the leaders. Fignon couldn't hold his wheel, while LeMond stomped harder on his pedals to catch the three leaders and led them over the summit into the last descent.

If this wasn't drama enough, a tragedy befell Bauer. He had been chasing closely behind LeMond and Fignon, and was about to link up with them when his rear tire flatted. He skidded to a halt, forlornly looking for technical support. The Canadian's chance of a rainbow jersey had again been cruelly plucked from him.

Then, as Fignon, too, joined the break, Konyshev rushed 15 meters clear, descending in an aerodynamic tuck. The Russian was soon joined by Claveyrolat. Then LeMond closed the gap, followed by Rooks, Fignon and the gritty Kelly: six men to contest a world title.

On the Mont Carmel climb, Fignon counterattacked, and again it was LeMond who closed him down. They were now into the final short descent ... and Rooks chanced his luck, racing 50 meters clear. But LeMond already was sensing victory, and he was the first to cross to the Dutchman. Kelly, a PDM teammate of Rooks for the rest of the year, was

*World Professional Road Championship • France • 1989*

next. Onto the flats, a vigorous Fignon pulled the other two riders back, and the six were all together again.

They passed beneath the red one-kilometer-to-go kite, where Fignon again dashed ahead. "I thought I was going to win; if I could have gotten only 60 meters' lead I'd have been world champion," he said later. "But it was LeMond who again sought me out."

Fignon was still leading as they turned the final bend, 300 meters from the line … and while everyone was thinking that the officials would soon be picking out a rainbow jersey to fit Kelly, the incredible, amazing, tireless LeMond bolted away on his 53x12.

Kelly took up the chase, inching nearer and nearer on his 53x13, but the earlier head wind had died away and Kelly seemed to be undergeared. Rooks and Konyshev were in the Irishman's wake, desperately trying to grab that extra something that would give them the gold medal.

It was a sprint finish as classic as the one at Como, Italy, in October 1983 at the conclusion of the Tour of Lombardy. The winner then by a whisker was Kelly over LeMond. This time LeMond had too much power. And a frustrated, disbelieving Kelly gave up when he saw that he was beaten … allowing Konyshev to slip by on his left to take the silver.

LeMond managed a split-second victory wave with his left hand before he braked, but his open-mouthed whoop of realization said it all. The cheers rang out from the stands to salute his extraordinary achievement. From oblivion earlier in the season, he had become the fifth man in history to win both the Tour de France and the world championship in the same season.

All the superlatives under the sun (or should it be the rainbow?) could not adequately express the American contingent's emotions as LeMond powered his way across the

**RAINBOW OVER THE ALPS**

line on the rain-soaked Avenue du Colombier at the end of this heart-stopping world professional road race championship. The American had gambled everything on leading out that final sprint against the five grittiest racers to survive the rigors of a remarkably rapid race on an afternoon of awful weather. He had gambled, and won.

A few minutes later, while a somewhat muffled rendition of the Star Spangled Banner barked from the public address, the faces of the three medalists summed up the sensational outcome. Up on the highest step, there was a luminescence in the twinkling blue eyes of LeMond, 28. On his right, a rider whose Rubicon was the Iron Curtain, Dmitri Konyshev, could not suppress the excitement of becoming the first Soviet in history to medal in a professional cycling championship. The palefaced 23-year-old smiled innocently down, not quite believing that he'd come so far in his short career.

At the other end of the podium, with the bronze medal hanging from his long neck, there was a forlorn, lonely look on the face of Sean Kelly, 33, the old warrior. Perhaps this had been his last, and best, chance of winning the only jewel missing from his collection of the world's most prestigious single-day races.

Just as heartbroken at the finish was the trouble-plagued Steve Bauer, who crossed the line, yes, in 13th place. Instead of the blond Canadian, it was his American friend LeMond who was world champion for the second time, six years after Altenrhein, and five weeks after his unforgettable Tour de France victory over Laurent Fignon. And once again the French star would probably have won if it hadn't been for the dogged determination and ultimate power of his American rival.

*World Professional Road Championship • France • 1989*

# OVER HILL AND DALE

## Three
## Peaks
## Cyclo-Cross
# England
# September 1984

Cyclo-cross is a branch of cycling that began in the early part of the 20th century as a form of winter training—riding across fields on a road bike, and carrying the machine when the terrain gets too muddy or steep. The first world championships in the discipline didn't happen until 1950, with Britain holding its first national cyclo-cross championships in 1954. One of the more notorious and most unusual events in England is the Three Peaks Cyclo-Cross, first held in 1961.

# England

SCOTLAND

*North Sea*

N. IRELAND

REP. OF
IRELAND

Dublin •

• Carlisle

• Middlesbrough

Three
Peaks

Bradford •

• Leeds

Liverpool •

• Manchester

WALES

ENGLAND

*Atlantic
Ocean*

London •

• • • • • • • • • • • • • • • • • • • • • • • • • • • • • • • • • • • • • • • • • • • • • • • • • • • • • • • • •

HAILSTONES WERE MIXED with the rain that blew horizontally across the barren summit of 2373-foot-high Ingleborough Hill. "Some of the worst conditions I've known," said John Rawnsley, in a broad Bradford, Yorkshire accent. And he should know. Rawnsley is the organizer of England's late-September Three Peaks cyclo-cross, and he has competed in all 24 editions of the race. He added: "This is my 98th time over the Three Peaks route. I do my 99th in the fell runners race in April, and I'm inviting some friends for the 100th trip next June—I'm walking that one."

When the thick, pea-soup clouds momentarily parted up on the first of the three peaks, sparkling views were revealed of the other two mountains—2419-foot Whernside and the table-topped Pen-y-Ghent, 2273 feet. At the height of the storm, 121 of the 122 starters in the 1984 Three Peaks were toiling up the steep trails and across the boggy plateaux of Ingleborough. The other starter had already turned back, his chain wrapped around his useless machine after the derailleur had broken at the start of the climb.

The first rider to appear across the summit's rock-strewn escarpment was a frail-looking figure in black. His name: Tim Gould. He was not even born when Rawnsley began his love affair with this rugged, yet romantic, corner of the Pennine Hills. Gould, aged 20, comes from Matlock, Derbyshire. His father, Harry Gould, was a road racer back in the 1950s, in the Langsett team of independents (a category of semi-professionals that disappeared in the mid-60s.) "Tim loves this race," Harry said, "that's why we come back every year." This was the fourth time Gould junior has taken part in the Three Peaks, his best showing having been second in 1983, when he finished five minutes behind Richard Bates, a fell runner turned cyclist [Hills are sometimes called fells in northern England], who has since retired from cyclo-cross racing.

*Three Peaks Cyclo-Cross • England • 1984*

One of Bates's Bradford RCC clubmates and another runner, Barry Peace, who was fifth in 1983, was second to the top of Ingleborough, and he was to prove a worthy opponent for the younger Gould. Anticipating trouble, a mountain rescue team had pitched a tent on the summit, with a radio link to the race start and communications center down in the valley at Helwith Bridge, where a rain-swollen River Ribble raced beneath the stone arch bridge beside the starting area.

Rough weather is notorious in these parts, and when we reconnoitered the course the previous afternoon, all three peaks were hidden by clouds. It has been known for riders to go missing, and it is now a race rule that every competitor carries a whistle and a "bivvy bag," so that a rider becoming lost or seriously injured can set up a temporary bivouac, or campsite.

There was obvious danger in descending 1000 feet in less than one mile through clouds, wind and rain—and that was the task facing the riders after they had pedaled, carried and hauled their bikes up the eastern slopes of Ingleborough. "I like going downhill, I like the descents ... that's the best bit," said Gould. And yet, even he crashed on this first hair-raising drop. "I was going down and all of a sudden it gets too rocky, and I couldn't slow down in time," he explained in his Derbyshire dialect. "I came off ... but I only did my brake lever in, that were all. And I was away again."

Others didn't come off as lightly as the young Matlock man. Pete Lewin of the Leicester Forest CC crashed over his handlebars and somersaulted down the mountainside. "I heard his head crack against a rock," said an eyewitness. "He was a bit groggy when he got up and there was some blood coming from a wound. He was too far down the hill to go back to the rescue post, so I told another rider to keep an eye on him as they continued down."

 **OVER HILL AND DALE**

Lewin had his head bandaged to stop the bleeding, but he was, of course, out of the race. Another faller on the first peak was one of the six pioneers who were riding (and carrying) mountain bikes around the 56-kilometer (35-mile) course.

"There was a concealed gully with water in it," explained bespectacled David Ferguson from the Blackburn, Lancashire club, Summit Cycling Club. "I hit it broadside and fell awkwardly and hurt my back. While I was lying on the ground, I thought, 'What the hell am I doing here!' I had preconceived ideas of what it would be like up there—but it becomes awesome."

One first-timer who fared better on Ingleborough was Mike Johnson, a member of the Coalville Wheelers near Leicester. "I was only sixth or seventh to the top," he said, "but I dropped down okay. I went straight by the others and I was third by the bottom. I had one close call, when my back wheel came up where my ears are, but I managed to hold it."

Johnson has a background in road racing and cyclo-cross, but he chose to compete in the Three Peaks running race before tackling this cyclists' version. He finished ninth in the even longer Welsh Peaks run, and he has also completed the grueling, two-day Karrimor Marathon in the Scottish Highlands. As a build-up to this big day, he was training 200 miles a week on the road as well as running 20 miles.

Yet the most thorough preparations do not always work out on the day, as Chris Singleton of the Halesowen Athletic & Cycling Club from Birmingham found out. "I came here to get in the top 10," said Singleton. "But I punctured at the bottom of the first peak, just as we came off the road. I'd already had three punctures on the ride from the train at Lancaster to get here, so I borrowed a spare from a lad in the bunk room. When I changed the tubular, I found out that was flat, too."

He added that his training had comprised a five-mile run every morning before work, and another two-and-a-

*Three Peaks Cyclo-Cross • England • 1984*

half hours in the evening that included road riding, cyclo-cross and running up and down steep, sandy hills near his home.

In contrast, Gould admitted that he did no special training, other than what he does to prepare for normal one-hour cyclo-cross events. He is training to be a chemical engineer and divides his time between attending university and working in industry.

"Since university in July, I've been training hard," he said. "But now I'm at work, so I only train a few hours each evening, mostly on the road. I try to do half-an-hour of running every day, but it usually works out every other day."

He is fortunate to have a cycling father who can organize the support needed for a race like this. After starting on a first cyclo-cross bike—"with six gears, 13 to 26, with a 42 at the front"—he changed onto his road bike after the Ingleborough descent—"so I could have a bottle"—before changing to a second 'cross machine to tackle Whernside. It was back on to the road bike for the 14 kilometers leading to the last climb, where he changed back to the original 'cross bike, which had been cleaned. A fifth change was made for the final three kilometers from Horton-in-Ribblesdale village to the Helwith Bridge finish.

"It's a good course," opined Rawnsley. This 56-kilometer version was being used for only the second time. The first 19 editions of the race saw variations of the 40-kilometer peak-to-peak-to-peak course used by the fell runners. The change has meant that the event record of 2:37:33 set by five-time winner Eric Stone—another Matlock native—is unlikely to be improved upon; but the course's extra 16 kilometers provide a much more "accessible" race, for both riders and spectators.

With 30 kilometers of paved road, 20 kilometers of rough trails and another six kilometers that the organizer

**OVER HILL AND DALE**

describes as "unrideable," the course favors an all-around rider rather than a specialist. The first vital section is the steep road climb out of Ribblesdale, before the race turns left up an even steeper stony track over a cattle grid. Even so early in the race, Gould was in the lead, having opened a gap on the road with Nigel Gilbert (South Yorkshire Road Club) and Andy Hurford (Velo Club Nottingham).

Running specialist Peace was well back in the chasing group—and he was not to get on terms with Gould at any point in the race. And the younger man was able to relax once he had established a near five-minute lead over Ingleborough.

While the riders scrambled over this first peak and negotiated the often muddy, mostly stony trail past the evocatively named Quaking Pot, to Cring Bottom, and on down to "base level" at Skirwith, the hundreds of spectators and helpers pedaled or drove through the torrential rain to Chapel le Dale. This is a center for the murky pastime of caving, and the busy Hill Inn is a popular gathering place of spelunkers, walkers and cyclists.

There is a kindred spirit among people who often have to battle the elements in this wild country, and it was particularly noticeable on race day. It's hard enough cycling on these "heavy" roads, without having to climb to the tops of three mountains with your bicycle. That commitment was greatly appreciated by the spectators, who applauded the men at the back of the race as warmly as they did those at the front.

A popular place for watching was the steep, grassy field at the foot of Whernside. After following a dipping farm lane from Chapel le Dale, the riders climbed a short steep hill—still on the tarmac—up to this field. This is where the more organized competitors like Gould and Johnson changed bikes, while others battled on through clinging mud at a gateway into the field. It was possible to ride up the first bumpy stretch, but then everyone had to shoulder their

*Three Peaks Cyclo-Cross • England • 1984*

bikes and run, jog or walk the next two kilometers to the 1800-foot-high ridge that leads to the summit.

There was a deep ditch to cross—either by a narrow, wooden bridge or across a mud-and-stone-covered pipe—and at the top of the field a high, drystone wall to climb. Most used a set of steep wooden steps to cross the wall, while a few manhandled their bikes over a wooden gate before climbing over. The route continued across a peat bog and another stream, before reaching the long, steep path to the ridge.

It was noticeable how everyone, including spectators, respected the countryside. Without the cooperation of the farmers and landowners, a race such as this would not exist; while the help of the National Park Authority and the local police is invaluable in making the event both safe and respected.

Even the weather cooperated, as the clouds had cleared for the climb—and descent—of Whernside. It was possible to ride most of the ridge trail to the top, where the riders turned and came back the same way to Chapel le Dale. Because of this retracing of the route, Gould knew exactly how far he was in front of Peace. It was still around the five-minute mark. Nonetheless, a crash on the tricky descent, or a mechanical incident could soon wipe out such a lead.

But Gould was taking no chances—he flew with the wind along the exciting, dipping and climbing stretch of road back to Horton. He was back on his all-chrome Cilo road bike, the tubulars singing on the tarmac that was wet from the storm. There were still clouds in the sky, but they now made dappled shadows on the delightful green land-scape of the Yorkshire Dales.

Ahead, Gould could see the familiar, flat-topped profile of Pen-y-Ghent. The final climb—because of the improved weather—would prove the easiest of the three. It follows to the summit a section of the famous Pennine Way, a long-dis-

**OVER HILL AND DALE**

tance trail that links the hilltops of this backbone of northern England. Gould used it to double his lead over Peace over the peak.

The Bradford RCC man was already being pressed by Johnson on the road section, but the situation soon became worse. "My back tub [tire] started to roll," said Peace, "so I changed bikes. And then the tub blew on the back wheel. I was looking for another bike and whipped a lad's machine—and then the front tub blew on that!"

All this was going on in front of Johnson, who was now only two minutes behind Peace. The younger man made a storming effort on the final three kilometers along the valley road back to Helwith Bridge, but he was still a minute down as he entered the farm gate that marks the race finish. In turn, Peace was an enormous 12 minutes behind Gould.

How did the young winner feel about his performance? "It was easier this year, to be honest. I wasn't pushed really … I was trying … but there wasn't someone two minutes behind to force me like last year."

Although Gould won by 12 minutes, the next seven finishers were all covered by a similar margin. Less than a minute behind Johnson came Russell Beresford (Norton Wheelers), who improved six minutes and nine places from his 1983 performance. He had no challengers for his fourth place, but there was a fine battle for fifth place between Tim Taylor (Macclesfield Wheelers), Nigel Lanaghan (Keswick Athletic Club) and Paul Gilbert (South Yorkshire RC). On Pen-y-Ghent, Taylor was passed by Lanaghan, a fell runner from the Lake District, who was taking part in this race for the first time. In the end, the on-the-bike sections defeated Lanaghan, who was passed by both Taylor and Gilbert before the finish.

A similarly close contest was being fought more than an hour back down the road between the two leading moun-

*Three Peaks Cyclo-Cross • England • 1984*

tain-bike riders, Phil O'Connor from south London and Christopher Igleheart, an American riding for the Summit CC team sponsored by Muddy Fox mountain bikes. Igleheart, a 33-year-old from Portland, Maine, has had experience of off-road racing at home, but he found the Three Peaks something completely different. "There's nothing like this in America," he said.

Igleheart and O'Connor had swapped places several times during the race, but the visitor appeared to have the mountain-bike prize in his pocket by the top of Pen-y-Ghent. Yet he was fading quickly. "I was told that he was just around the corner," said O'Connor, "but I could hardly believe it when I turned the corner and saw him there."

Racing a mountain bike for the first time, the Englishman dropped the American by more than four minutes by the end, where he arrived in 85th place in a time of 5:03:04. The two shook hands and Igleheart, who had taken 88th place, gasped, "That was the hardest event of my life. I need a beer...."

Rawnsley was pleased that the mountain bikes had taken part. "And I think I'll get an American team next year. We have to put on something special, it being the 25th anniversary."

He was also hoping that a return will be made by the team of Swiss amateurs from the RV Wetzikon-Assos, a club that annually invites a team from Bradford to compete in their annual cyclo-cross classic, near Zürich. Their Albert Manz, who won the Three Peaks race in 1981, was the rider who finished two minutes behind Gould in last year's event.

What is certain is that the bearded Rawnsley will be back to tackle his 101st trip around the Three Peaks. He is in his late 40s, as is Neil Orrell, from the Zodiac Cycle Racing Club of Lancashire. They are the only two riders to have completed all 24 editions of this, "the toughest cyclo-cross race in the world."

 **OVER HILL AND DALE**

# RACE OF THE FUTURE

**Tour de l'Avenir**

## Portugal-Spain-France-Italy

## September 1986

While the Tour de France grabs the attention of the whole world, few people take note of the Tour's little brother, the Tour de l'Avenir—the Tour of the Future. First held in 1961, it is a race that has frequently lived up to its name, having been won by men who went on to win the Tour de France: Felice Gimondi (1964), Joop Zoetemelk (1969) and Greg LeMond (1982). The 1986 Avenir saw an epic battle waged between two young Americans, Roy Knickman and Alexi Grewal, and a little-known Spanish cyclist named Miguel Induráin.

# Portugal-Spain-France-Italy

IT SHOULD HAVE BEEN the perfect moment to talk to Roy Knickman. We were in room 219 of the Carena Hotel at Gap, capital of the High Alps region in France, only 48 hours from the end of the 24th Tour de l'Avenir. Knickman was lying in bed reading Milan Kundera's "The Unbelievable Lightness of Being." On the bedside table was the race leader's yellow jersey that the 21-year-old American had been racing in a few hours earlier. But there was something wrong with the jersey. No numbers. They had been removed at the village of Laragne-Monteglin, 71.5 kilometers from the end of the 11th stage. A mystery illness had forced Knickman to quit a race he had been leading for eight days, and seemed destined to win. Now, instead of following in the wheelmarks of Greg LeMond, who won the Tour de l'Avenir in 1982, this native New Yorker was going to have to wait for his break-through into the big time of European racing.

Despite feeling sick and a little depressed about his retirement from the race, Knickman was ready to talk and tell us how he had won the yellow jersey and almost kept it to the end. But first of all, we wondered how he found him-self on the start line in Porto, Portugal, only two days after competing at the world championships.

"I talked with Michael (Fatka) about the end of the sea-son during the Coors Classic," explained Knickman, who race's pro for Fatka's team, Levi's, in the United States, and for the French squad, La Vie Claire, in Europe. "He finally said I could do what I thought best. So instead of riding the Cititour in New York [a major U.S. one-day race], I came to the Avenir. l thought it would do more good for my career."

Knickman plans to spend most of 1987 living and rac-ing in Europe, giving priority to the shorter stage races, "and I would like to go back and do the Tour of Italy and be a team G.C. rider, not as a domestique." This does not seem

*Tour de l'Avenir • Portugal-Spain-France-Italy • 1986*

an impossible goal for Knickman, who proved in this Tour de l'Avenir that he has the makings of a true all-around rider.

To prepare himself for this end-of-season test, he trained particularly hard during the previous two weeks. "I had three or four easy days to recover from the Coors before training for the world's," he continued. "I was doing 140-mile rides at about 24 mph, sometimes in the mountains. Andy (Hampsten) and I rode together for seven hours around the world's circuit (at Colorado Springs), one day. In the race itself, I tried to ride with pressure, always at the front of the pack. l blew up twice during the race, but I think I succeeded in what I did. So I was really positive for the Avenir."

Knickman placed a respectable 14th in the Avenir's 4.8-kilometer prologue time trial in the packed streets of Porto, 20 seconds behind stage winner Miguel Induráin, the tall 22-year-old Spaniard who is a time trial specialist. "I knew then I was on good form," said Knickman, "because it was raining and I went at two miles per hour around the corners. My manager told me off for being too cautious.

"It rained again the next day, the first stage, and I crashed. l was beginning to think that this wasn't a race for me. l was going fast in the 53x12, when we hit some railroad tracks. l tried to do a bunny hop over them, but I hit the rails somehow and flipped, and spun down the road on my side."

The wounds were still prominent 10 days later when we spoke. Scabs covered the wide grazes down his left calf, thigh and hip. "I was picking grit out of it for three days," he pointed out. "I didn't have my Spenco second skin with me; otherwise, it would have healed more quickly."

Remarkably, it was the day after his crash that Knickman attacked and took over the yellow jersey. He explained how his new La Vie Claire teammate, Norwegian Jaanus Kuum, played a part in his breakaway: "I was about 20th

**RACE OF THE FUTURE**

over the first long hill. I climbed it easily in a 42x18. On the descent, Jaanus and I played games, attacking in turn, just to test out the opposition. I picked a good spot and went away with a Spanish guy [Enrique Carrera]. It was the longest stage of the race and there were still about 180 kilometers to ride, so the pack didn't bother too much. There was a lot of cross-tail wind. I felt good, and rode it like a training ride. The other guy wouldn't work, so I put him in the gutter for 30 kilometers. I was in my 12 sprocket. In the end, he said he would work. Our lead was up to 10 or 11 minutes by then. The pack started to chase, but I just laughed and kept the pressure on. We were still eight minutes ahead at the finish in Salamanca."

It was the sort of break that riders dream about achieving, but with 10 days of racing to go, the hardest part lay ahead, including stages in the Pyrenees and the Alps. "I had come to the race to ride for Jaanus and Guido (Winterberg), but now I had to defend my lead. At first I thought I had no chance of winning, but things started to fall into place. I figured I'd be okay."

Knickman didn't have an easy task. At the start of the fifth stage from Palencia to Vitoria, in Spain, the peloton split into four groups in a fierce crosswind, just as the American stopped with a puncture. With a little help from his teammates, Knickman worked his way across from one group to the next, but he took 50 kilometers to regain the leaders. "I knew I was going well because at the end of that stage I got away in a small break with Alexi (Grewal) and picked up some more time."

Knickman had trouble sleeping, though, because of his cuts. "I woke up one night and started reading my 700-page book of Stephen King short stories, which are pretty scary. (While reading one) I had to get up and go to the bathroom. I was standing there when I felt this warm liquid on my

*Tour de l'Avenir • Portugal-Spain-France-Italy • 1986*

ankle. I looked down and there was blood all around my feet on the floor. It was just like re-living the Stephen King story: I thought I was going to bleed to death! My wounds had dried while I was in bed and then cracked...."

Knickman still held a commanding lead at Pau, now in France, before the start of the 134-kilometer eighth stage, which was considered the toughest of the race, climbing the Aubisque and Soulor passes, with a finish on the Luz-Ardi-den mountain.

"I didn't know what to expect," Knickman continued. "I hadn't been climbing well earlier in the year, but all things are relative. I was still getting over a knee problem at the Giro, and I have changed my position. My saddle has been moved back 3.5 centimeters, about an inch and a half, during the season, and I'm using a bike with shallower angles. Now, I look like a normal bike rider! It's much better on descents. The bike seems to steer itself around the corners.

"I've also switched my style of climbing. Instead of being at the back of the group and getting dropped, I start the climb in the front. I treated the Aubisque as just another hill and climbed it on the 22 cog. The rain and wind made it difficult, but I only lost two minutes or so on the climb. I lost more time coming down. The descent was hell: misty and cold. I stopped for a rain jacket. Carrera, who was still second on G.C., was pulling his feet out of the pedals and going around the corners with his feet on the ground.

"An Italian [Marco Votolo] went over the edge. His bike flew into the air and landed 1000 feet down the mountain. They didn't find it for two days. When I came along, he was climbing back over the edge, with blood all over him.

"I eventually caught up with Alexi and Guido in the valley. We were told to make Alexi [who was on a rival French team, RMO] ride by our manager, so he pulled for 20 kilo-

 **RACE OF THE FUTURE**

meters. I felt good on the 15-kilometer Ardiden climb, which I rode with Guido."

At the summit, where he finished behind Kuum, Grewal and Induráin, Knickman was still the overall leader by more than five-and-a-half minutes. He felt that he had overcome the biggest hurdle. He said he felt good in the rain during the next stage—short and hilly—before a 300-kilometer transfer by car to Avignon. And the following day's 27.5-kilometer time trial at Carpentras should have given Knickman the opportunity of increasing his overall lead on everyone—except perhaps Induráin, who had won the time trial in each of the previous two Tours de l'Avenir.

In the morning, Knickman rode the course that circled the Côtes de Ventoux vineyards and contained one climb of two kilometers, a similar descent and one or two tricky turns in the tangerine-tiled Provençal villages. It was a perfect, sunny autumnal day … but it turned hellish for the American in the yellow jersey.

"I didn't feel right from the beginning," Knickman recounted. "I had cramps and burning in my legs and I knew I wasn't doing a good ride. My stomach was upset in the morning, and I could only eat cereal for breakfast and some spaghetti for lunch. I had no energy."

The result was that the 21-year-old Knickman finished the stage in a disastrous 54th place, 3:08 behind stage winner Induráin. He was still the race leader, but with only 2:18 of his advance intact.

Knickman's sudden illness, which the doctors diagnosed as a cold, but was a much more serious virus, became worse overnight. He could eat only a bowl of soup for dinner and knew that he didn't have much hope of surviving the stage to Gap. "I felt okay on the first little hill, but then the pace started getting faster and faster, and I began dropping to the back of the peloton. Alexi said to me, 'You don't

*Tour de l'Avenir • Portugal-Spain-France-Italy • 1986*

look too good today.' I was dropped soon after that. I didn't think it would look good for the race leader to suddenly abandon, so I rode along on my own to the feed zone. They handed me my musette, but I turned in the road and gave it back to them. I'm really disappointed."

With Knickman's disappearance, the general classification suddenly took on a more open look, going into the final two days. Induráin was the new leader, followed by Frenchman Patrice Esnault (at 1:10), Grewal (at 1:20) and Kuum (at 1:40); with two more French pros in touch, Jérôme Simon of Peugeot (at 3:06) and Bernard Richard of Fagor (at 3:12). Ahead lay an alpine stage of 109 kilometers, crossing the redoubtable Col d'Izoard to Briançon.

"The stage is a bit short for me," said Olympic champion Grewal, before the start in Gap. He was wearing the white-green-and-blue jersey of his new team, RMO, under directeur sportif Bernard Thévenet, the former two-time winner of the Tour de France. "I prefer a stage with two or more passes," continued Grewal, "so that it's a battle of strength at the end. With just one climb, I'll have to go flat out and see what happens."

After almost a year's absence from racing before this season, Grewal said he was finally feeling strong. And although the Coloradan may not have been a hit with the management of his previous team, 7-Eleven—"all they were good for was the money," he commented—he had made a big impression on Thévenet. The RMO team boss said, "Alexi has developed much self-control—we call it *sang froid*—in the time I have known him, since June. We came together in an unusual way. I had a call from his sister Neena, who lives near me in Grenoble, just after the 7-Eleven team was pulled from the Tour of Spain. She told me that Alexi wanted to race in Europe, and asked if it was possible for him to take part in the Dauphiné. We arranged a

**RACE OF THE FUTURE**

meeting, and I agreed to take him in the RMO team for the Tour of Luxembourg, the Midi Libre and the Tour de l'Aude. I was pleased with his performances: King of the Mountains in Luxembourg and 10th overall in the Midi Libre. He was tired and abandoned in the Tour de l'Aude. And then, four weeks ago, he called to see if he could ride the Avenir. I agreed, and I've signed him up for the whole of the 1987 season."

Thévenet added that the Olympic champion still has a few things to learn: "He has to learn to be less nervous in the races, and he must also get some contact lenses. He would be leading this race now, if it hadn't rained in the Pyrenees. He had to remove his glasses to make the descent of the Aubisque, and he also stopped to let some air out of his front tire. He is so shortsighted that he could see only 10 meters in front of him. He was four minutes behind Induráin and Kuum after the descent, but he passed Kuum and almost caught the Spaniard before the Ardiden finish."

Unlike many coaches, Thévenet has realized that Grewal prefers advice to orders. "He likes to think about something and act upon it in his own time," said the French directeur sportif. This observation proved beneficial for the Carpentras time trial stage of the race. Thévenet noted, "Alexi was riding time trials with straight arms. We went riding together before the time trial, and I showed him how to bend his arms to obtain a more aerodynamic position. As a result he changed his position and did an excellent ride, placing fifth, only 51 seconds behind Induráin."

Grewal agreed with his new guru. "That was my best day of the whole Tour," he said, obviously pleased with his performance. But, we wondered, could he displace Induráin from the yellow jersey on the Izoard?

For this vital stage, on which any of the first five was in with a yellow-jersey chance, the weather was perfect: warm

*Tour de l'Avenir • Portugal-Spain-France-Italy • 1986*

sunshine and a breeze blowing from the left, as the peloton headed out toward the Serre-Ponçon lake, the largest reservoir in Europe. What no one expected was the instant series of attacks by the Soviet team, which resulted in more than 46 kilometers being covered in the first hour. The speed and the crosswind produced a 13-man break, led by three of the Soviets and including two of the top five (Simon and Richard). After they had passed through the feed zone at Guillestre—strangely deserted compared with its flag-waving, crowd-jammed self when the Tour de France passes through—only nine were left in the lead, with a three-minute advantage on a peloton that was quickly shedding the non-climbers.

Despite being in the depths of the overall classification, the Soviets Viktor Demidenko and Oleg Laroshenko continued to make the pace in the dramatic, yellow-rocked Queyras canyon. There was talk of a deal having been done with the Fagor or Peugeot teams, in an attempt to give Richard or Simon the yellow jersey. The hopes of La Vie Claire were left with Winterberg—who was in the break—because Kuum was suffering from the same symptoms as roommate Knickman, and he was destined to retire the next day.

When the climbing became more serious where the route turned left out of the canyon, the Soviets were dropped, and Simon went clear with Winterberg and a Portuguese, Casimiro Moreda, while Richard temporarily lost contact. Behind, an energetic Grewal was setting the pace and had pulled a dozen men to within 2:08 of the leaders.

The steepest part of the Izoard does not begin until about seven kilometers from the 7500-foot summit, but a long, straight five-percent grade through the scattered Alpine village of Arvieux always causes problems for the weak. It was here that Simon—much shorter and lighter than his cycling brothers Pascal and Regis—made his bid for

**RACE OF THE FUTURE**

victory. Winterberg matched his jump, but he soon drifted back to the black-haired Richard, one minute behind. Further back, Esnault surprised Grewal with a sharp attack, but the bespectacled American soon responded—"It took only one attack," he said—and was immediately 80 meters ahead of Induráin.

Throughout the remaining kilometers of the steep climb, Induráin remained locked to the rear wheel of the Colombian Abelardo Rondon, who put everything into his effort, sweat pouring profusely from his brow. Again, it seemed that a deal had been made, although the race leader simply said "Rondon and I are just good friends." Whatever the truth, Rondon topped the climb ahead of Induráin, but lost almost two minutes to the Spaniard in the last, downhill 17 kilometers.

On this sparkling alpine afternoon, through the dusty decor of the Casse Desert, famed for the Tour de France escapades of Fausto Coppi, Louison Bobet and Thévenet, Grewal turned on a super show. Sitting high in the saddle, the Olympic champion surged away from Esnault on the steepest part of the climb, clicked past Winterberg and Richard, and then closed a one-minute gap on Simon in the final three kilometers.

Grewal was first over the crowd-lined summit and quickly lost Simon on the steep, serpentine descent. Esnault, Gayant and Richard were scattered back down the road, with Induráin cresting the pass on Rondon's wheel, 1:19 in arrears. Grewal's overall deficit, remember, was 1:20. Would he be able to press home his advantage?

The epic battle turned to the powerful Induráin's advantage, however: He successfully picked off the riders in front of him, until he and the other four passed the five-kilometers-to-go board, only 39 seconds after the solo leader. The gap continued to close ... but there was one last hill to

*Tour de l'Avenir • Portugal-Spain-France-Italy • 1986*

climb, angling up through the medieval streets of Briançon, the highest town in Europe. The climb enabled Grewal to keep his stage victory, although the fifth-placed Induráin was only 26 seconds behind, his yellow jersey intact. Grewal lay flat on the street for two minutes after his arrival, and needed another 10 minutes of riding to compose himself for the presentations. "I knew it was now or never," he said, "and I gave it everything. I attacked in a 39x14, and climbed the steep parts in the 17 or 19 cogs. I couldn't have gone any harder. I don't have the yellow jersey, but I'm pleased that I have made a good comeback. And there are two more climbs tomorrow morning...."

But Grewal, now in second place, would have a hard time making up 54 seconds on a rider like Induráin, whose formidable chase down the Izoard showed that he has courage as well as considerable talent. Indeed, it was the American who faltered on the next morning's half-stage to the Italian ski station of Sestriere. There were two climbs, but the race was much too short and fast for Grewal to contemplate another attack. Waiting in the sunshine at the finish line in Sestriere, a convalescent Knickman said, "I thought Alexi could still win." But instead, the new RMO team leader lost time to his main rivals and dropped to third place.

All that remained of the two-week race was a 91-kilometer plunge down to the Piedmont plain, with the whole pack streaming into the streets of Turin on a perfect late summer evening, and the first European Community-sponsored Tour de l'Avenir (and possibly the last) was over. The race had promised so much for two Americans, but it was perhaps fitting that a talented young cyclist from Spain—one of the new countries in the 12-nation European Community—should emerge the winner.

 **RACE OF THE FUTURE**

# A CLASSIC TIME TRIAL

## Grand Prix
## des Nations
# France
# September 1984

Before the world road championships added an individual time trial to its schedule in 1994, the famous Grand Prix des Nations time trial was regarded as the foremost test for time trialists. Today, it is still regarded as a classic event, held every year in late September. The 1984 edition was one of the best, pitting the two top French riders, Bernard Hinault and Laurent Fignon, against the world-beating Irish stars, Sean Kelly and Stephen Roche. The event took place at Cannes, on the French Riviera.

# France

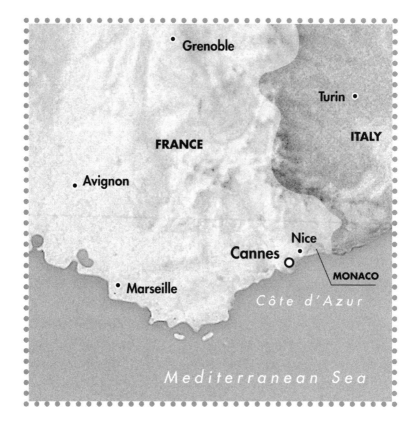

Grenoble

Turin

ITALY

FRANCE

Avignon

Nice

Cannes

MONACO

Marseille

Côte d'Azur

Mediterranean Sea

IF YOU STAND by the 12th century look-out tower high above the yachts moored in the harbor of fashionable Cannes, your eyes will be drawn along the curving, palm-lined promenade that leads to La Croisette—a peninsula that took its name from an ancient cross erected here. The cross has long since been replaced by a casino, the Palm Beach, where the attraction in September 1984 was a pop group, The New Seekers.

Following the line of the peninsula to the south, you will see three low-lying islands, one of which is named St. Honorat. It was here, in an austere stone-built monastery that the patron saint of Ireland, St. Patrick, spent nine years of his life receiving his religious training. Fifteen centuries later, two Irish habitués of a quite different discipline—professional bike racing—traveled to Cannes with the intention of teaching the continentals something about the art of time trialing.

At his first attempt in the Grand Prix des Nations—which is regarded as the world time trial championship—Stephen Roche finished second to Swiss specialist Daniel Gisiger. That was three years ago. The Dubliner's second attempt, in 1983, again saw him challenging Gisiger for victory, but he faded badly in the closing kilometers to place fifth. This year, Roche was determined to win—"although there won't be much between the first five," he said a few days before the Cannes rendezvous....

The second challenging Irishman, Sean Kelly, is three years older than his compatriot, but Kelly's aptitude for racing against the clock has only emerged in the past three seasons. It first appeared on a crisp, sunny afternoon in March 1982, just along the Mediterranean coast from Cannes, on the final stage of Paris-Nice.

*Grand Prix des Nations • France • 1984*

Kelly needed to beat the race leader, Gilbert Duclos-Lassalle of France, by at least five seconds to win this seven-day, stage-racing classic. The last stage was the traditional 11-kilometer haul up the Col d'Eze mountain road—one of the more demanding time-trial courses in France. Not only did Kelly beat Duclos—by an impressive 44 seconds—he also won the stage. And 10 days later, Kelly achieved an even more remarkable result: He defeated French ace Bernard Hinault by half-a-minute in the time-trial stage of the Critérium International, a two-day race that was won overall by a certain Laurent Fignon, in his first season as a professional.

Since then, Kelly has rarely been beaten in time trials, and it seemed a good idea when he entered the Nations for the first time last year. Unfortunately, it coincided with one of the Irishman's rare "off" days, and he crept home in 14th place out of 18 starters. This year, it was a far more confident Kelly who traveled to Cannes, after placing third in the Paris-Brussels classic. He also had his lead in the Super Prestige Pernod competition to defend—and his newly forged reputation to uphold.

Another man looking to this classic time trial to enhance his star status was Fignon. He had shown true time-trialing ability in his 1983 and '84 Tour de France victories—but his public and the French media were looking to him to prove his undoubted ability in other arenas. Fignon had failed at the world championships, and the Nations was to be his final race in Europe in 1984....

For Bernard Hinault, the task was not to prove himself, but to show that he had fully recovered from his 1983 tendinitis injury, and that his second place at the 1984 Tour de France was just a forewarning of his return to the role of number one cyclist in the world. He may not have said it openly, but it was clear that the disparaging remarks made

**A CLASSIC TIME TRIAL**

by Fignon during the Tour de France had hurt Hinault's pride; and this was another factor in his determination to re-prove himself.

It was a disappointment for the organizers—*L'Équipe* and *Le Parisien* newspapers associated with the city of Cannes—that world hour record holder Francesco Moser decided against competing. "It's been a long season for me," the Italian star explained, "and I guess I'm not getting any younger."

As for Greg LeMond, he had already returned home to California. So there were no Americans, Britons or Italians on the start list of 14 selected riders, but the international concept of the event was retained by the presence of three Swiss—Gisiger, Jean-Mary Grezet and Urs Freuler—the use-ful Dane, Kim Andersen, and the 1980 winner, Jean-Luc Vandenbroucke of Belgium. The race's "open" status was provided by two amateurs: Alex De Bremaeker, a Belgian specialist, and Helmut Wechselberger, the well-known Aus-trian who finished seventh in this event two years ago.

The reason why there is so much prestige attached to doing well in the Nations is the event's history. There was a great tradition attached to the original course in the Chevreuse valley, south of Paris, where the bike fans of the French capital gathered at the end of each season to see their heroes battle against the clock. The race was created in 1932, to fill a void: There was no direct time-trial clash between the world's top riders.

At first, the race was over 140 kilometers, a distance that remained until the mid-1950s. But after World War II, there were fewer and fewer star riders who were willing to expose themselves to such a long, difficult test, after a rac-ing season that included more and more events. So the dis-tance was reduced to 100 kilometers, which gave the Nations a new lease of life—until the mid-1960s, when the

*Grand Prix des Nations • France • 1984*

same problems arose, and the organizers chopped the distance to 73 kilometers. There were some fine races, and superb winners, such as the record nine victories of Jacques Anquetil between 1953 and 1966. But when traffic density made it impossible to continue the race in the Paris area, there was a complete rethink.

Outside sponsorship was found to allow starting money to be paid to the top riders, and the distance was increased to 80 kilometers. The first of these new-look Grand Prix des Nations was held in 1973, at the holiday resort of the Merlin property company (the new main sponsor), at St. Jean de Monts on the Atlantic coast of France, where Eddy Merckx was the clear winner from two other Tour de France stars, Luis Ocaña and Joop Zoetemelk.

This success persuaded *L'Équipe* to further increase the distance to 90 kilometers, and the race was transferred to Angers, a town in the Loire Valley where better crowds could be expected than in remote St Jean. The race remained at Angers for three years, until the present agreement was made with the Cannes municipality in 1977. The 90-kilometer distance was retained, but it was now stretched over two laps of a circuit that is much hillier than any of the previous courses.

Three consecutive victories by Hinault insured the race's success, publicity-wise, but it was difficult to convert the cosmopolitan inhabitants of one of France's most expensive stretches of real estate to the joys of bike racing. Still, the advantages of remaining at Cannes in late September include the generally warm, fine weather, the minimal problems with traffic, and the whole-hearted backing of the local authorities. This also happens to be the hometown of the race director, Félix Lévitan.

When Hinault did not compete in 1980, the race was given a more competitive look—as was confirmed by the victory of Vandenbroucke, ahead of Gisiger and Moser. The

 **A CLASSIC TIME TRIAL**

following year, a less than enthusiastic Hinault was beaten into fourth place by Gisiger, Roche and Hans-Hendrik Oersted of Denmark; and this fact encouraged more riders to consider accepting invitations to the race in the past three editions. The Nations has perhaps not regained all of its former popularity with the public, but it has certainly reestablished itself as a respected classic. And with live television coverage, there are probably more people aware of the event now than in "the good old days."

The wins claimed by Vandenbroucke and Gisiger (in 1981 and 1983) also showed that the race could be won by time-trial specialists who were not as good at climbing as Hinault. Although there is a total of 1270 feet of climbing on each of the two laps, there are no enormously steep grades. The circuit tends to favor those who can "pace" their uphill efforts to allow maximum output on the long downhills and the virtually flat 15 kilometers along the coast road.

AFTER A HOT, sunny Saturday when the bathers of both sexes were happy to go topless on the exclusive beaches of Cannes, Sunday, September 23 dawned wet and wintry. The bronzed surf bums employed by such five-star hotels as the Carlton, Martinez and Gray-Albion, still manicured the exclusive sands along the Croisette croissant; but the ominous black clouds and a gale-force wind from the northwest signaled a day of heavy showers and infrequent, bright intervals. The one compensation for the riders was the direction of the wind: favorable along the coastal highway, and therefore not too difficult on the twists and turns in the hilly interior.

Most of the leading contenders had prepared for this 49th Grand Prix des Nations in a similar manner: daily sessions of motorpaced training, combined with just one or two races since the world championships in Barcelona. The excep-

*Grand Prix des Nations • France • 1984*

tion was Kelly, who had won four stages and the overall title at Spain's Tour of Catalonia, prior to his third placing in Paris-Brussels just four days before the Cannes rendezvous.

In contrast, Hinault, Fignon and Roche had used Paris-Brussels as training, with Roche retiring from the 301-kilometer-long classic at the second feed zone, 100 kilometers from the finish. "I wore lots of clothes to sweat out this cold I've had for a week," said the Dubliner before starting the Nations. "I'm feeling fine and I hope I can win."

Roche spoke with hope rather than confidence. Kelly was more guarded, and did not risk making a forecast. He was clearly tense before the start, and when asked how he thought he would fare, he replied: "We'll talk about that after the finish."

Fignon, too, was unsure of his form for his first attempt in a time trial of this length. He expressed confidence in his preparation program, but to direct questions, he said, "If I don't win, it won't be the end of the world." The winner of the past two Tours de France seemed almost too relaxed to face such a difficult test. He knew it was his last race of the season and he was already talking about his preparations for 1985. This was not the attitude of Hinault, who realized he had much to prove.

Interestingly, Hinault had adopted the carbo-loading method of dietary preparation used successfully by runners in their build-up to a marathon. There are few occasions when a pro cyclist can afford the time to prepare so thoroughly for a specific event. However, Gisiger had used carbo-loading for his 1983 Nations win, while Moser proved the merits of the method in breaking the world hour record last January.

In any time trial, it is an advantage to know what times you have to beat. Indeed, Fignon said he was going to base his effort on the man who would begin three minutes ahead

**A CLASSIC TIME TRIAL**

of him: Roche. The Frenchman had used the same method to win his three time trial stages of the Tour de France a few months earlier. Both Kelly and Roche were ahead of Fignon, but Hinault and Gisiger had the advantage of starting in the final two slots. With no clear-cut favorite, the race was open in more senses than one.

Before the big guns began firing, the course was opened by a 12-man field for the one-lap amateur Grand Prix des Nations. This gave an indication of what to expect: At the first time check (atop Vallauris hill after 13.4 kilometers), the eventual amateur winner Bernard Richard of France clocked 21:13. Only three professionals were to beat his time.

The first pro to get close to Richard's split was Andersen, who was on form after winning the Grand Prix d'Isbergues the previous Sunday. His 21:17 was equaled by Kelly, who had set off from the starting ramp in fairly lethargic style. The same couldn't be said about his pursuer, Roche, who made a fast, nervous getaway as if the finish were at the other end of the bay. The younger Irishman was soon into his fluid style, and he romped up the four-kilometer climb, through the crowd-lined village of Vallauris, to reach the first time-keeper in 20:45—already 32 seconds up on Kelly.

Fignon, on a Gitane Delta time-trial bike (the others used regular road machines) and wearing a yellow, teardrop-shaped helmet, was 20 seconds slower: It was going to take more than gadgetry and precise schedules to win this race. It was going to take the determination of a Hinault, who made a ferocious, wild-eyed start, clearly intent on showing his best form to his youthful opponents. At 29, he still has the drive of his younger days, partly explained by his well-chosen racing program for 1984. He said at the beginning of the year that he would race only 100 times through the season: This was his 104th outing.

*Grand Prix des Nations • France • 1984*

Riding out of the saddle for most of the long climb, Hinault went through the 13.4-kilometer marker in 20:50, just five seconds down on Roche. And when Gisiger smoothly churned by in 21:16, we knew that Hinault really meant business.

The middle section of the Cannes circuit is the most typical of a time trial course in France, with constant turns and ups and downs, winding through both wooded and open countryside, and passing through two or three small villages. On this 16.6-kilometer stretch (just over 10 miles), Fignon made his expected reply, completing the distance in 21:40. Although this was the fastest, it recouped him only five seconds on Roche and four seconds on Hinault. Kelly lost a few more seconds, and was now 38 seconds down on leader Roche.

From this check at La Roquette, the riders zoomed down a steep, hairpin descent to La Bocca, before pounding back on the flat road to Cannes with the wind behind them. While Kelly and Gisiger again lost half-a-minute, Roche and Fignon continued at a similar pace to each other, but that pace lost Roche 11 seconds—and the lead—to a marvelous-looking Hinault.

Richard, the amateur winner, completed his lap in 1:02:02. The first pro to better this was Andersen, who cut through the final turn as if on rails, riding his low-slung red Rossin bicycle to post 1:01:34. A less comfortable looking Kelly, who was snatching at his pedals in characteristic fashion, improved this by eight seconds; but less than two minutes later, a super-smooth Roche purred through in 1:00:25. This was the fastest lap recorded in eight years on the Cannes circuit and confirmed Roche as one of the world's top time trialists—but would he be able to maintain his effort for another lap?

Fignon came through 19 seconds down on Roche, but both their times were eclipsed by Hinault's 1:00:18. Since his

*A CLASSIC TIME TRIAL*

comeback from injury, the former king of time trialing had not won a single race against the clock—perhaps this grey September day would see the end of that unwanted streak.

There was a great roar from the thickening crowd when Hinault's lap time was announced, but the fans would have to be patient to see if their hero could maintain his form for another hour. The TV cameras were now in action—on motorcycle and helicopter—and they soon focused on Hinault tackling the Vallauris climb for the second time. He looked just as strong as he had a lap earlier but, remarkably, he did not gain anything on Roche, who was still only seven seconds behind at the hill summit.

In contrast, Fignon lost a further 23 seconds on the climb, where Kelly began a strong surge. The Irishman's 21:15 for this 13.4-kilometer stretch was only five seconds slower than the two leaders. He did even better on the winding roads to La Roquette. Making light work of the strong crosswinds and false flats, he caught his three-minute man, Duclos-Lassalle, on the fast, twisty drop to Mouans-Sartoux. The time checks confirmed the strength of Kelly as on this one stretch he took more than 40 seconds out of both Roche and Fignon. With 14.5 kilometers left, Kelly had moved 21 seconds ahead of Fignon, and he was only 25 seconds down on Roche.

But while Roche and Fignon weakened, Hinault kept up his form—just a second slower than Kelly on this difficult stretch—and his ultimate victory seemed virtually assured. The 29-year-old Breton was not going to throw it away now. He quickly left behind Vandenbroucke, whom he had caught just before La Roquette, and the TV motorcycle joined him for the final flourish, riding alongside the crashing waves of an unseasonably aggressive Mediterranean.

Rarely have we seen Hinault looking so aerodynamic. His back was flat, his head on the same level, his style com-

*Grand Prix des Nations • France • 1984*

pact and effective. "I've been experimenting with my position," revealed Hinault, who was riding a conventional bike with Reynolds 753 tubing, and his aero' brake levers the only concession to wind-tunnel technology. "We had already found that I was better with the saddle put back by half a centimeter, and after discussions with Paul Köchli [his La Vie Claire team coach] on Thursday, I asked the mechanic to fit a stem one centimeter longer. I tried it out as the night fell, and found that I was even better stretched out...."

So effective was his new position and burning ambition that Hinault blazed these final 14.5 kilometers in only 17 minutes 17 seconds—an average speed of well over 50 kph! It was a splendid way to finish a race that he described as "the one which has pleased me most since I won the world championship at Sallanches in 1980." He then added: "Never perhaps have I known such intense emotion as today."

While Hinault had raced to victory in 2:00:50, Kelly's 2:02:24 impressively moved him into second place, much to the chagrin of Roche, beaten by his compatriot by just 12 seconds. "I'm used to it," said Roche. "It's not the first time I've been beaten by him! I died a bit after the hill on the second lap, and came back at the end. But I was coughing up phlegm from the cold I've had...."

While Roche was disappointed, Kelly was very pleased. He had shown his ability in such a long time trial, and he had clinched the Super Prestige Pernod trophy. Could he have done better? "I didn't prepare at all for it," Kelly replied. "I should prepare a bit, maybe for a fortnight...." He might also ask for a little help from St. Patrick.

 **A CLASSIC TIME TRIAL**

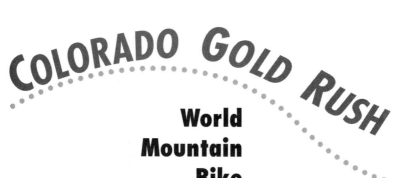

# COLORADO GOLD RUSH

## World
## Mountain
## Bike
## Championships
# United States
# September 1990

Mountain biking is the newest branch of competitive cycling. It was founded in the late-1970s, when a group of enthusiasts in Marin County, California, modified old-fashioned cruiser bikes to race each other down a trail on the side of Mount Tamalpais. By the early-'80s, the machines had evolved as specialist mountain bikes, with compact frames, smaller wheels, fat tires and ultra-low gears for going uphill. This enabled the enthusiasts to race cross-country on all types of terrain. For a few years, unofficial "world championships" were held in both America and Europe. The first official world's came to Durango, Colorado, in September 1990.

# United States

NED OVEREND has never looked better as an athlete than he did on September 16, 1990. Just before 3:30 p.m. on a warm, mainly overcast day, the mountain-bike legend cruised into the short, finishing straight at Purgatory Resort, near Durango, Colorado, more than two minutes ahead of his nearest challenger, Thomas Frischknecht of Switzerland, to win the most prestigious title of his career: the senior men's cross-country at the inaugural Union Cycliste Internationale world mountain bike championships. Before crossing the line, Overend raised both arms high to acknowledge the roar of approval from a large, exuberant crowd. Then, as if for his own satisfaction, the 35-year-old from nearby Durango punched the air with his right fist, then with his left.

Like the other hundreds of off-road racers who had traveled from 25 countries to compete in Colorado, Overend knew that this first official world off-road championship meant so much more than the two unofficial world titles he'd won at Mammoth, California, in past years. And joining him among the day's gold-medal winners was another Colorado resident: Juli Furtado. Furtado's victory over Sara Ballantyne in the senior women's cross-country was the biggest upset of the championships—and it was a win earned on merit, not luck. Furtado went out fast, as she has often done in the past. But this time, she didn't weaken or, more importantly, crash. The Yeti rider was strong on the climbs, more controlled on the downhills, and showed greater vitality than all her opponents. In contrast, Ballantyne, like many of the other off-road stars, had a jaded, end-of-season look.

Of the 10 world championships contested at the Purgatory Resort, the American riders won eight gold medals, five

*World Mountain Bike Championships • USA• 1990*

silver and six bronze—a total of 19 medals. The other 11 medals were divided among Great Britain (one silver, two bronze), Switzerland (two silver, one bronze), Canada (one gold, one silver), France (one gold), Belgium (one silver) and New Zealand (one bronze).

The cross-country races completed a successful week of mountain bike racing that impressed visitors and captivated the many new spectators. Although there were a few loose ends noticed by seasoned observers of other cycling world's, the organization masterminded by Durango promoter Ed Zink operated like clockwork. Events started on time, the rugged San Juan Mountains were majestic, the weather was clear and warm … and the racing was superb.

THE FOUR-LAP, 52-kilometer senior men's cross-country didn't go completely the way of Overend and the American national team. Although Overend (and the other team leaders) had a front-line berth on the starting grid, his U.S. teammates Rishi Grewal, Tim Rutherford, John Tomac, John Weissenrieder and Dave Wiens all lined up in the depths of the 130-man field. And when one of the inexperienced Austrian riders fell after 150 meters—just as the grass-covered start narrowed into the first uphill trail—Overend was nearly dragged into the 20-rider pileup.

"I didn't want to get caught in the traffic," Overend said, "but I didn't get in my toeclips fast enough. So the crash happened in front of me. My front wheel got hit by a guy who went down, but I managed to go wide, to get around."

By the time the men emerged at the top of the first, curving uphill—riding one behind the other like a Tour de France peloton—Overend was back in 18th place. The line was led by Italian roadman Claudio Vandelli, ahead of Belgium's Filip Meirhaege, a fast-starting Grewal, Italian off-

**COLORADO GOLD RUSH**

road champion Mario Noris, and Britain's Tim Gould. Others who'd already worked their way into the top 20 included Weissenrieder (ninth), Tomac (10th), Frischknecht (13th), Italian road sprinter Paolo Rosola (15th), Wiens (19th) and AlpineStars' Mike Kloser (20th).

This first lap didn't follow the pattern of the following laps. Instead of plunging to the right to begin the principal, excruciatingly steep climb, the riders continued uphill on a broad, dirt trail, to join the climb at the second of its four turns.

By the initial 9700-foot summit—before the course cut through the trees and headed for the top far turn—Vandelli was joined by Frischknecht, Gould, Overend and Tomac. Fiercely determined, Tomac then launched himself into the longest part of the descent—down the terrifyingly bumpy Swire's Gulch—to dramatically take the lead from Frischknecht and Overend.

To make such death-defying downhills, Tomac explained that he "corrals the adrenaline." And contradicting the conventional wisdom, the Yeti-7-Eleven pro clearly wanted to make the downhills more crucial than the uphills on this particular day. Whether he was right we will never know because Tomac flatted just as he hurtled back to the 8950-foot base level. And as the Durango-based rider spent a frustrating two minutes changing his tube, a dozen riders flashed by him—headed by Frischknecht, Overend and Gould.

These three—the ultimate medalists—were bunched together when they completed their first lap. They were followed across the line by a fading Vandelli, Kloser, Grewal, an emerging Paul Thomasberg (Giant), Noris, Weissenrieder … and Tomac. Shouting at the riders ahead of him to move out of his way, the demonstrative Tomac was clearly determined to overcome his losses as quickly as possible.

*World Mountain Bike Championships • USA• 1990*

But, now, the race was becoming an uphill battle, an exercise that suited the leading trio much better than their pursuers. And for the remaining three laps, the riders would descend the switchbacks from the first uphill, and head across the lower mountainside, before starting the main climb. Overend spun out his granny gear on this vital pitch, while former world junior cyclo-cross champion Frischknecht shouldered his bike and ran alongside the American. Gould used a combination of riding and pushing to overcome the near-30 percent grade.

By the top, the three leaders were 1:30 ahead of a still surging Grewal, who was followed at five-second intervals by Tomac (up to fifth), Weissenrieder, Kloser, Thomasberg and Vandelli. At the front, Overend was still more afraid of Gould than Frischknecht, having finished almost a minute behind the 26-year-old Englishman in the non-championship uphill race, earlier in the week. However, it was now Gould's turn for mechanical problems.

"I dropped my chain on an uphill, and couldn't get it back on," he later lamented. "I lost about 15 seconds to the other two. But I couldn't do anything about it." That same lap, descending Swire's Gulch, Gould again dropped his chain—but was able to lift it back before emerging into a short, muddy, section of single track below Purgatory's ski lift No. 6. The two front riders were now 45 seconds ahead of him.

Behind them, Ritchey's Rutherford had emerged from nowhere into fourth, two minutes down, followed by Coors Light-GT's Grewal, and Tomac, while Vandelli had now been replaced by Noris as the top Italian challenger. Also moving up on this second lap were Tom Rogers of GT (up to eighth), Fat Chance-Campagnolo's Don Myrah (11th), and Mongoose's Max Jones (15th). The next few minutes

**COLORADO GOLD RUSH**

saw national team members Rutherford and Wiens both drop out of the reckoning.

Rutherford came to grief on the descent, while Wiens was having all sorts of problems. First, his chain dropped and jammed between his chainrings. "I sorted that out," said Wiens, "and I was only just behind Max (Jones). Then my rear tire flatted, and I was about five minutes down when I restarted. And as I was descending the switchbacks, stuck behind some slow Mexicans, I fell over and broke my pedal...."

While these minor dramas were being played out, the most crucial phase of the whole race was taking place ahead. Now on their third lap, and ascending the principal uphill for the second time, the 35-year-old Overend and 20-year-old Frischknecht were again alongside each other. When the Swiss remounted after running up the steepest pitch, he was still with the American. Then, Overend started to open up a slight lead—first one meter, then two. He was three seconds ahead at the climb's second turn, and Frischknecht could do nothing about it.

"I didn't want to back off on that third lap," stated Overend later. "I was working pretty hard. I suspected I'd be stronger than (Frischknecht)." Riding in the saddle, with his chain on the middle chainring, Overend was working at his maximum. He was clearly more comfortable in the thin air than either of his immediate challengers.

And at the fourth of the climb's turns, before disappearing into the pine forest, the U.S. champion was 15 seconds clear of Frischknecht, and 1:20 ahead of Gould. Next came the surprising Noris with Rogers (at 2:00), followed in the next minute by a still determined Tomac, a cool Thomasberg, a gasping Grewal and a consistent Myrah (who had won the three-lap qualifying race, four days earlier).

*World Mountain Bike Championships • USA• 1990*

However, the strongest-looking climbers at this stage looked like the pair riding in 16th and 17th positions: Tom Collins of Marin, and Durango Wheel Club expert, Travis Brown. These two continued to move forward, and passed three more riders on the course's back loop. And before the finish, they would also overtake a fading Weissenrieder, and an exhausted Grewal—who pulled out of the race. Meanwhile, Overend continued to open up his lead on Frischknecht: one minute by the end of lap three, 1:30 by the main climb's summit, two minutes before heading back down Swire's Gulch for the last time … and 2:36 at the finish.

After completing this final lap, the tired, but happy Swiss uttered, "I almost died," before rolling on his back, and kicking his muddied, cramping legs into the air. Frischknecht then added, "Ned was clearly the best. He's the right champion."

Both Overend and Frischknecht explained that they'd taken things easy on the final descent, anxious not to fall or sustain a flat. As a result, Gould maintained the 3:24 deficit he'd held at the top of the main climb, while others closed in. The most notable of these were Thomasberg—who overtook Noris and Rogers to claim fourth place ("My best ever race"); and Jones—who went past Myrah, Tomac, Noris and Rogers, to finish fifth.

TAKING THE LEAD on the first climb, and extending it throughout the three-lap 39-kilometer senior women's race, the short, powerful racer in the stars-and-stripes jersey rode to an easy victory. However, the winner wasn't the expected Sara Ballantyne, but her national teammate and Boulder neighbor, Juli Furtado. It was the upset of the championships, and a result that left Ballantyne tight-lipped, and doing her best to put on a brave face.

 **COLORADO GOLD RUSH**

After finishing 2:27 behind Yeti's exuberant Furtado, Specialized ace Ballantyne hugged her younger colleague, and said, "This is good for you." And trying to explain her own disappointment, the 29-year-old Ballantyne told reporters, "I was waiting for her to collapse. I usually wait until she falls on a pile of rocks—but not this time. She had a good race." However, Ballantyne admitted that, unusually for her, she had some cramping on the inside of her thigh muscles, on the last lap. And friends said that the hot favorite was ultra-nervous before the race, and was able to eat only half a pancake for breakfast. And that nervous energy possibly cost megawinner Ballantyne the victory in the race she most wanted to win.

From the start, when Canada's Elladee Brown made a brief appearance in the lead, the race quickly became a battle between Furtado, Ballantyne … and a third Boulder resident—world road race silver medalist, Ruthie Matthes of Ritchey. These three were well clear by the top of the main climb, on its easier ascent; and by the end of lap one, Furtado had already pulled 45 seconds ahead of the other two, with Susan DeMattei of DiamondBack a further minute behind, in fourth.

Matthes surprisingly outclimbed Ballantyne on the second lap, and briefly held second spot, before dropping back again around the course's back loop. DeMattei was holding strongly in fourth, while fifth spot was taken briefly by yet another U.S. national team member, Julia Ingersoll of KHS. Ingersoll overtook both Brown and West Germany's Susi Buchwieser on the main climb on this second lap … but she never looked like catching DeMattei or Matthes.

Afterward, Ingersoll exclaimed, "This wasn't a mountain bike race. It wasn't technical. It was one giant hill climb." On the final lap, while Furtado continued to extend

*World Mountain Bike Championships • USA• 1990*

her lead, Buchwieser, only 19, showed remarkable stamina. The powerfully built West German recaught Ingersoll, raced by a suffering DeMattei, and was only 30 seconds behind bronze medalist Matthes at the finish. Buchwieser's recovery showed that the Americans may not have everything their own way in future years ... although 23-year-old Furtado also has plenty of time for improvement.

Since leaving the U.S. alpine ski team, Furtado has had remarkable success in cycling. She was national road champion in 1989, and has improved consistently since turning to full-time, off-road racing in mid-July. "I've trained really hard for the past month," explained Furtado after her win. And her methods were clearly better than Ballantyne's, who had twice flown to Europe and back to clinch her overall title in the Grundig World Cup. The resultant jet lag, and the pressure from her sponsors and supporters, meant that, for once, Ballantyne had to settle for silver instead of gold.

 **COLORADO GOLD RUSH**

# HOME IS OUR HERO

## Nissan International Classic
## Ireland
## September 1985

In the mid-1980s, Irish cycling was at its zenith. Sean Kelly was the No. 1-ranked rider in the world, thanks to his domination of Europe's one-day classics, and Stephen Roche was on the verge of his extraordinary 1987, when he became only the second rider in history to win the Tour de France, Giro d'Italia and world championship in the same year. In celebration of their favorite sons, the people of Ireland flocked to the roadsides to witness the first Nissan International Classic, a five-day race that started and finished in the heart of Dublin.

# Ireland

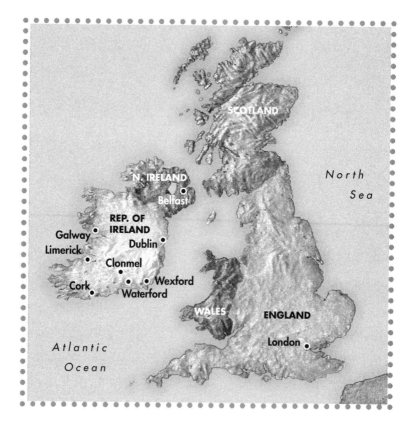

SCOTLAND

N. IRELAND

Belfast

North Sea

REP. OF IRELAND

Galway

Limerick

Dublin

Clonmel

Wexford

Cork

Waterford

WALES

ENGLAND

London

Atlantic Ocean

HEARN'S HOTEL in Clonmel, County Tipperary, had never experienced a day quite like this one. It was a warm Friday morning in late September. The street was filled with people jammed between the brick walls of the hotel and the Town Hall opposite. So dense was the crowd that forcing a way through to the hotel entrance was almost as difficult as trying to get a quote from a stage winner at the Tour de France. There were dozens of children outside, pressing their noses against the hotel's windows and waiting around its broad front door. "Who won the race?" they piped. A reply of "Kelly first, Roche second," elicited an excited cheer of shrill, young voices. They had not known the result of the just-finished race because it was a time trial, which is not the easiest of events for an uninitiated spectator to understand. And the margin by which Sean Kelly won this third stage of the five-day Nissan International Classic was something that even Stephen Roche had difficulty understanding.

Roche was tipped to win the time trial. After missing the vital break on the race's opening stage—won by Kelly—and losing all hope of overall success, Roche restored his fans' confidence by making a brilliant solo attack 24 hours later, to take third place on the second stage, to Kelly's hometown of Carrick-on-Suir.

Kelly's homecoming was every bit as emotional as expected, with the town's 5000 population tripled for the occasion. The stage had kept Kelly in the yellow jersey, equal on time with the two dangerous Dutch riders, Adri Van der Poel and Teun Van Vliet. "I'm confident that I can beat Van der Poel by a few seconds," said Kelly, "but I am not sure about Van Vliet. l don't know how good he is in a time trial."

Kelly knew that he had to race at his best if he was going to win this time trial. The course measured 13 miles

(21 kilometers) from Sean Kelly Square, Carrick, along the rolling N24 highway to Clonmel. There was barely a breath of wind in the Suir valley. The morning mist drifted back and forth across a pale, watery sun. It was warm and humid—not ideal time-trialing weather— and not at all like most days when Kelly had ridden this route on training rides with the Carrick Wheelers, the cycling club he joined as a skinny teenager.

"There is usually a strong west wind blowing against you on that road," said Bobby Power, a Carrick Wheeler who achieved a high amateur standard as a racer. "I can remember Sean riding with us when he was 17. He would come out and torture himself. To make a ride harder, Sean would always wait for people who punctured and help them back to the group. One time, we waited for Sean's brother Vincent on the hilly coast road to Dungarvan. We rode back to find Vincent, and eventually passed the place where he stopped. He had obviously turned for home. We were about six minutes behind the others by then, and it took us more than 15 miles to catch them, working bit-and-bit. Another day, Sean waited so many times that he was dead and had to take a shortcut home. He told me later that he only just made it."

Power also recounted a more recent incident: "Sean was back home for a short time between races. He rode a local race with us for training, but with about five miles to go, he decided to chase two riders who were a minute up. I went with him. We came to a little rise and Sean suddenly stood on the pedals and left me. The road was dry, but he made the wheel spin, just burning up the rubber. You've got to be on a motorbike to turn on that kind of power." It was this potential power that Kelly would need for a time trial that would probably decide the outcome of this inaugural Nissan race.

 **HOME IS OUR HERO**

Most of Carrick was in the triangular-shaped Sean Kelly Square to see the start of this historic stage. The crowd chanted, stamped their feet and cheered all 75 riders, as they set off at one-minute intervals. Some were clearly more serious than others. Englishman Tony Doyle, who was building up to the six-day track season, was one of the serious ones. He had missed the stage-one break and knew that the time trial, his specialty, offered him one of his few chances of success. The world championship pursuit silver medalist was riding a low-profile bike with a rear disc wheel and a small, spoked front wheel. Wearing an aerodynamic helmet and a serious expression, Doyle was the first to break the 26-minute barrier, recording 25:33, a speed of 30.643 mph (49.315 kph). It looked as though it would be a tough time to beat.

Before Roche mounted the starting ramp, the closest to come to Doyle's time were the 20-year-old British hope Joey McLoughlin (25:50) and Belgian star Ludo Peeters (25:40). Roche was confident. He was the only rider using two disc wheels, the front one smaller than the rear, on his low-profile machine. He started like a rocket and averaged more than 32 mph (51.6 kph), completing the first five miles in 9:21. He has a delightfully smooth style, his upper body not rocking like most cyclists. On the downhill and flat sections, he turned a 53x12 gear (119 inches) at a steady 100 rpm. On the uphills, he stood on the pedals or shifted down to 53x13 (110 inches). It was impressive to watch.

Roche caught two riders: veteran British pro Keith Lambert of Falcon and Dutch rider Henry Manders of Kwantum. Lambert blew his cheeks out in astonishment, when passed by Roche after only four miles, while Manders hung out his tongue to indicate his respect. Roche completed the first 10 miles in 18:44, with a fastest mile in 1:45, and a slowest of

*Nissan International Classic • Ireland • 1985*

1:59. He slowed slightly over the final three miles, but his eventual 24:58 was clearly a ride of the highest quality.

Shortly after Roche began his time trial, Kelly, warming up, came riding slowly in the opposite direction. The race leader was sitting up and taking a drink, when he looked across at his friend and rival with a quizzical expression. Kelly was using a normal aluminum-framed Vitus with a rear Mavic disc wheel.

Once Kelly began, in contrast to the robot-like style of Roche, he displayed the energy described by Power. He used all of the wide road, "taking left-hand bends on the right side of the road," according to one witness. At halfway, he was about level with Roche, but then, as Kelly said later, "I could see Van der Poel and Van Vliet up ahead on the road, and I did everything to get on to them."

Kelly's "everything" took him 23 seconds ahead of Roche at 10 miles (reached in 18:11), at which point he was closing fast on the two Dutchmen. The rest of the race was captured beautifully by the motorcycle-mounted TV camera of RTE, which followed Kelly as he sped like a hurricane past the astonished Van Vliet. Within another half-mile Van der Poel was fighting for Kelly's back wheel, and the pair engaged in a hectic sprint for the finish line. First across the line was the Irishman, who was saturated with sweat that poured profusely down his face. But what time had he done?

Van der Poel, a fine rider in a medium distance time trial such as this, had recorded 25:10, only 12 seconds slower than Roche—which meant that Kelly's time was an extraordinary 24:09, a speed of 32.420 mph (52.173 kph). It was the fastest time trial longer than 20 kilometers that any cyclist has ridden in the sport's history. And he had done it on a course that climbed more than it descended.

**HOME IS OUR HERO**

The only performances on a par with Kelly's Tipperary time trial are those by two world hour record holders. Francesco Moser raced at 31.676 mph (50.977 kph) to win the 42-kilometer final stage of the 1984 Giro d'Italia; and Ole Ritter of Denmark went faster than both Moser and Kelly with a 33.691 mph (54.219 kph) performance in a 19-kilometer stage of the Tour of Sardinia in 1971. But the Dane had a tail wind on the Sardinian course, which started at a 738-foot elevation in Sassari to finish at sea level in Port Torres. On the same course two years earlier, Ritter had been more than two minutes slower in less favorable conditions.

Kelly's time trial victory was the athletic highlight of the week—and it effectively won him the race. After the stage, sitting in Hearn's Hotel over a lunch of omelet, rice and salad, while children gaped at him through the windows, Kelly was delighted to learn of his speed. "I've not been able to ride a good time trial all year," he admitted. "But today, for the first time I could really hurt myself at 100 percent. I knew I had to ride hard to beat Van der Poel and Van Vliet, and riding at home must have given me the incentive to go that fast."

There had been some other good performances on this memorable day, not least of which were those by Spenco's Nigel Dean (seventh in 26:12) and Roche's teammate Paul Sherwen (26:18). "I haven't tried as hard as that in a time trial since 1980, when I came fifth in a stage up Mont Faron in the Tour Méditerranéen," noted Sherwen. That ride clinched him fourth place overall in the French stage race; this one kept him in fifth place....

The hierarchy in this Nissan Classic had been established on the opening stage from Dublin to Wexford. On paper, there was nothing difficult about the 98-mile route that skirted the Wicklow Hills to the west in a large arc.

*Nissan International Classic • Ireland • 1985*

There were two hill primes: one no more than a gentle rise to the Kildare-Carlow county boundary after 42 miles; the other a short, steep ramp on a tricky 3.5-mile finishing loop. Intermittent rain and a strong head wind discouraged early breaks; and the 76 starters were still grouped when Kelly set the race in motion on a patriotic note, by winning the first, hectic hot-spot sprint in the wide, dipping main street of Naas.

The organizers had done a good job to assemble 18 teams for this revamped Irish tour: six continental pro teams, six national amateur selections and six sponsored British squads. La Vie Claire and a Danish amateur team were welcome late additions, but there were problems with two pro formations about to disband. Safir withdrew and La Redoute, Roche's team, was able to compete only because temporary sponsorship was given by battery manufacturer Ever Ready Ireland. It was unusual to have four men per team, instead of the usual six or seven, for an international stage race, and it was obvious that temporary alliances would develop through the five days. This was to prove a contributory factor in the first-day split.

Beyond Naas, the race turned south, and then southeast at Castledermot, a village of stone cottages, tin-roofed barns, a beautiful ruined abbey and rich fields—where the "National Ploughing Championships" would take place later in the year. The change of direction meant that the wind was now blowing from the riders' right, encouraging them to attack. As we looked back down the narrow, winding road, the most visible jerseys were the yellow-and-white ones of Dries Nissan riders Teun Van Vliet and Hennie Kuiper. Van Vliet attacked two or three times, before getting clear with British pros John Herety (Ever Ready-Marlboro) and Steve Jones (Raleigh-Weinmann) just after the prime hill.

**HOME IS OUR HERO**

"Van Vliet was flying," said Herety, "and I couldn't have lasted much longer when we were caught. It was one long line on the descent and I could see the bunch splitting. I thought this could be a danger. Just then my teammate Steve Fleetwood punctured and we waited for him. That was when the break went."

Herety's team leader Graham Jones had trained hard for this race, desperate to prove his stage-racing capabilities after a season of British criteriums. But he missed the 10-strong break—that was caused by another Van Vliet thrust—and tried to bridge the 15-second gap through the twisting streets of Tullow. With him went Joey McLoughlin from the rival ANC team. "But Joey wouldn't work," explained Herety. "He said his teammate Gary Thomson was in the break. That was stupid because with two men in the break, they could have had the team race sewn up."

No others got close to the 10 breakaways, who began working in close harmony despite representing 10 different teams. Besides Van Vliet, those working the hardest were Kelly, Van der Poel, Dean, Kim Eriksen of La Vie Claire and Johnny Weltz, the Dane who won a silver medal in the world amateur road race championship three weeks earlier. Also in the break were Thomson, French amateur Philippe Magnien, Tony James of Falcon and Sherwen—who had covered the move for team leader Roche.

Sherwen soon found himself an unwelcome passenger on an express speeding through archetypical Irish countryside of patchwork fields, narrow fern-lined lanes and white-painted farmhouses nestling among green hills. The break's lead mounted from 30 seconds at Ardattin to 90 seconds at pretty Clonegall, where a farmer with a small white dog tucked inside his jacket were among the spectators watching the racers pour over a stone, hump-backed bridge spanning

*Nissan International Classic • Ireland • 1985*

a fast-flowing salmon stream. When the leaders emerged from the back roads at Bunclody, 26 miles from Wexford, their advance was over three minutes. Another seven minutes would be added before the finish in Wexford.

The fight for the first yellow jersey was begun by Van der Poel, who accelerated clear just after crossing the broad River Slaney, two miles out of the town. Kelly moved to the front of the line to control chasing operations, but the tall 26-year-old Dutchman, fresh from winning the Paris-Brussels classic, began the two laps of the finishing circuit with a 10-second lead on the others. He was caught on the first climb of the hill, which reared up between stone walls to a school at the top of the circuit. The second time up, the students and teachers saw a darting attack by Kelly himself. "It wasn't a flat-out effort," said Kelly. "I attacked because I didn't want anyone to get away before the sprint."

It was a brilliant tactical move by the Skil team leader. Eriksen, a long-jawed Dane, was the first rider to bridge the gap, on the descent between rain-soaked crowds to the seafront. Then the pace slowed and the parrying started for the uphill finishing sprint of 300 yards.

Kelly's wife Linda was among the head-craning spectators noisily awaiting the outcome. Thomson had been dropped on the hill; Magnien quickly disappeared from the picture; and Van Vliet went backwards when Van der Poel made his expected jump. But Kelly matched the Kwantum rider and came bursting through to win the stage. He would be wearing the yellow jersey home to Carrick-on-Suir the next day.

The thousands of Kelly fans who congregated on Carrick's Main Street and Seskin Hill were fully expecting their homecoming hero to win the second stage, but a win to order is not easy in cycling. It proved a fairly lively stage,

**HOME IS OUR HERO**

despite being the longest: 115 miles. Roche attempted a breakaway in Waterford, after 36 miles, much to the delight of a Tour de France-size crowd; but he was reeled in before the town's famous crystal glassworks were reached. Then, in the sea mist at Dunabrattin Head, Graham Jones and new pro Paul Watson climbed with the gulls for a brief flight from the peloton. "The Belgians and Dutch chased us down," said a dejected Watson, who had quit the Belgian Fangio team midway through the Tour de l'Avenir two weeks earlier, and was racing here for Roche in the Ever Ready-La Redoute team.

Ironically, it was Fangio team leader Eric Van Lancker who counterattacked, and when he was joined by Kwantum's Leo Van Vliet, there was no reaction from the other continentals. With Milk Race winner Van Lancker setting a fierce pace up the hills, they arrived in Carrick 30 miles later, four minutes ahead of the peloton. There was no danger of either of them taking the race lead, but that Kelly stage win was now out of the question. The crowd cheered the two European riders anyway.

Their cheers were much bigger, of course, for Kelly. When he arrived at the head of the pack to start four laps of a five-mile finishing circuit, the crowd's roar could probably be heard at his parents' farm, five miles away. They greeted Roche almost as warmly, when the Dubliner made a brilliant solo over the last 11 miles to take third place, two minutes behind stage winner Van Vliet, who left Van Lancker on the final climb. Twelve seconds behind Roche, there was a ferocious sprint between Kelly, Van der Poel and Teun Van Vliet that was narrowly taken by Van der Poel. The rest of the field was scattered around the tough circuit, after being humbled by the 16-percent grade of Seskin Hill. "I used to *walk* up it on my ride home from school," said Kelly.

*Nissan International Classic • Ireland • 1985*

After the excitement of the Carrick finish and the Cionmel time trial, there was a feeling that the rest of the race might fall flat. It was a feeling that was soon forgotten. At the tiniest villages and on the smallest of hills, there were still crowds of Tour de France proportions to watch the spectacular fourth stage from Clonmel to Cork that took place on the afternoon of the time trial.

There was some early action in the stage that culminated in a breakaway on The Vee, the race's highest hill that climbs through the beautiful Knockmealdown Mountains above Ballyporeen, the ancestral home of President Reagan. The break was started by Brian Holm, another of the Danish world championship riders. He was joined by British pros McLoughlin and Malcolm Elliott, continentals Henry Manders of Kwantum and Dirk Durant of Fangio, and Magnien.

It would have been a potentially winning combination without Magnien, but the experienced French amateur was still dangerous on general classification, and, after Holm had snaffled the mountain prime at the 1112-foot summit, Frenchman Frédéric Vichot led the chase for Kelly to bring the field together in the dark, damp, delightful dale of the River Blackwater. Crossing the river into Fermoy—before another huge crowd—Elliott won a rapid sprint from Irish amateur Raphael Kimmage, to take a firm grip on the hot-spot leader's white jersey.

There was no more serious action until Kelly and Roche led the still compact group into Cork along a hilly back road, to join the top end of a dramatic two-mile finishing circuit in the city. The riders had to climb the 25-percent grade of St. Patrick's Hill four times, all the while watched by a massive crowd. It was the perfect stage for another Kelly-Roche show. The two Irish stars were soon part of a 13-strong group that left the rest struggling. And they

**HOME IS OUR HERO**

matched every move until the start of the final lap, when Roche brilliantly countered an attack by Van Lancker and sped clear to a fine stage victory. He arrived with 10 seconds to spare on Kelly, who sprinted away from Van der Poel and a gutsy McLoughlin for the second Irish one-two of the day.

Roche and Kelly were by now on the crest of a very high wave, and the next morning, on the fourth day, they gave a repeat performance for an even larger audience at Limerick. Graham Jones—still seeking a win—made a well-timed attack on the five-mile finishing circuit. "I got the gap," said a frustrated Jones, "but Roche came up to me and jumped me with only two miles to go." Roche went on to a popular victory, Jones was absorbed by the pack in the last 200 yards, and Kelly blasted down Limerick's widest shopping street to take an exciting second place from British pro criterium champion Dave Miller, London amateur Nick Barnes and Van der Poel.

The fourth day's second 66-mile stint proved uneventful—until the finishing circuit in Galway, where Jones again attacked, and was again countered. Kwantum's Ludo Peeters joined the Ever Ready man. But Teun Van Vliet and Van der Poel crossed the 50-yard gap on the last lap, and Van Vliet immediately broke away on a short hill to earn an opportunist win. He was followed into Eyre Square at the end of a gloriously sunny day by Van der Poel, Peeters and Jones, with Kelly taking another rapid downhill sprint for fifth.

The Irish nation was hoping that the man in the yellow jersey would climax this first Nissan Classic with a stage victory in Dublin. This would certainly have pleased the impressively large crowd that clung to the barriers and buildings along the length of the Irish capital's world famous O'Connell Street ... but there was no arguing with a clinical stage victory by the cold-eyed Van der Poel. The Dutchman

*Nissan International Classic • Ireland • 1985*

benefited from an initial policing job by Peeters on optimistic attacker Neil Martin of Bilton-Condor, Roche's brother-in-law, before streaking away around Parnell Square a mile from the line. With first place gone, Kelly took no chances on the final U-shaped turn, and was clearly beaten in the second-place sprint by Elliott and the rapid Dutch amateur Rob Harmeling.

The enormous crowd mobbed around the winners' podium placed in front of the white-pillared Post Office Building, where the Irish Republic had its origins 70 years ago. Perhaps September 29, 1985, will become as famous a date: the day that national hero Sean Kelly won the first Nissan International Classic and converted his country to the sport of cycling. "Home is our hero," proclaimed his Carrick-on-Suir fans, happy that he didn't take the long way home.

 **HOME IS OUR HERO**

# A CLASSIC FINALE

**Tour**
**of**
**Lombardy**
Italy
October 1968

Every year, the European road season comes to a close among the falling leaves of northern Italy's lake district, at the fabled Tour of Lombardy. This one-day classic, dating from 1905, now closes the annual UCI World Cup competition; until the mid-1980s, it marked the end of the Super Prestige Pernod contest, a season-long series that encompassed all of the classics, as well as the major stages races and grand Tours. The race's mountainous course makes it one of the toughest on the calendar, while the high-class field in 1968 made it one the most spectacular editions on record.

# Italy

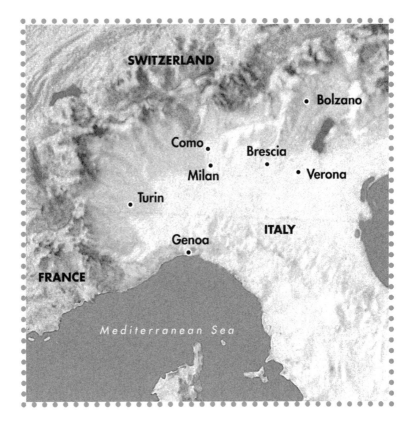

"BE OUTSIDE the Ristorante Tirreno near the Central Station in Milan at eight o'clock on Saturday morning."

These were my "starting instructions" from Signor Michelotto, assistant organizer of the 62nd Tour of Lombardy for the biggest Italian sports daily, *La Gazzetta dello Sport*. It was Thursday afternoon and we were in the *Gazzetta's* impressive *organizzazione* office, where they were busily sorting out bundles of programs and typing out lists and instructions—probably routine work compared to their year-long task of promoting the three-week Giro d'Italia (Tour of Italy). But back to that other Tour I had come to see....

The Tour of Lombardy is no longer a true Tour (or circuit), as it was for its first edition in 1905. And as it was in the 1940s and '50s, when the springboard for the legendary Fausto Coppi's five solo victories was the steep northern side of the infamous Madonna del Ghisallo pass, with the race ending at the Vigorelli velodrome in Milan. Now, the *arrivo* is 50 kilometers to the north, in Como, where I was staying the night before this 1968 edition. To make my 8 a.m. rendezvous in Milan, I had to catch the 6:41 a.m. train from Como, and I was wondering whether I would be on time as the crowded commuter special crawled through a thick mist, with its bell clanging in a mournful monotony. I need not have worried, and by 8:10 I was sitting snugly in the back of a dark green Alfa Romeo 1750 sports car, on the way to the actual start of the race at the State University, five miles north of the city center.

We passed several riders on the busy highway, and arrived at the same time as German star Rudi Altig, who was wearing his light-blue Salvarani team wool track-suit and a plastic racing cape to combat the cold mist. The weather only added to the confusion that typifies the start of a big

*Tour of Lombardy • Italy • 1968*

race—with press cars, bikes, riders and fans all gathered haphazardly in front of the University campus. It was now 8:25 and the *partenza* was scheduled for 8:45.

From the list of 160 officially engaged to ride, there was only one *inglese*, Derek Harrison, and so I went off in search of him. An announcer was jabbering away in Italian, still asking riders to sign on, as I made my way through the dense crowds. Once onto the University grounds, things were better. The team cars were parked in a line around the main building. I was looking for Harrison's Frimatic team wagon. No sign of it.

There was the Pelforth team car, with Tour de France champion Jan Janssen sitting relaxed by its side, while further on multi-world champion Rik Van Looy was talking to Belgian teammate Willy Derboven, one of Van Looy's old "Red Guard." And just on the corner was the Bic team car with Lucien Aimar, resplendent in his French national champion's tricolor jersey, measuring the wheelbase of his bike with a folding metal ruler and angrily telling off his mechanic. Pre-race nerves, I suspect. A smiling Charly Grosskost, the flamboyant French rider, looked much happier, with his feet up inside the car, as he chatted with another French standout, Bernard Guyot, who was leaning down from his Lejeune mount. Still no sign of the Frimatic team! Next came Italian Franco Bitossi and his Filotex henchmen, whom I had seen the day before in Como, buying grapes at the end of a morning training run. I was around the back of the building by now—and, finally, there was the only Englishman riding the Tour of Lombardy!

I said it was a surprise to see him there. Harrison agreed: "I packed up for the year last week after Paris-Tours, and then on Monday night got a phone call to go to De Gribaldy's at Besançon ... to travel down here! Still, it was a

 **A CLASSIC FINALE**

great drive coming over the Alps in the sunshine yesterday." He went on to say that he had been in the hospital for four weeks following his Tour de France crash, and recuperated for a further two weeks before getting back on his bike; since then, he had only been racing for about a month. "I find it impossible even to finish a hard criterium at the moment, let alone a classic. I only lasted 150 kilometers in Paris-Tours—but it was 30 mph most of the time! I've only come here to make up the team and see what the race is like."

Clearly, he was unprepared for the *Giro di Lombardia,* and was still adjusting the height of his bars when I left him, with a soigneur asking if he wanted some embrocation on his legs.

As I ran back to the main road, the announcer was calling the riders to the line amid a scene of panic, with cars revving up and my two Italian companions impatiently waiting to get into the line of preceding press cars. Preceding, because the Tour of Lombardy is equivalent to a mountain stage in a major stage race, with a total of 10,000 feet of actual climbing to be done. This comparison is even more true now that the finish is at Como, the last major climb being in the city itself. And the quality of the recent winners—Gianna Motta, Tom Simpson, Felice Gimondi and Bitossi—only confirms the opinion that a "sprinter" is unlikely to win today's Lombardy. In fact, it has now developed into a race as cherished as Paris-Roubaix, mainly because of the nature of the bumps—little ones (cobblestones) in the French classic, as opposed to big ones (mountains) in the Italian. A quick glance down the program to see who was riding only proved the point—Eddy Merckx, Herman Van Springel, Walter Godefroot (the 1-2-3 at Roubaix), plus Raymond Poulidor, Janssen, Altig, Gimondi, Van Looy, Motta, Bitossi, Michele Dancelli, Jo De Roo, Ward Sels, Ger-

*Tour of Lombardy • Italy • 1968*

ben Karstens, Georges Van Coningsloo, Dino Zandegu and Valère Van Sweevelt (all winners of major classics)—a full list indeed!

Such a classy field was gathered not only to dispute the Tour of Lombardy but also the finale of the Superprestige Pernod competition. This was the situation in this season-long contest that takes in all of the world's major classics and stage races: 1. Van Springel, 194 points; 2. Gimondi, 180; 3. Godefroot, 165; 4. Janssen, 158; 5. Merckx, 141.

Any of these five could still pull off the first prize of $5000—and the prestige that goes with it! The points at stake in this final counting event were for the first 10 finishers, as follows: 60, 40, 30, 20, 15, 10, 8, 6, 5, 4. For fifth-placed Merckx to become the new holder of the Pernod trophy, he had to win this race, with Van Springel in eighth place, or worse—a possibility. While a result of 1. Gimondi, 2. Van Springel would give the same result in the Super-prestige ratings. Therefore, to retain his position at the top, Van Springel really had to win a classic—something that he had still not done!

When lining up, each team is obliged to have only one of its riders in the front row. so that every sponsor represented in the event has an equal chance of figuring in films of the start! This was one of the special instructions printed in the informative race brochure; as it happened, a rather abortive regulation, since there would not be many films taken in this thick morning mist. It was now 8:45 precisely, on Saturday, October 12, 1968, and the 62nd Giro di Lombardia was underway. A field of 142 *coureurs* sped off into the gloom.

*8:47 a.m.* The first attack. And these were not unknowns: Van Looy (Willem II), Ferdinand Bracke (Peu-

**A CLASSIC FINALE**

geot), and Raymond Riotte (Mercier). Three kilometers later they were back in the fold, but they had set the tone for a rapid start: 46 kilometers were covered in the first hour, as many as in the flat Paris-Tours a week before! Italians Bordrero (Molteni), De Pra (Salvarani), Lievore (Kelvinator), Andreoli (Filotex) and Franchini (Germanvox-Vega) were all among the most ardent of those early attackers.

The wide highway had now given way to a two-lane road, and the mist had already succumbed to a weak sunshine. Crowds waited at the roadside, especially at intersections where cross traffic had been halted. I was surprised to see that cars were still coming the other way on the race route; and as we climbed gradually to Inverigo (16 miles), the line of press cars was slowed by a ponderous truck lunging away in front—with the race only a few minutes behind. The police motorcyclists were more than a match for these conditions, however, and they always seemed to wave other traffic off the road before the race arrived.

*9:20 a.m.* The riders were all back together as they turned left at the top of the easy Inverigo climb. There followed a quick swoop on the still wide road that curved to the right and then rose again to the village of Anzano (20 miles). It appeared we were in Motta country now, testified by a huge "Forza Motta" banner and a life-size model of the Italian star astride a racing machine…. A crowd of several hundred lined the streets as we turned sharp right, then left, and began a steep winding descent on a bumpy back road.

*9:30 a.m.* "Polidori, Panizza, Riotte and Wagtmans have a 200-meter lead," the race radio informed us, followed by the urgent order to press cars: "*Accelerare, accelerare….*" The 50-mph line of swaying cars was too close to the four attackers. But soon, there were only three, Wladimiro Panizza (Pepsi-Cola) having dropped back to the bunch. We were

*Tour of Lombardy • Italy • 1968*

now nearing Erba and the start of the long climb to Sormano and the Ghisallo. At Erba, Giancarlo Polidori (Pepsi), Rini Wagtmans (Willem II) and Riotte had a 40-second lead, and so this was the first serious action. The first 25 miles had been covered in 48 minutes!

The race now entered the Assina valley, which culminates at the Madonna del Ghisallo, 10 miles and 1600 feet higher. With the sun warming the still morning air, we motored ahead, through Longone, where an idyllic vista opened up over the tiny Lago di Segrino, a jewel of a lake shimmering between tall Lombardy poplars and towering mountains. The road then climbed between the stone and stucco houses of Canzo, and instead of taking the old 12-percent village street of Asso, climbed from the rushing waters of the Lambro river on a wide, horseshoe-shaped bypass.

We parked at the top by a metal guardrail and looked down through the haze for signs of action. At 9:49 a.m., the white-blue-and-purple-clad trio emerged from between the imposing, square houses below, as they slowly tackled the first really steep slopes of the day. They were not going that slow, however, as it was a full minute before the still intact peloton of 130 men also burst through into the sunshine, a throbbing mass of colors stretching out into a giant string of beads, as the pace quickened at the front. The three fugitives were still moving smoothly as they passed us ... but just around the corner, after plunging through a short tunnel, was the turnoff to Sormano.

The riders made a six-mile loop here, tackling a steep, hairpinned road to the village of Sormano, perched in the trees 800 feet above us, before dropping back to the valley on another road. After only 30 miles of racing, this "Wall of Sormano" is a severe test for those riders "just along for the ride." In a post-race press conference, chief organizer Vin-

 **A CLASSIC FINALE**

cenzo Torriani criticized the lack of fight shown by the majority of riders, saying that he had "not engaged 160 riders so that three-quarters of them could have a free day's outing to Milan." Maybe Signor Torriani's Sormano climb is one of the chief reasons for this lack of fighting spirit. As Harrison later remarked: "I was not the first one to get shot off. I carried on after the descent, but then a group of Italians appeared coming the other way, taking off their numbers. They shouted to me— "Arrison, Como!' In other words, this was the last shortcut to the finish at Como, and quitting the race later on would have meant a six-hour trip in the bus for abandoned riders."

From the racing angle, the picture is completely different, because the Sormano-Ghisallo duet serves to split the big field up and leaves in command only those riders with aspirations to victory. Indeed, Polidori, Wagtmans and Riotte were all absorbed on the Wall by a group of race favorites and men on form. This was the order of the leaders at the Sormano summit: Panizza (Pepsi), Ricci (Mercier), Poulidor (Mercier), Bellone (Mercier), Campaner (Mercier), Moser (Pepsi), Dancelli (Pepsi), Michelotto (Max Meyer), Merckx (Faema), Delisle (Peugeot), Karstens (Peugeot), Vandenbossche (Faema), Gimondi (Salvarani), Altig (Salvarani), Bitossi (Filotex), Motta (Molteni), Van Springel (Mann-Grundig), Carletto (Salvarani), Janssen (Pelforth), Adorni (Faema), Houbrechts (Mann) and Galbo (Max Meyer).

On the steep, switchback descent back to the start of the original climb, a partial regrouping took place and 40 men were together to attack the remainder of the Ghisallo climb. A TV car was waiting a mile from the top, a crash-helmeted cameraman strapped securely on its roof, waiting to film the leading riders over the summit. The first man in his viewfinder was another of the adventurous Frenchmen from

*Tour of Lombardy • Italy • 1968*

the Mercier team, Francis Campaner. He had gained 30 seconds on the group, with teammate Walter Ricci shadowing Moser in between. This morning, there was only a sparse gathering outside the Madonna del Ghisallo cyclists' chapel—a shrine that houses the old bicycles and race jerseys of Italian legends like Coppi, Bartali and Girardengo.

Instead of the usual view of distant peaks, a thick white blanket of mist still shielded Lake Como, 1800 feet below. On the breathtaking descent, we realized that Campaner, the 22-year-old Frenchman from near Bordeaux, was out to make a name for himself, as it pays to impress your directeur sportif at the time of signing contracts for the following season! And it seemed that his team were backing him to the hilt. By the foot of the descent, at Bellagio (47 miles), he had stretched his lead to 50 seconds, while Jean-Pierre Genet, a more experienced Mercier team man, was now sitting on the chasing Neri (Max Meyer).

A dozen miles now separated us from Lecco and the start of the next big climb, the Colle di Balisio. Those miles were probably the flattest of the whole race, and also the most sinuous. It was an old corniche road hugging the edge of the mountains that dipped almost vertically into the mirror-like lake, frequently plunging through unlit tunnels hewn out of the rock. As we slowly cruised along this narrow, bumpy back road, we soon spotted the brave Campaner plugging away on his own, with Neri and Genet coming up fast, and the bunch now a minute back. Around a few more bends and then we could see the two chasers flashing between the trees across a small bay, and about to catch the leader. It was now 11:54 a.m., and my time check made the trio only 30 seconds up on the bunch.

As the small industrial town of Lecco came into view at the end of the lake, the road became straighter and wider,

 **A CLASSIC FINALE**

and the crowds were the biggest we had seen that day. Left across a steel-girder bridge over the Adda river and the seven-mile Balisio climb began immediately, rearing up through the town on the smooth pink cobblestones in which this region abounds. The race radio told us that the breakaways had stretched their lead to 50 seconds at the entrance to the town ... but the massive crowds now lining the route would surely see a change in that.

After one or two turns between the houses and high stone walls, the road left the town to climb straight up a steep, green valley. The sun was now beating down, but the rugged grey mountains that rose up to 8000 feet in front of us were still partly lost in the haze. Although Genet and Neri were quickly dropped, it seemed that the stars were still content to watch each other and not unduly exert themselves. This was a real brute of a climb, and the cobbles continued the whole way up, the last three miles being steeply hairpinned with the tifosi gathered three-deep on the "open" side of the road, so that they could see the riders toiling up toward them for several minutes. At the top, young Campaner was again on his own and 20 seconds clear of a small group headed by Dancelli and Bitossi.

The Frenchman had been away for 30 miles, so it was no surprise when he was quickly caught by Bitossi on the wide, straight road that started the rather gentle descent. We were now in the high-level Valsassina, a charming grassy valley that is a ski center in winter, its bright wooden chalets competing with new apartment blocks in the village of Barzio across the green meadows. Ahead of us was the first feed zone at Introbio (72 miles). In most countries, this means a roughly 400-yard stretch of road where all the team cars pull up and their occupants hand up cotton musette bags to the riders; but here, the feed zone was three miles

*Tour of Lombardy • Italy • 1968*

long, and musettes could be handed up at any point on that stretch. However, most of the road was gradually descending, and the majority of team managers had gathered on a short hill that climbed up to the village of Introbio itself.

The race had been going for three hours, and a glance at the profile map showed that there were still 93 miles remaining, with four big climbs packed into the last 40. There was to be another feed at Porlezza (118 miles), but a missed musette here could mean a missed victory on that strength-sapping finale.

Consequently, Bitossi was more interested in eating than attacking, and had probably gone out front to be sure of getting his own special rations. Two men who had already been written down in our notebooks took advantage of the situation, and soon Genet and 23-year-old Italian Panizza had moved out to a clear lead. The Mercier and Pepsi-Cola teams again! Could this mean that their respective team leaders, Poulidor and Dancelli, had pretensions to victory? The sympathetic Frenchman certainly had little to show for his season's efforts—other than an impressive string of criterium wins—while the former Italian champion was in the same boat. Both men would restore their waning reputations with another classic win, and both of them had the ability to pull it off.

"Merckx has attacked on the descent in company with Neri."

Now here was a man with more than enough ability, too. Merckx had already won Paris-Roubaix earlier in the year, and in this race had finished second in 1966 behind Gimondi—as opposed to Poulidor's two third places in the previous two editions of this season-closing classic. Another look at the map showed that 30 miles of flat lakeside roads immediately followed this descent. Was Merckx out to

 **A CLASSIC FINALE**

steal a march on his rivals by linking up with the obviously fit Neri, Panizza and Genet, before discarding them when the climbing started again; or was this just a reminder to them that, although he had lost his rainbow jersey to Faema teammate Vittorio Adorni a few weeks earlier, he was still as strong as ever?

This descent to Bellano was the most dangerous of the whole race. After continuing for a few miles on the wide, smooth road, it suddenly degenerated into an unsurfaced track. We were heading down a steep valley, and the "road" was carved out of the left side, plunging through frequent unlit tunnels and always with a precipitous slope down into the tree-lined chasm to the right, and a rocky cliff to the left. After this *discese precipitose* (as the program called it), it was a pleasure to emerge into the bright sunshine and drop down to Como's blue lake via a series of modern, built-out hairpins that ended in a vicious bend to the left over a rail crossing.

*12:03 p.m.* Bellano. Genet and Panizza were 45 seconds up on Merckx and Neri, the front of the decimated bunch at one minute. All told, there were only 68 riders left in the race. We had motored along the lake so that our driver could grab a bite to eat, and we were waiting at the end of a long, flat straight just before Colico (92 miles). After a while, the momentary silence was broken by the growl of the police motorcycles, and we saw the Genet-Panizza tandem appear in the distance. I took a time check and it was almost two minutes before we moved off in front of the break, and still no sign of the bunch. This confirmed the radio flash that Merckx and Neri had been caught a short way after Bellano, and this had obviously meant that the group had reformed and slowed down after making contact. So the Merckx salvo was just a damp squib!

*Tour of Lombardy • Italy • 1968*

For the next dozen miles, we cruised along in front of the two leaders—the gangling Genet's rolling style contrasting with the tiny Panizza's rhythmic pedaling. They were both holding the tops of their handlebars, soaking in the hot sun, but even so were maintaining a steady 25 mph. We heard from behind that another Mercier man had gone away, this time 22-year-old Ricci. But nobody joined him and he was soon replaced by Italian Carlo Chiappano (Salvarani), who was quickly joined by former Tour de l'Avenir winner Mino Denti (Faema). We were now on a marsh at the northern end of Lake Como, where the flat road sat on a levee, with tall poplars on either side. We could have been in Belgium ... but a quick glance to the right and the 10,000-foot peaks of the Alps re-affirmed that we were still in northern Italy! Over a metal bridge, left, and we joined a narrow, winding road hugging the western shore of Lake Como. At Sorico (98 miles), the leading pair was 1:45 ahead of the chasing duo, with the bunch still two minutes behind.

The 100-mile point was passed in three minutes over the four hours, and the race was now really warming up as two Belgians joined the chase: Merckx's Faema lieutenant Martin Van den Bossche and Van Springel's Mann-Grundig teammate Daniel Van Rijckeghem. Through Domaso and Gravedona, the crowds were growing all the time, packing the normally sleepy streets. At Dongo (105 miles), Genet and Panizza were 1:00 up on Chiappano and Denti , 1:25 up on Van den Bossche and Van Rijckeghem, and 1:40 ahead of the main group. With eight miles to go to the start of the final series of hills, the domestiques still ruled the roost; but just as we heard that the chasers had joined up to make a foursome (including two Faema men!), Dancelli showed that he was really out to put on a show. He left the peloton,

**A CLASSIC FINALE**

followed by watchdogs Altig (Salvarani), Franco Balmamion (Molteni) and Tony Houbrechts (Flandria).

We had now driven ahead to a two-mile cobbled hill twisting up away from the lake between the dusty vineyards at Menaggio, and we were waiting near the top, looking down toward the crowd-lined hairpins. The radio announced that Merckx was having trouble and changing bikes, and with the climb just about to begin, this meant a quick acceleration of his rivals that even caught Janssen napping. In no time, Gimondi, Motta, Bitossi, Poulidor, Michelotto, Van Springel, Bellone and Laghi (Germanvox) had caught all the men in front, and the unfortunate Genet had been dropped (and shortly retired).

As they came into our view, Altig, Gimondi and Motta were setting a terrific pace at the head of the line of 15 fugitives. Behind, Merckx was chasing furiously. He had already reeled in Janssen; and Delisle (Peugeot) and Poli (GBC) were also benefiting from his rapid back wheel. As they got nearer to us, we could see that Altig was riding very strongly, and assumed that Gimondi must have told him to go away, so that he would have an easier task behind.

Altig was clearly approaching the form that won him Milan-San Remo earlier in the year; and by the top of this comparatively short climb, he was 35 seconds clear of Mercier's Gilbert Bellone of France, and Belgians Houbrechts and Van Rijckeghem, with the front of the reformed group a minute back. But before the descent proper came, there were three little ups and downs, which were enough for Bitossi to make a counterattack. As for Merckx, he sent the faithful Martin Vandenbossche after him as a shadow. The second feed was waiting at the bottom of the hill in Porlezza (120 miles), but Altig had no time to waste and he was soon powering his way alongside Lake Lugano in one of his famed solo

*Tour of Lombardy • Italy • 1968*

escapades.

It was strangely silent flitting through the shadows with only the trees and water for company, before Osteno was reached. It was then back into the sunlight, reaching hoards of spectators and a sharp left turn for the cobbled delights of the Passo d'Intelvi. Already the fine Rudi had drawn 50 seconds clear of Bellone, Houbrechts and Van Rijckeghem, who had Bitossi and Van den Bossche hot on their heels. But what was this? "The chasing group conducted by Gimondi and Motta is at 2 minutes, 40 seconds."

Were we going to see a repeat of last year's race, when Bitossi attacked at Menaggio, dropped his two companions on the Intelvi and stayed away to win by half-a-minute at Como?

We were now cruising slowly up the steep, winding hill clinging to the side of a beautiful grassy valley, where the sun cast long shadows from the thin trees and thick crowds. We stopped just above a tight turn to the right, right after the halfway point and looked down toward a small pastel-colored hamlet nestling in the trees. Altig soon appeared, smoothly negotiating the pink cobblestones. Next came Bitossi and Vandenbossche, having dropped the other three, 1:05 down on the German. Then it was the bright yellow jersey of Van Rijckeghem at 1:10, the bright red of Houbrechts at 1:15, and the violet of Bellone at 1:30. The cheers of the crowd were quickly reaching us, and the driver had to pull away just as we spotted the dozen-strong Gimondi group and timed them through, still at 2:40.

For the next two miles through the banner-waving thousands, we kept a short distance in front of Altig in his seeming triumphant progress: his fair hair shining in the sun, his eyes clear, his square, red face dripping with sweat, hands on the tops with the arms horizontal supporting that

 **A CLASSIC FINALE**

big torso in streamlined majesty, and those powerful legs nimbly turning a small gear. As the summit came into view, our driver accelerated onto a wider road through even denser crowds, to ensure that there would be no interference with the riders on the drop back down to Lake Como at Argegno.

As we plummeted down this road through the ancient villages of San Fidele, Castiglione and Dizzasco—it was more like a bobsled-run than a road—we heard that Bitossi's progress was even more startling than Altig's. He was timed over the top only 35 seconds in arrears (with Vandenbossche still with him); Van Rijckeghem and Houbrechts had dropped to 1:30 back; while the group was just two minutes behind. That group now consisted of Van Springel, Gimondi, Motta, Merckx, Bracke, Delisle, Janssen, Dancelli, Bellone, De Roo (Willem II) and … Poppe, right-hand man of Van Springel.

On the final section of the descent, a glance to the right revealed a long crocodile of people massed on the other side of the canyon-like Intelvi valley, lining another steep hill back to the distant heights. Yes, it was full tilt into Argegno (135 miles, 30 to go), over a stone bridge, up a short drag to an almost 180-degree turn to the right, then up a steep, cobbled lane, for another 25 minutes of climbing, through Schignano, to Castiglione, on the other side of the valley! This was where the Salvarani tactics came unstuck, because Altig was caught by Bitossi and Vandenbossche as soon as this second part of the Intelvi double feature began.

Meanwhile, the Gimondi platoon had dropped to 2:15 in arrears, with Houbrechts-Van Rijckeghem about to be absorbed. It was clear that Altig was tiring quickly and so it would be up to Gimondi to try to bring back the fleeing Bitossi. Think back to those Superprestige placings: Van

*Tour of Lombardy • Italy • 1968*

Springel (first overall) only had to defend; Gimondi (second) needed a win really to pull it off; Godefroot (third) had been dropped; Janssen (fourth) was not having a brilliant day so far; and Merckx (fifth) had his faithful Vandenbossche sitting comfortably on Bitossi and in with a chance of victory. The Salvarani plan had misfired badly, and it would be now doubly difficult to shoot down trigger-man Bitossi.

Once again we motored ahead and parked just beyond Schignano village, with a clear view across a small side valley to the latter part of the climb, zigzagging across the green slopes. Altig was still with the other two, as they slowly climbed out of the trees below. We waited another two minutes, but still no sign of the others. Altig lost contact on the last stretch of the narrow road before Schignano, and the race looked won for Bitossi or Vandenbossche. A short drop, a bend to the right, and another short hill brought us to Castiglione again—and that second dizzy descent to Argegno. With 50 seconds lost by the top, Altig folded dramatically on the downhill and was back in the bunch by the lake, where the gap was still 2:10.

Only 12 miles remained before reaching Como, where the final climb and descent awaited. As car after car hooted its way noisily past to get to the finish, we hung back until the Filotex-Faema duo rounded a bend emerging from one of the short tunnels on this lakeside ride. Bitossi looked comfortable, confident in the knowledge of having made a similar situation successful 12 months before. The tall 27-year-old Vandenbossche, his balding head contrasting vividly with the dark locks and sideburns of the Tuscan, was in a difficult position. He had managed to stay with Bitossi for 30 miles already, including those two backbreaking climbs, so he should be capable of staying the same way until the finish. A classic win was therefore in his grasp, as the Italian

 **A CLASSIC FINALE**

probably did not know much of the Belgian's sprinting ability, which is quite considerable. What we saw was the action
of a devoted team man to Merckx. Vandenbossche was not
working with Bitossi, as he could have done. Instead, he
came through for his turn, but made no effort to increase the
25-mph tempo.

Just as we joined a new, very wide stretch of highway
that rose gently above by-passed villages on the lake, the
radio announced that Janssen and Van Springel had broken
away. So the wily Dutchman had something in hand! He was
making another late bid to retain his Super Prestige title, and
I wondered if glory was going to be snatched from Van
Springel's grasp as dramatically as three months' earlier in
the Tour de France, when the closing Melun-Paris time trial
saw Van Springel lose his yellow jersey to the Dutchman.

The talented pair's rapid acceleration halved the leader's
gap in five miles and took them 25 seconds clear of the
group. Gimondi's chances were now very remote—and they
were completely destroyed a few seconds later, when Merckx himself took up the chase and quickly bridged to
Janssen and Van Springel.

I was still watching Bitossi and Vandenbossche rolling
along when suddenly the other three burst onto the scene as
if they were in another race, such was their speed. Merckx
was leading his companions at an extraordinary speed—
they averaged over 30 mph to make up their two-minute
deficit within six miles! At the same moment came the news
that Altig had retired.

The rest were 40 seconds behind, but Gimondi was trying to rally them. By then we had reached the incredible
crowds gathered in Cernobbio, where only a 10-foot-wide
gap was left in the center of the wide road. And as a short
drag took us to the top of the bumpy cobbled drop into

*Tour of Lombardy • Italy • 1968*

Como itself, the lead of the five in front had risen to one minute. Half of the city was closed to traffic to make possible the final 7.4 miles of the race. And it looked as though half of Como's 70,000 population—as well as much of the population of Milan and every town within motoring (and cycling) range—was out to see the final act of this great Lombardian velodrama.

SO THE SCENE IS SET, as the autumn sun slants across the quiet north Italian town on a warm Saturday afternoon. There are only five left on stage from the original cast of 160. There is 28-year-old Franco Bitossi, the only Italian and the hero of the day, expected to repeat his fine performance of the previous year. There is the cunning Dutchman Jan Janssen, also 28, the one they all fear in the sprint. There is the Quiet One, Herman Van Springel, 25. And then comes the villain and chief disturber of the peace, 23-year-old Eddy Merckx, with his henchman Martin Vandenbossche. Gathered to see this unrepeatable show is a live audience of many thousands, with countless millions glued to television screens all over Europe.

The five enter hurriedly from the north, heralded by the Longines loudspeaker car bringing news of their progress. As police whistles blow, Merckx leads his companions around a broad right-hand sweep and out of view under a steel railway bridge. The scene is now plunged into shade, as tall, stone houses shield the sun from the first steep slopes of the San Fermo ridge. It goes straight up, and the wicked Eddy makes the rest suffer as he recklessly attacks. It is too much for his faithful servant Vandenbossche, and he leaves the stage.

But the already battle-scarred Italian hero Bitossi parries this body blow and manages to hang on to the villain. The reactions of the Quiet One, Van Springel, are not as quick,

 **A CLASSIC FINALE**

and it is some time before he realizes that he is not suffering as much as the straining Dutchman, and looks to see that his tormentor and the hero are only 100 yards in front. The upward grade has now decreased in severity, and the leading pair has swung off to the left, riding steadily through a corridor of massed humanity. As they pass under a new concrete viaduct that carries a motorway high above, Van Springel realizes that he still has a part to play, and rejoins the performance. The trio calls a momentary truce, to ensure that the dangerous Janssen does not have a chance to reply. At San Fermo della Battaglia, Van Springel is now making the pace from Bitossi and Merckx, and Janssen is left behind, at 300 yards.

The way is clear for the grand finale. There is a broad, straight descent for two miles; then comes a left turn and a mile of flat main road, before a short, fast drop to Camerlata roundabout; and then the final mile and a half down a steep curving highway into Como. The hero Bitossi is now watching every move of his dangerous Faema rival, confident that he, the points winner of the Tour de France, has the best sprint of the three.

Meanwhile, Dr. Mann's personal client Van Springel has done some more thinking, and realizes that he will stand no chance in a three-up rush for the line. He is still feeling strong, but his only chance is to get away from them as soon as possible—if he is to win his first classic. It's now or never. The flat section has been reached before the final descent, and Merckx leads from Bitossi and Van Springel. Van Springel then jumps down the far side of the road. Bitossi spots him, but expects Merckx to respond to the attack. Merckx, though, has had a very tiring day, having had to chase hard following a machine change, chase hard after Janssen and Van Springel when they attacked earlier, and

*Tour of Lombardy • Italy • 1968*

just having made a violent attack himself. There is a moment's hesitation and by now the under-estimated Van Springel has 100 yards in hand. With the grade again pointing downward, Merckx is not willing to make any more bellicose actions that would take the Italian up to Van Springel to contest the sprint.

At last, Van Springel is riding with the conviction of a winner, and his rapid progress is unstoppable as he pedals his 53x13 triumphantly down the wide black street toward the deep blue lake. Straight over the police-controlled traffic lights, a sharp left turn around the corner of the Stadio Sinigaglia and left again through the wide gate onto the vast concrete track. A roar of greeting erupts for the yellow-jerseyed Belgian, as he starts his lap-and-a-half of the 429-meter bowl.

Fifteen seconds pass before Bitossi and Merckx appear to an equal buzz of excitement from the packed stadium. Half a minute later, Herman Van Springel freewheels over the line, his arms held aloft in the traditional victor's salute. He has won his 13th race of the year, out of 141 he has contested ... but he has also won the most important victory of his career so far: that Super Prestige Pernod Trophy.

As expected, Bitossi easily outsprints the unhappy Merckx, much to the approval of the hometown audience. Janssen and Vandenbossche come in singly, respectively 53 seconds and 1:15 respectively behind the winner; before the Gimondi troop of eight enters to another roar from the excitable fans. Much to their approval, local boy Motta takes sixth place by several lengths from Gimondi and Dancelli, and our cycling classic ends as delirious supporters swarm around their idols, even though they have suffered defeat by that quiet foreigner, Herman Van Springel from Flanders.

 **A CLASSIC FINALE**

## SEEKING EL DORADO

**World Hour
Record
Attempt**

# Colombia
# October 1995

Many of the world's' greatest cyclists have at some point in their careers attempted, or broken, the most difficult record in the sport: the world hour record. Italian Fausto Coppi did it in 1942, two years after the first of his five Giro d'Italia victories, riding 45.798 kilometers in the allotted 60 minutes. That mark was beaten by French great Jacques Anquetil in 1956, a year before the first of his five Tour de France wins. Then, in 1972, at the height of his career, Belgian legend Eddy Merckx broke the record by the widest margin in 74 years, with a distance of 49.432 kilometers. Another five-time Tour winner, Spanish phenomenon Miguel Induráin pushed the record over 53 kilometers in 1994; and then lost it to Giro winner Tony Rominger of Switzerland, who topped 55 kilometers. Near the end of his career, Induráin returned to the arena....

# Colombia

IN A FOLD of the Andes mountains, high above the city of Bogotá, Colombia, sits a remote lake, the Laguna de Guatavita. It was here, about 1000 years ago, that the Muisca Indians worshipped a gilded god by tossing gold pieces into the lake's deep waters. The stories of fabulous riches and hidden gold created the legend of El Dorado—a legend that brought the Spanish to the area in the 16th century. Their arrival marked the founding of Bogotá ... but they never found the gold.

More than 400 years later, drawn by tales of fabulous world records being set at the brand new Velódromo Luis Carlos Galán in Bogotá, another Spanish party came to Colombia's capital city. Its goal was to recapture the world hour record for five-time Tour de France champion Miguel Induráin.

On paper, everything looked good in the days before his designated October 15 record attempt. It had been said that, on a Bogotá track that saw four (short-distance) world records beaten during the world track championships two weeks earlier, Induráin would not only beat Tony Rominger's awesome record of 55.291 kilometers, but put it in the archives for the rest of this century.

The nine-man entourage that accompanied Induráin to Colombia knew that success would be very difficult. The Banesto team's publicity director Francis Lafargue admitted that the goal of trying to win two world championships and set a world record in the space of 12 days placed a heavy psychological burden on Induráin. Speaking a few days before the record attempt, Lafargue, who is one of Induráin's closest friends, said, "While he may not be attempting the record in the best circumstances, it would still be a pity to miss the opportunity. But Miguel is very strong in the men-

*World Hour Record Attempt • Colombia • 1995*

tal department. And it was he who said, 'If I am still strong ... why not?'"

Another who accepted the magnitude of his rider's challenge was Induráin's sports doctor Sabino Padilla, who had been monitoring the Spanish champion's condition every day since he began altitude training in Colorado, six weeks earlier. Padilla spoke about the "unknown factors," and was concerned that although his rider would benefit from the reduced air resistance at this altitude, he might experience breathing problems from the reduced-oxygen levels.

Another factor was the unusual micro-climate of Bogotá. To avoid the winds that regularly pick up here by 8:30 each morning, Induráin's record attempt was scheduled for 6 a.m. But the pre-dawn starting time on this Sunday in Colombia wouldn't deter thousands of fans from driving, biking and walking through the dark, and causing a bizarre 5 a.m. traffic jam outside the velodrome.

This noisy crowd's palpable enthusiasm, along with the confident mood of the Banesto team personnel, certainly reinforced Induráin's determination to take back the record he first claimed on September 3, 1994. Yet the pressure also made him more nervous of failure than one would expect from this impeccable champion....

After winning the 43-kilometer world time trial championship and taking silver in the 265.6-kilometer road race only a week before, Induráin had moved into Bogotá's Capital Hotel—a brand-new 10-story building, five minutes from the velodrome. Once there, Padilla programmed his rider's conversion from mountain-climbing roadman to world-class track racer. He had five days to get ready ... but things didn't begin well.

Although Induráin—who was accompanied by his brother Prudencio—could train on the road on Tuesday

**SEEKING EL DORADO**

and Wednesday, rain on the first day stopped them riding on the track, while strong winds prevented any serious tests on the second day. Even on the Thursday—three days before the record attempt—an overnight dew left the track damp until 7:20 a.m. Then, real preparations could finally begin. This was also the morning when Induráin and his team had to decide if the attempt would go ahead as planned … or whether they would return to Europe on the next plane.

At 7:42 a.m., Induráin began his first 15-minute test, pushing a gear of 62x14 on his mark IV Pinarello Espada. He went through 14 kilometers in a handy 15:41—10 seconds faster than he had covered the same distance in his 53.050-kilometer record-breaking effort at Bordeaux, France, 13 months earlier. That was a promising start; and when a half-hour later he recorded 15:31 for the same 14-kilometer distance, using a slightly smaller 61x14 gear, the whole team was encouraged—even though Rominger went through 14 kilometers in 15:12 during his record-setting ride last November 5. But Induráin had done well enough for the Sunday-morning record rendezvous to be confirmed.

With the decision made, Induráin could now focus on preparing himself mentally for this ultimate challenge. First, however, he had to assure himself that he was capable of maintaining an average speed of 56 kph on the 333.3-meter concrete velodrome. So on both the Friday and Saturday mornings, the two Induráin brothers woke up at 4 a.m., breakfasted at 4:30, and drove to the track at 5:15. Just behind them came a requisitioned Postobon team car, with their two road bikes on board.

After warming up for about half-an-hour on the Saturday morning, Induráin transferred to the latest version of his high-tech Pinarello Espada aero' bike, paced by the team

*World Hour Record Attempt • Colombia • 1995*

mechanic on a Honda motorcycle. He then circled the track for 20 minutes at a paced 60 kph, cruised to a halt, removed his aero' helmet, and walked to an infield tent at 6:50 a.m.

Before Induráin re-emerged, bright sunshine came out from behind the clouds cloaking the nearby mountains. With the air heating up and no wind, conditions were perfect for a new speed test. Induráin warmed up for five minutes, paced by brother Prudencio on his road bike, and was soon up to top speed.

If he were to break the record the next day, the Spaniard would have to complete 166 laps at an average lap time of 21.7 seconds. Now, riding the modified Espada bike that mirrored his regular time-trial position, he was lapping at speeds even faster than required. For 3000 meters, he averaged 21.4 seconds a lap—exactly on the 56-kph schedule that he would aim for the next morning.

Remaining on the track, again warming up behind Prudencio, Induráin began a second test 10 minutes later. This time, he raced just three laps at top speed—completing the kilometer in 62.5 seconds, an average of 57.6 kph. Clearly, in these perfect conditions, man and machine were ready. And in a 15-minute trackside press conference—before a media gathering of about 100 reporters, photographers and TV cameramen—Induráin was quietly confident of the task facing him Sunday morning.

After such a successful morning of tests, most observers were confident that Induráin was going to break the record. His attempt was the front page story in *Il Tiempo* (The *New York Times* of Colombia), and, in conjunction with the RCN national radio and TV networks, the newspaper offered big cash prizes for readers who came closest to guessing the distance Induráin would ride. Furthermore, despite the attempt being scheduled for a breakfast-time screening in

**SEEKING EL DORADO**

Bogotá (along with it being broadcast live around Europe), a packed stadium was expected the next morning.

Besides all the pressure from the public and media, there was also a huge bonus awaiting Induráin should he top Rominger's mark. It was expected that a successful bid would see the Spaniard collect double the estimated $415,000 purse he earned when he broke the record in Bordeaux last year.

"Miguel told us after the Tour de France that he would like to do the record. So he told us then to start preparing," said Lafargue, explaining why the purse had doubled. "When we did it last year, it was just after the Tour and hard to get everything ready...."

The principal sponsors for this new attempt were the French TV network Canal-plus, Campofrio meats from Spain, and Ardila Lule—the wealthy Colombian family that owns the Postobon food and beverage company, and Leona brewery.

"The priority is a sporting achievement," Lafargue emphasized, "but it's also a commercial operation. And we have the best cyclist in the world for sale. So it's normal that we get a lot of sponsors for the world hour record. He is not hard to sell."

Induráin's popularity in Colombia is almost god-like, as attested by the thousands who poured into the Bogotá velodrome before dawn that Sunday. They were there for the heralded event ... but also to pay homage to the man who is a sporting superstar in Hispanic nations.

The day had started at 3:30 a.m. for Induráin, and unlike on the previous days, he had time to shave before breakfast and still leave for the track by 4:30. The track was dry enough to warm up on, thanks to the velodrome floodlights having remained on all night. But there had been gusts

*World Hour Record Attempt • Colombia • 1995*

of wind through the night, and the temperature was a few degrees below the usual 48-degree mornings in Bogotá—which lies just north of the equator, and thus has almost constant temperatures throughout the year.

After an initial warm-up on his road bike, Induráin, still wearing tights and a jacket, climbed aboard the high-tech Espada track machine, and at 5:30 a.m., he began lapping the track behind his pacing motorcycle. This final warm-up lasted 15 minutes, until Padilla—satisfied that Induráin's pulse was again operating at the 185 beats per minute of the previous tests—signaled it was time to stop.

At 5:50 a.m., the Spanish champion was back in the tent on the infield, while helpers gave the concrete surface a final mopping, and placed the foam markers on the inner side of the track's datum line, ready for the record attempt. By now, the stands in the 5200-capacity velodrome were almost full, and there was a great awareness that we were all about to witness a significant moment in cycling history.

Within five minutes, Induráin reappeared in his racing uniform—a skinsuit specially manufactured by Nalini at an alleged cost of $10,000, and made from a Swiss-woven "argento" ski-race fabric that is claimed to be lighter and more aerodynamic than Lycra. As Induráin nervously waved to the crowd, his mechanic ran up to him with his bike and helmet, while a mob of photographers strained to get the best shots before the champion began a final warm-up.

After four minutes of slowly circling the oval like a lion stalking its prey, Induráin stopped at the beginning of the 67-meter-long home straight, where his record attempt would start. It was 5:59 a.m. and the sun back-lit the clouds above the Andes with a golden tinge. Was this a sign that a Spaniard was finally going to find El Dorado?

**SEEKING EL DORADO**

The sun was out, but it was still cold. The thermometer on the electronic scoreboard flashed 6 degrees Celsius—only 43 degrees Fahrenheit. And as any physics student knows, cold air is denser than warm air; so some of the advantage of using this high-altitude venue was being lost, a fact that would make Induráin's Herculean task even tougher.

However, compared with his 1994 attempt, Induráin was clearly better armed. His carbon-fiber monocoque Espada IV bike was a better fit, although fractionally less aerodynamic. This was offset by a more aero' helmet, made by Vetta, the front of which extended below his nose and incorporated shaded lenses to see through. It gave Induráin the look of an iron-masked conquistador. And now it was time to do battle....

On Bordeaux's indoor track last year, the Spaniard rode a 59x14 gearing, which he pedaled at an average cadence of 100.9 revs per minute. Rominger used a slightly bigger 60x14. Now, Induráin was on 62x14, and again aiming at the 101-rpm cadence he would need to break the record.

Despite that heavier gear, he started much faster than before. From the standing start, Induráin took half-a-minute to ride the first lap, but then settled into an awesome rhythm, completing each of the next two laps in 20.5 seconds. He hurtled through the first kilometer in 1:10.958— almost four seconds faster than his 1994 opening, and fractionally slower than the lower-geared Rominger.

Induráin continued at this elevated 103-rpm cadence for another three laps, to complete his second kilometer in a phenomenal 1:03.141. At this rate, he would break the world 4000-meter record of 4:20.894 set indoors by Graeme Obree two years ago....

It was clearly too fast a start, and so Padilla signaled Induráin to ease off slightly. Even so, the next two kilometer

*World Hour Record Attempt • Colombia • 1995*

times were both between 1:04.5 and 1:05, giving Induráin a 4:23.520 split at 4000 meters.

Then, after riding the next kilometer in 1:05.658, the Banesto rider went through the 5000-meter point more than a second faster than Rominger—in a time of 5:29.178. This is the fastest ever recorded at this distance. When the Union Cycliste Internationale dropped the world 5000-meter record from its books two years ago, it was held by Olympic champion Chris Boardman with 5:38.083.

But despite his excellence so far, Induráin's riding was becoming more erratic. He was wavering off his line, particularly around the bankings, and the extra distance he was covering inevitably pushed up his lap times. As a result, instead of a required pace of 1:05 per kilometer, he was turning in 1:06s and then 1:07s. The result was a 7.64-second deficit at 10 kilometers....

By the 15-kilometer mark, Induráin was 22 seconds (a whole lap) behind Rominger; at 20 kilometers, the deficit was 33.5 seconds; and at 25 kilometers, 44 seconds, or two laps back.

Throughout this period, and despite the evidence of the big digital clock on the scoreboard, the crowd continued to urge on its hero, chanting, "Mi-guel! Mi-guel,! Mi-guel!" At the same time, Induráin's helpers, especially Padilla and team director José-Miguel Echavarri, waved frantically for their rider to increase his pace.

But the demands had become too great: Induráin was clearly fighting a losing battle. Still, he wasn't going to give up until defeat was inevitable. That point came after he'd completed 85 laps—just beyond 28 kilometers and 31 minutes into his attempt.

So when it came to racing full throttle at high altitude in search of Rominger's record, Induráin was just not ready.

**SEEKING EL DORADO**

Following his attempt, the 31-year-old Spaniard said, "I accept with serenity this defeat." Despite his dignity, it was a defeat—not only for Induráin, but also for the much-touted concept of attacking cycling's most-coveted, and most difficult, world record at 8400 feet above the level of the sea.

At the subsequent press conference, no excuses were offered. There were several explanations, however, regarding why Induráin couldn't maintain the record-breaking pace he had started at. The rider himself summed it up best by saying, "I'm upset because we've been working for a long time at altitude. Today, I wasn't in the groove to break the record. One day, one is capable of doing it; the next day, that's not the case."

This last comment clearly referred to the fast tests he'd made 24 hours earlier, when the air was warmer and the conditions calmer. But trying to break this record outdoors and at altitude proved too great a task, even for the best cyclist in the world. Like the Spaniards who came seeking El Dorado four centuries ago, Miguel Induráin's quest for the world hour record had finally failed.

*World Hour Record Attempt • Colombia • 1995*

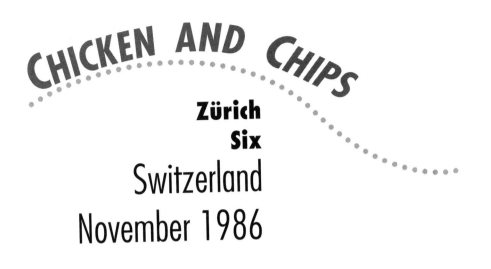

# CHICKEN AND CHIPS

**Zürich**
**Six**
Switzerland
November 1986

To the European sports fans who flock to watch indoor track racing through the winter, six-day racing is fast, flashy and glamorous. But behind the scenes, there is a blue-collar lifestyle. Racers lead a treadmill existence, fighting illness, racing up to 200 miles a night, sleeping through the day, and then driving across the Continent to the next event. The rewards can be considerable, but so are the demands.

# Switzerland

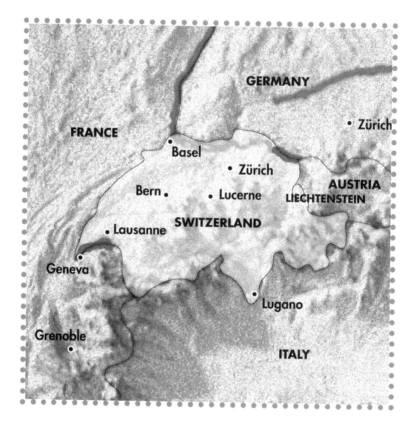

LESS THAN ONE HOUR remained of the second day in the 34th Zürich Six-day Race. The yellows, reds, blues, greens and blacks of the racers' silken shirts merged into a kaleidoscopic blur, as they rattled around the steeply banked, 250-meter wooden velodrome at the Hallenstadion, in Switzerland's biggest city. World professional pursuit champion Tony Doyle was flowing in and out of the 17-team pack, pedaling his 49x15 fixed gear at over 53 kph, riding within a few millimeters of other flying wheels, a crash always a touch of tires away. One would assume that it took every ounce of a rider's energy and concentration to stand the pace in this session of Madison racing—a nonstop, two-man relay—but as he circled the wall-of-death turn during one of his brief, resting laps, Englishman Doyle shouted down his dinner order to his helper: "Etienne! Chicken and chips!" The time was three minutes before 3 o'clock in the morning of Wednesday, November 26, 1986.

Doyle was into his 39th day of racing of the winter season, which began only 42 days before. "I've already spent a whole year of my life racing around six-day tracks," calculated the 28-year-old Brit, who first entered this anachronistic, cutthroat branch of cycling six years ago. "The race directors treat us like animals. They all think their race is the only one that matters, and they make it as tough as they can. The organizer of the Berlin and Dortmund races is an ex-prisoner-of-war. It's his ambition to see everyone on their knees at the finish."

Berlin and Dortmund provided Doyle with his first six-day victories in October 1983, when he teamed up with the Australian ace Danny Clark, a former Olympic silver medalist. This formidable pair repeated the Berlin-Dortmund double this winter. And of the six races he had ridden before

*Zürich Six • Switzerland • 1986*

Zürich, Doyle had won four. Clark's record was five wins out of six races; but on this cold November night, the 35-year-old Aussie was temporarily on the sidelines, suffering from what the doctor had diagnosed as a possible stomach ulcer.

When we visited him earlier that night, Clark was resting in his home-for-the-week: one of 17 tiny trailers parked in the moon's shadow of the gaunt, rectangular stadium. The trailer's windows were covered with thick brown paper, inside and out. "The sunshine was waking us up," explained Doyle. Indeed, sleep is hard to come by when you go to bed just before dawn and have breakfast just before dusk. Clark was subdued, but showing signs of recovery. "The doctor has given me this medicine. I have to take it for six weeks," he said with a resigned air. "I had something similar at Bremen five years ago. I carried on racing then and I wasn't right for the rest of the season. I think it's my nerves. I've won five times this winter, and Tony's won four. I was worried about keeping our position at the top."

Clark's concern over his status seemed strangely misplaced. He has been competing in six-day races for 15 years, and his 39 career victories put him fifth on the all-time list— behind Belgian Patrick Sercu, Dutchmen Peter Post and René Pijnen, and Belgian Rik Van Steenbergen. "Danny has always been a nervous sort," said Doyle. "When I started racing in six-days, it should have been Danny helping me build up my confidence. But I was having to look after him."

It is Doyle's confidence in his own ability and his utter professionalism that have enabled him to become the most consistent performer on the six-day circuit. Starting with that Berlin victory three years earlier, the Ever Ready-sponsored professional had notched up 10 wins by the start of the Zürich race. He seems to thrive on this treadmill existence: racing every night, sleeping in the daytime, grabbing

**CHICKEN AND CHIPS**

meals like that early-morning plate of chicken and french fries, and flying on to the next town to start it all over again.

Few people can comprehend the physical and mental demands of a six-day rider's life, and that is why we joined Doyle during a critical phase of his winter season. After his wins with Clark in Germany, he flew south for the first of two French six-day races, at the recently rebuilt velodrome in Grenoble. He was teamed with Francesco Moser, the 35-year-old Italian who had twice broken the sea level world hour record a few weeks earlier. "Moser isn't a great six-day rider," commented Doyle. "He's much too nervous. He doesn't like lots of riders around him. But the sport needs some superstars to ride the sixes to bring in the crowds. That's why he gets paid more than anyone."

Whatever Moser's inadequacies in this branch of the sport, he helped Doyle win the Grenoble race. It was Moser's 13th six-day victory, Doyle's ninth. They finished a lap ahead of the 1984 Grenoble winners: local man Bernard Vallet and the Danish expert Gert Frank. For most of the riders, that race was the perfect preparation for the prestigious Paris Six which began nine days later. But Doyle traveled first to Munich in southern Germany, where he again changed partners, this time riding with another experienced Aussie, Gary Wiggins. Although this pair won the difficult Bremen Six in January 1985, Wiggins was short of form at Munich and they finished only fifth, 14 laps behind winners Dietrich Thurau ... and Clark. There was a time when the tall, bronzed, blond-haired Thurau could name his fee for any six-day race in Europe. But the promise he showed early in his career was never fulfilled and, at 32, he is negotiating a difficult period in both his professional and private life.

The Paris race confirmed the dominance of Clark and Doyle, although they were again paired with different part-

*Zürich Six • Switzerland • 1986*

ners. Clark eventually won the race, teamed with Vallet, while Doyle finished second, on the same lap, with another French road-race star, Charly Mottet. After his lap of honor, receiving his prizes and packing his bags, Doyle was ready to drive his own car the 200 or so miles to Ghent, Belgium, where another race was due to begin the following evening. "One of the cycling magazines thought it would be a good idea to send a reporter along to interview me during the journey," said Doyle, "but after three questions, he went to sleep." Apparently, the world pursuit champion's demanding schedule is not to everyone's tastes.

The 46th Six Days of Ghent was typical of the modern approach to this traditional sport, with six to seven hours of racing each evening, ending at 1 or 2 a.m. This is a light menu compared with the average West German six-day, and it enabled Doyle to stay with his Belgian soigneur Piet DeWit in Brussels, a half-hour's drive away. He found this more comfortable than staying at the Ghent Sports Palace, which is not the most glamorous of locations: The 1940s-built stadium has not been modernized since it was remodeled after a fire 20 years ago. The rooms where the riders change are tiny, windowless cells, with plain concrete floors and walls.

One of the race sponsors at Ghent is Heineken, and not surprisingly, the spectators are encouraged to drink the sponsor's beer. There are bars set up on the infield, where the price of entry is only 200 Belgian francs (about $5), whereas trackside seats vary from 450 to 700 francs ($11 to $17). "They even turned up the heat so the public drank more beer," noted a snuffle-nosed Wiggins. "Now the riders are all going down with colds and flu. In some of the German sixes, they make us race another half-hour, if there are people still drinking at the bars."

 **CHICKEN AND CHIPS**

Bands and a beauty contest help keep the crowds enter-tained at Ghent; while other sixes, such as Paris, provide laser shows and performances by leading pop singers and orchestras. Through all the hoopla, the racers have to remain concentrated on their demanding schedule of sprints, Madisons, elimination races and derny-paced events. Even after a 10-minute round of prime sprints, a rider needs to change his sweat-soaked shirt, and have a rub down from his soigneur. At the end of a 30- to 90-minute Madison session, the rider's helper will have ready a sponge, a bowl of clean water, a drink of honey-sweetened tea, and perhaps a bowl of fruit and rice to eat. Depending on the exact program, the teams race 200 to 300 kilometers every night. As Doyle pointed out during the second evening in Zürich, "Over the past six weeks, I've ridden the equivalent of the Tour of Italy followed by the Tour de France."

At Ghent, Doyle and Clark dominated the race, despite the start of the Australian's stomach upset during the final weekend. They made sure of winning by earning a bonus lap for the best overall performance in the series of nightly record attempts. This included a track record for a flying-start kilometer in 58.9 seconds, and a standing start 2000-meter, two-man pursuit in 2:10. On the last evening, they were challenged strongly by two teams: the Belgians Stan Tourné and Etienne De Wilde, who won here in 1985; and world keirin champion Michel Vaarten, who was teamed with the Ghent-domiciled Dane, Gert Frank. Whenever one of these three teams made an attack, the other two soon chased. Clark-Doyle easily held their one-lap lead through the last session, with the only real challenge coming from Tourné-De Wilde 40 laps from the end of the 90-minute Madison. Doyle, riding more strongly than Clark, contained the Belgians' lead to a half-lap, about 80 meters, with some

*Zürich Six • Switzerland • 1986*

strong pulls at the head of the peloton. The aggressors eventually tired, but their five-kilometer-long effort kept the
crowd on its toes until the dying minutes.

A few seconds after 7 p.m., Clark symbolically won the
final sprint to confirm his team's victory. He and Doyle were
presented with the winners' yellow jerseys, laurel leaves and
flowers, before their first lap of honor. Doyle's wife Ann—on
a rare visit to see him race—was at the trackside to receive
the flowers. A second victory lap was made with the green
jerseys as points winners—and there was a second kiss for
Ann Doyle.

As the crowds drifted away into the damp November
night, Doyle trudged through the narrow corridor beneath
the track to his room. He showered a body scarred by another recent crash, blew dry his cropped hair, and changed into
blue slacks, sports shirt and navy overcoat. He exchanged
some words with his trainer, gave a few quotes to a journalist, and arranged a rendezvous later that night with some
agents to discuss future contracts. It was 7:50 p.m. His last
call was in the stadium manager's office, to collect his
appearance fee and share of the prize money. He then drove
to Brussels with his wife for their dinner meeting at the
Sheraton, and discussed business for several hours. By the
time he got to bed at 3:15 a.m., Doyle's mechanic Steve
Snowling was halfway across Germany in a car crammed
with 17 wheels, three frames, three big boxes of tools, suitcases, a compressor and the rest of his paraphernalia. "All
that stuff only goes into the car, because I've got it down to
a fine art," said Snowling.

Also driving across Europe were Wiggins and fellow
Australian Tom Sawyer. "We left Ghent at about 10 p.m. and
decided to drive via Luxembourg to shorten the journey by
120 kilometers," said Wiggins. "We arrived at the French

**CHICKEN AND CHIPS**

border at about one o'clock in the morning, and couldn't get across. I'd vaguely heard that people needed visas for going into France; it's only European Community nationals who don't need them. We were turned back and had to find a different route through Germany. We didn't arrive in Zürich until 7:15."

Wiggins had driven all night and slept most of the day, before starting another six-day that night. Meanwhile, Doyle was up fairly early in a cold, drizzly Brussels, where he had a short ride to the Zaventem airport for a late-morning Sabena flight to Zürich. Snowling was already working on the bikes when Doyle arrived at the Hallenstadion, in the suburb of Oerlikon, only 10 minutes drive from Zürich's Kloten Airport, where bright sunshine made the prospect of another week of indoor racing a less than thrilling prospect.

There was not much time for the mechanics, soigneurs, runners and riders to set up their bikes, changing rooms, trackside cabins and trailers, before their first dinner in the sparsely furnished restaurant where they would take all their meals during the next six days. Surprisingly, the riders had to pay for all these meals at prices which would have not embarrassed the fanciest restaurants in London or New York.

"I put weight on in the winter because of the rubbish food we have to eat," said Doyle. "I get through about 8000 calories of food every day during these races." His pre-race meal was typically substantial, and served (not by choice) in the following order:

- Milky rice pudding
- Canned fruit salad
- A mixed salad
- A three-egg omelet
- Veal steak with spaghetti and carrots

*Zürich Six • Switzerland • 1986*

This was washed down with a bottle of mineral water and two or three cups of coffee.

On this first night of the Zürich Six, the racing would not start until 10:30 p.m. The crowd of 9300 packed the stadium many hours earlier, attracted by a 10-event sports personality competition similar to TV's "Superstars." This one starred Olympic decathletes Dailey Thompson and Jürgen Hingsen, whose appearance fees far exceeded the fees paid most of the six-day riders. The bike race began with an immediate 60-minute Madison, which proved a particularly demanding event for men who were tired from traveling and lack of sleep and had no time to warm up around the wooden velodrome. The crowd roared encouragement for the home team of Urs Freuler and Daniel Gisiger, who ended the night with the yellow jerseys as race leaders, with Tourné-De Wilde and the Hermann brothers from Liechtenstein on the same lap. The chase proved difficult for the groggy Clark, and even Doyle's strong riding couldn't prevent them losing a lap. Doyle was sharing a trackside "cabin" with Wiggins and Sawyer, tended by soigneur Etienne llegems—who helps the 7-Eleven team during its European schedule.

"My soigneur Pierrot doesn't come to Zürich because the sleeping accommodation is so bad," said Doyle. The soigneurs sleep on hospital-type beds, among the drying washing and assorted débris of the riders' changing rooms. Ilegems said that some places were worse. "In Madrid," he recalled, "there were no beds for us. We asked for mattresses, but they never came. We slept the first night on a blanket placed on the concrete floor. The next night we took bedrolls from the cabins."

After the first Madison race in Zürich, the evening continued until midnight with a series of sprints. The pros then had a 90-minute break, while racing continued with ses-

 **CHICKEN AND CHIPS**

sions of the concurrent amateur six-day and professional motor-paced event. Doyle, Sawyer and Wiggins trooped off to their massage room for a meal prepared by Ilegems—toasted ham rolls, canned rice, fruit salad, yogurt, mineral water and tea. They chatted to pass the time away. Other times, they will read books or listen to a Walkman. "I'm just finishing Jilly Cooper's 'Riders'," said Doyle.

In the small hours of this Tuesday morning, the immediate talk was about the toughness of the Madison: almost 54 kilometers of racing in one hour. "Everyone is burnt out because the racing is so hard. It took us about 10 minutes to take a lap tonight," said Doyle, who had tried out slightly-longer-than-usual, 167.5-millimeter cranks on this wide 250-meter-long track. "The cranks didn't feel right. I'll tell Steve to put the 165s on tomorrow."

"I was seeing circles in there. I could only follow and not attack, and we lost three laps," noted Wiggins, who seemed more concerned with his health. "We can feel cold air coming in a door when we're at the top of the track in one corner. I'm having to wear a thermal undervest to keep warm."

The 34-year-old Australian looked tired from his long, overnight drive from Belgium. "I slept over 14 hours today in three goes," he said. "I normally sleep about seven hours. And we don't get much chance to sleep here. Our caravan is right next to the rubbish shoot for the stadium. And I guess we'll get woken up in the morning when the garbage trucks come around, or the trucks delivering the beer."

Doyle contemplated a question of how it felt to have reached the top echelon in six-day racing. Did he feel like a true star? Like another Peter Post or Patrick Sercu? "Not really," replied the tall, pale-faced Englishman. "You can't get arrogant living in England. There is little recognition from the media and no respect for performances in the sixes. If I

*Zürich Six • Switzerland • 1986*

go to the (cycling) clubroom, I'll still get asked if I'm going on the club run that weekend, or the freewheeling contest, whatever. Out training on the road, kids will still shout, 'Your wheel's going 'round mister,' or 'Get off and milk it!' There's virtually no acclaim in Britain," he observed.

He said that his 1987 season would be based around defending his world pursuit title at Vienna in August, and that his preparation might include some of the shorter international stage races. It's often forgotten that Doyle is a highly accomplished road racer, and it's likely that he could have become a top name in the classics, if he had not devoted his energy to track racing. But few men can claim his degree of success in the six-day arena, and he is the first British rider ever to become one of the inner circle of highly paid experts. If he does not receive the respect he deserves at home, he clearly has it from the continental crowds and his fellow professionals.

Doyle's immediate concern was the chances of Clark rejoining him in the race. (He didn't, and Doyle ended the race in fourth overall, re-teamed with Swiss rider Jörg Müller, two laps down on winners Freuler-Gisiger.) The world champion returned to the massage room to tell us: "Danny can't come out for the rest of the night. He's lost three kilograms [almost 7 pounds] since yesterday. He looks bad. He won't even be able to leave his teeth to science." He paused and then quipped, "They're false."

The talk turned to the state of six-day racing as a sport. They mentioned the big crowds they had at Munich—over 95,000 paying spectators in the six days—and contrasted this with the scarcity of people watching some of the early-morning sessions at Zürich. "One night, half an hour before the end of racing, we counted just 27 people in the stands," said Wiggins. "Or 28, if you included a drunk who was fast

**CHICKEN AND CHIPS**

asleep." None of the three riders could fully understand why the Zürich organizer Joseph Voegeli—who also promotes the Tour of Switzerland in June—insisted on the early-morning sessions. They only knew that they had to do exactly as Voegeli ordered. "If you don't toe the line," they echoed, "he'll throw you out of the race. It happened to the Betz brothers last year. It was a strange story. Werner Betz had eaten some red beets with a meal, and during one of the late night sessions, he thought he was passing blood when he went to pee. The doctor advised him not to continue riding that night, but he forgot to tell Voegeli. When Voegeli found out, he told Heinz Betz and his brother to get out of the stadium and never to come back. Even though Werner was the European motorpaced champion last year, Voegeli wouldn't allow him to come back here to defend his title this week."

Voegeli's intransigence is well-known, as is his strong ego. That evening, we were given another insight into the character of a race director who gives no favors. While sitting in the track restaurant, Steve Snowling said, "Guess who that man is sitting at the next table wearing the blue overalls, with a pass hanging around his neck. He's one of the cleaners here … it's Voegeli's brother."

For most of the motor-paced sessions and the Madisons, the big boss, wearing a tailored dress suit and silver tie, could be seen standing in his "patch" at the end of the back straight, a glass of white Swiss wine at his side. He was pleased that Swiss riders were so well-represented at his race. Besides Freuler-Gisiger, the Swiss were represented by six other teams: the youthful Müller-Joho, Hafliger-Winterberg, Bruggmann-Marki and Machler-Achermann combinations, and the experienced Dill-Bundi and Ledermann pairing.

But even the presence of these local riders brought little enthusiasm from the few hundred people left in the stadium

*Zürich Six • Switzerland • 1986*

for the night's remaining Madison race. It was approaching 3 a.m. The 12-man brass band was persevering with its repertoire of traditional tunes, after a session at the coffee bar. A flower seller drifted along the row of trackside tables, trying to get rid of a last bouquet of red roses to diners finishing off a last bottle of wine. A mixed party of beer drinkers was singing and giggling. A couple was jiving to the oompah music of the band. "They look like a bunch of carrots," joked Doyle, referring to the band players in their orange and green outfits. The resting riders sat by their cabins with blankets over their knees, awaiting the end of the night's very last sprints, when only one from each team was on the track. A few riders were yawning. Wiggins came in for his rest; sweat was flowing from his nose and neck. He removed his soaked thermal vest and donned something dry.

The images were similar 24 hours later. Outside, a damp-looking moon was in its last quarter. The streets of Zürich were deserted. The buses and trams would be leaving their depots in two hours' time to start another long day of transporting the Swiss about their pretty city. A city that the 34 riders in the six-day would not see before flying out, for the luxury of a few days at home before the single-night Six Hours of Copenhagen race in Denmark, followed by the Maastricht Six in the Netherlands a few days later. Inside the Hallenstadion, Tony Doyle was circling the 30-degree banking. He shouted down to his helper, "Etienne, chicken and chips!"

 **CHICKEN AND CHIPS**